HOW MANY TIMES WERE YOU SEDUCED TODAY?

Chances are, you don't know the answer. As far as advertising men are concerned, you're not supposed to know. Their job is to arouse you without your suspecting it.

This very day, every time you looked at a TV commercial, or an ad in print, you very probably were being sexually assaulted by devices your conscious mind cannot detect.

Now for the first time, in this eye-opening book you can find out what is really being done to you, how it is being done, and how you can protect yourself against a media that is manipulating your mind for your money.

After you read SUBLIMINAL SEDUCTION, you will see things you never saw before in every ad you look at.

SUBLIMINAL SEDUCTION

Ad Media's Manipulation of a Not So Innocent America

Wilson Bryan Key

A SIGNET BOOK

SIGNET
Published by the Penguin Group
Penguin Books USA Inc., 375 Hudson Street,
New York, New York 10014, U.S.A.
Penguin Books Ltd, 27 Wrights Lane,
London W8 5TZ, England
Penguin Books Australia Ltd, Ringwood,
Victoria, Australia
Penguin Books Canada Ltd, 10 Alcorn Avenue,
Toronto, Ontario, Canada M4V 3B2
Penguin Books (N.Z.) Ltd, 182–190 Wairau Road,
Auckland 10, New Zealand

Penguin Books Ltd, Registered Offices:
Harmondsworth, Middlesex, England

Published by Signet, an imprint of New American Library,
a division of Penguin Books USA Inc.

This is an authorized reprint of a hardcover edition published by
Prentice-Hall, Inc.

First Signet Printing, December, 1974
28 27 26 25 24 23 22 21 20

 REGISTERED TRADEMARK—MARCA REGISTRADA

Printed in the United States of America

Contents

All of my recommendations, therefore, can be reduced to this one: study the modes of the media, in order to hoick all assumptions out of the subliminal nonverbal realm for scrutiny and for prediction and control of human purposes.
MARSHALL McLUHAN

It may be impossible to resist instructions which are not consciously experienced. There seems to be a close parallel between these (subliminal) phenomena and those associated with post hypnotic suggestion and neurotic compulsive responses.

N. F. DIXON

The real catastrophe is the prospect of total moronization, dehumanization, and manipulation of man.

HERBERT MARCUSE

Media Ad-vice:
An Introduction

by Marshall McLuhan,
Director, Centre for Culture and Technology
University of Toronto

Customer in antique shop: "What's new?"

Professor Key has helped to show how the deceits of subliminal advertising can be a means of revealing unexpected
truth: the childlike faith of the ad agencies in four-letter
words points to our obsession with infantile bathroom images
as the chemical bond between commercial society and the
universal archetypes.

The old journalism had aimed at objectivity by giving
"both sides at once," as it were, the pro and con, the light
and shade in full perspective. The "new journalism," on the
other hand, eagerly seeks subjectivity and involvement in a
resonant environment of events: Norman Mailer at the
Chicago Convention, or Truman Capote writing *In Cold
Blood*.

In the same way, the old history—as Michael Foucault explains in *The Archeology of Knowledge* (Pantheon Books,
New York, 1972)—sought to show "how a single pattern is
formed and preserved, how for so many different successive
minds there is a single horizon." But now the problem of the
"new history" is "no longer one of tradition, of tracing a line,
but one of division, of limits. It is no longer one of lasting
foundations, but one of transformations that serve as new
foundations. . . ."

The study of advertising as contemporary cultural history,
of history on the hop and in the hopper, of history as process
rather than as a product, such is the investigation of Professor Key. Advertising is an environmental striptease for a
world of abundance. But environments as such have a way

of being inaccessible to inspection. Environments by reason of their total character are mostly subliminal to ordinary experience. Indeed, the amount of any situation, private or social, verbal or geographic, that can be raised and held to the conscious level of attention is almost insignificant. Yet ads demand a lot of attention in our environmental lives. Ads are focal points for the entire range of twentieth-century knowledge, skills, and technologies. Psychologists and anthropologists toil for the agencies. So, Professor Key has drawn our attention to the use made in many ads of the highly developed arts of camouflage.

T.S. Eliot long ago pointed out that the camouflage function of "meaning" in a poem was like the juicy piece of meat carried by the burglar to distract the house-dog of the mind so that the poem could do its work. Professor Key explains that the proclaimed purpose of the ad may, at one level, be just such a decoy so that the ad may do its work at another level of consciousness.

Secrets Within Banality

Today many people feel uneasy when serious attention is paid to objects and subjects that they are accustomed to classify as "trash." They feel that the base commercial operation of ads is beneath any claim to their awareness or analysis.

Such people, on the one hand, have little heeded the lessons of history and archaeology which reveal how the midden-heaps of the ages provide the wisdom and riches of the present. And yet, on the other hand, they know how their snobbish "freeze" (or surrender) in the presence of the horrid vulgarities of commerce is exactly what is needed to render them the cooperative puppets of ad manipulation. The ad as camouflage often uses the blatant appeal to hide more subtle and powerful motivations than appear on the surface.

Shakespeare's oft misquoted remark about "one touch of nature" that "makes the whole world kin" really concerns the eagerness of men to swallow a flattering bait. He is not suggesting that natural beauty is a social bond!

> One touch of nature makes the whole world kin:
> That all with one consent praise new-born gawds
> Though they are made and moulded of things past,

And give to dust that is a little gilt
More laud than gilt o'erdusted.

Men are united only in their eagerness to be deceived by
appearances.

The wise gods seal our eyes;
In our own filth drop our clear judgments; make us
Adore our errors; laugh at us while we strut
To our confusion

Thus part of the business of the ad is to seem frank, open,
hearty, and direct. The business establishment long ago
founded itself on ebullient attitudes of trust and confidence
which were part of the discovery that "Honesty is the best
policy" and "Crime doesn't pay." "Policy," of course, is the
Machiavellian term for "deceit," so immediate and overt
honesty can be camouflage for ultimate exploitation, in ads
as in politics. However, we live today in the first age of the
electric information environment, and there is now a sense
in which we are the first generation that can say, "There is
nothing old under the sun."

Since Sputnik (October 17, 1957), the planet Earth went
inside a man-made environment and Nature yielded its ancient reign to Art and Ecology. Ecology was born with
Sputnik, for in an electric information environment all
events become clamorous and simultaneous. An old adage at
IBM is: "Information overload equals pattern recognition."
At instant speed the hidden becomes plain to see.

Minds Are Quicker Than Eyes

Since the mind is very much faster than light (it can go
to Mars and back in an instant, whereas light takes minutes),
the hidden structure of many old things can now become
apparent. With the new information surround, not only
specialisms and monopolies of knowledge become less useful,
but the world of the subliminal is greatly reduced. Whatever
the practical uses and expediency of the subliminal may have
been in the past, they are not as they were. Even the future
is not what it used to be. For at electric speeds it is necessary
to anticipate the future in order to live in the present, and
vice versa.

Necessarily, the age of instant information prompts men

to new kinds of research and development. It is, above all, an age of investigation and of espionage. For in the total information environment, man the hunter and scanner of environments returns to supervise the inner as well as the outer worlds, and nothing is now unrelated or irrelevant.

T.S. Eliot has two statements that directly concern our new simultaneous world of "auditory" or "acoustic" space in which electric man now dwells on the "wired planet." The first passage is from his discussion of "Tradition and the Individual Talent," explaining that "the whole of literature of Europe from Homer and within it the whole of the literature of his own country has a simultaneous existence and composes a simultaneous order." It is the character of auditory space, which we make in the act of hearing, to be a sphere whose center is everywhere and whose margin is nowhere, for we hear from all directions at once.

In the magnetic city of the new electric environment we receive data from all directions simultaneously, and thus we exist in a world sphere of resonant information that is structured and which acts upon us in the auditory pattern. Eliot had regard to the role of the individual talent faced by this new kind of richness of tradition and experience. So it is not strange that our time should witness a revival of many forms of oral culture and group performance, any more than it is strange that we should see on all hands the awakening and cultivation of occult traditions, and new concern with inner life and visionary experience.

For these are resonant things hidden from the eye. The wide interest in every kind of structuralism in language and art and science is direct testimony to the new dominance of the nonvisual values of audile-tactile involvement and group participation. In fact, it could be said that there is very little in the new electric technology to sustain the visual values of civilized detachment and rational analysis.

Mr. Eliot's second statement on the world of the simultaneous concerns the "auditory imagination":

> What I call "auditory imagination" is the feeling for syllable and rhythm, penetrating far below the conscious levels of thought and feeling, invigorating every word: sinking to the most primitive and forgotten, returning to the origin and bringing something back, seeking the beginning and the end. It works through meanings, certainly, or not without meanings in the

ordinary sense, and fuses the old and obliterated, and
the trite, the current, and the new and the surprising,
the most ancient and the most civilized mentality.

Eliot here speaks of the mind's ear, the subliminal depths
and reach of the corporate tongue bridging countless generations and cultures in an eternal present. Eliot and Joyce
accepted language as the great corporate medium that en-
codes and environs the countless dramas and transactions of
man. Their raids on this vast inarticulate resource have made
literary history on a massive scale.

Meantime the enormous new environment of advertising
has sprung up as a service for the consumer who hardly
knows what to think of his newly bought cars and swimming
pools. It is well known to the frogmen of Madison Avenue
that those who read or hear the ads are mostly those who
have already bought one of the objects displayed. "Ask the
man who owns one," or "You feel better satisfied when you
use a well-known brand." The fact is that the ad world
is a colossal *put-on* as much as the world of fashion or art
or politics or entertainment. The stripper puts on her audience by taking off her clothes, and the poet puts on his
public by stripping or dislocating the familiar rhythms and
habits of expression.

How about the adman's rip-off? He must move on more
than one level in order to obtain the interplay that involves
the public. The poet lets us look at the world through the
mask of his poem while wearing us as his mask: "hypocrite
lecteur, mon semblable, mon frère," said Baudelaire to his
reader. The adman shows us the world through the mesh or
mask of his product while playfully putting on our cash and
credit as his own motley. But that there may be another
level of reinforcement, the ads sometimes provide a barrage
of optimistic innocence along with an undercurrent of guilty
joys and fears upon which the blatant, gesticulating commercial rides piggyback. It is the quest of Professor Key to un-
conceal this hidden ground of the ad as figure, and to reveal
the conflict between them.

Scuba Diving into Hidden Backgrounds

It may be that the impulse of the admen to use the hidden
ground of our lives in a furtive way in their ads is no mere
surrender to base impulse and greed for power. By replaying

the hot glamorous images in a cool scatological pattern, the subliminal message becomes a dramatic irony of the superficial and conscious one.

The subliminal replay of the open appeal thus offers an offbeat jazz quality of quarter notes sourly commenting on the full notes, by way of a wry twist. It is the role Freud himself played as diver into the dirty unhygienic depth beneath the dewy Romantic sentiment. At the extreme point, Freud the diver got a signal: "Surface at once. Ship is sinking." When he came up for air he wrote about "Civilization and its Discontents." After a long session in the dark unconscious, Freud recognized the visual and literate world as the location of civilized values and awareness. The dark within is the world of tribal or acoustic man who resists civilization as do our dropouts. Professor Key brings out the struggle between these worlds as inherent in the very structure of the not-so-humble ads that provide the directives and the competitive taste patterns of our commerce and our entertainment.

Bugging and Sleuthing have become a universal Business, like education. The electric age is the age of the hunter. It is the age of simultaneous information. The simultaneous ends the subliminal by making it as much a structural part of consciousness as former specialism or monopoly or secrecy. The age just behind us was the opposite of the electric age. The mechanical and industrial society was the age of steam and hardware and highway and monopoly and specialism. It was a visual world.

The age of the electrical and simultaneous is the age of environmental and ecological awareness. Structurally speaking, the simultaneous is acoustic rather than visual. We hear from all directions at once, and that is why the reign of the subliminal is ending. The subliminal or the hidden can be present to the hearing when it is not accessible to the eye.

It makes much sense when N. F. Dixon writes in *Subliminal Perception* that experienced psychologists of our sense lives have bypassed the subliminal and the auditory in favor of visual investigation. For the psychological, as much as for any other establishment, the commitments are to the preceding age of the visual. However, the new age is also subliminal to its predecessor. It is, therefore, easy to know that the eye may be solicited by lines it cannot see, and our judgments warped by motives that are not in consciousness nor in the habitual patterns of our nervous systems, "for the whole environment is full of subliminal influences which experienced psychologists have systematically neglected."

It is only fair to add that the electric environment is man-made and new, and experienced psychologists, quite as much as the rest of the population, continue to adhere to the older and familiar and visually structured world of the hardware age in which they invested all they had. For the visual is the world of the continuous and the connected and the rational and the stable.

Since we have now put an electrical environment of resonant information around the old visual one, our daily adaptations and responses are at least as much to the new acoustic environment as to the old visual world. If one were to ask, "Which is the better world?" it would be necessary to explain that the values of an acoustical and musically oriented society are not those of the classically visual and civilized society.

Predictions of the Past

For good or ill, we have phased ourselves out of the older visual society by our electric technology that is as instant as light. If we want to get back into a visually ordered world, we shall have to recreate the conditions of that world. Meantime we have a new environment of instant information that upsets and "pollutes" all the patterns of the old visual sequences. Nothing is "in concatenation accordingly" in the simultaneous world of sound. Effects now easily and naturally precede causes, and we can freely predict the past.

At the speed of light our space-time coexistence tends to give us the whimsical manners of the girl in Professor Butler's limerick:

> There was a young lady named Bright
> Who moved with the quickness of light;
> She went out one day
> In a relative way,
> And returned the previous night.

At electric speed, the goals and objectives of the old sequential and visual world are irrelevant. Either they are attained before we start or we are out of date before we arrive. All forms of specialist training suffer especially. En-

gineers and doctors cannot graduate in time to be relevant
to the innovations that occur during their training period.

Change itself becomes the only constant. We seem to live
in a world of deceits and fake values where, for example,
those engaged in news coverage are often more numerous
than those making the news. But the creation of a total field
of world information returns man to the state of the hunter,
the hunter of data.

To the sleuth, to Sherlock Holmes, nothing is quite what
it seems. He lives, like us, in two worlds at once, having
small benefit of either. Caught between visual and acoustic
worlds, physicist Werner Heisenberg enunciated the "Uncertainty Principle." You can never perform the same experiment twice. Heraclitus, living in the old acoustic world
before Greek literacy, said, "You can't step in the same
river twice." And today in the electric world we say, "You
can't step in the same river," period.

In the Renaissance, when the old acoustic world of
medieval and feudal order was quickly being overlaid by
the visual order of the printed word, there was an epidemic
concern about deceit and imposture. Machiavelli invented a
new art of lying by stressing an extrovert mask of bluff,
hearty sincerity. Iago tells us that he will wear his heart on
his sleeve for daws to peck at. Othello demands "ocular
proof" of his wife's infidelity, and is deceived by the same
"proof." Shakespeare's great plays are devoted to the theme
of the deceits of power. Hamlet is caught out of role. He
is a medieval prince adapted to the medieval world of acoustic involvement and personal loyalty. His world of ideal musical harmony collapses into one of visual distraction and
mere appearancs:

> Now see that noble and most sovereign reason
> Like sweet bells jangled out of tune and harsh

His dilemma is stated also by Ulysses in *Troilus and Cres-
sida*:

> Take but degree away, untune that string
> And, hark! what discord follows; each thing meets
> In mere oppugnancy: the bounded waters
> Should lift their bosoms higher than the shores,
> And make a sop of all this solid globe.

Other Side of the Looking Glass

The auditory man is an ecologist because he imagines everything affecting everything, because all happens at once as in a resonating sphere. The clash between the medieval ecologist and the Renaissance man of private aims and goals is playing in reverse today. The new technology is acoustic and total. The old establishment is visual and fragmentary. All this concerns Professor Key's study of the deceits of the admen.

These admen teams operate on the frontier between the worlds of eye and ear, of old and new. They are trying to have the best of both worlds by wearing both masks. Ben Jonson, Shakespeare's great contemporary, devoted much of his work to the presentation of the deceiver and the deceived, stressing the inherent appetite of most people to wallow in deceit as a delectable diet:

> Still to be neat, still to be drest,
> As you were going to a feast;
> Still to be powdered, still perfumed
> Lady, it is to be presumed,
> Though art's hid causes are not found,
> All is not sweet, all is not sound.

This could be an anti-advertisement today if equal time were allowed to query the counsel of each ad. Saving the appearances mattered more and more during the Renaissance and after. Molière's *Misanthrope* and *Tartuffe* are built on the assumption that truth is a matching of inner state and outer behavior. The fact that truth is making not matching, process not product, can never satisfy the visual man with his mirror held up to nature.

By contrast, Walter Pater plunged his readers into the forbidden world of the unconscious when he presented them with the image of Da Vinci's "Mona Lisa." He sought the truth on the other side of the looking glass:

> The presence that thus rose so strangely beside the waters, is expressive of what in the ways of a thousand years men had come to desire. Hers is the head upon which all 'the ends of the world are come,' and the eyelids are a little weary. . . . Set it for a moment

beside one of those white Greek goddesses or beautiful
women of antiquity, and how would they be troubled
by this beauty, into which the soul with all its maladies
has passed?

(*The Renaissance*)

Pater is fascinated by his image of a sick "soul with all its
maladies," spurning the slick white Greek goddesses of ra-
tionality. Pater has flipped, fashionably, out of the visual and
back into the medieval acoustic world. "All art," he said,
"constantly aspires toward the condition of music."

It is this music that began to be heard in the Romantic
depths of the starved and rationalistic psyche of the visual
cultures that reached from the Renaissance to the Victorian
age. Pater's pen portrait of "Mona Lisa" continues in a
plangent tone that might win the applause of any ad copy-
writer:

> She is older than the rocks among which she sits; like
> the vampire, she has been dead many times, and learned
> the secrets of the grave; and has been a diver in deep
> seas, and keeps their fallen day about her; and traf-
> ficked for strange webs with Eastern merchants: and, as
> Leda, was the mother of Helen of Troy, and, as Saint
> Anne, the mother of Mary; and all this has been to her
> but as the sound of lyres and flutes, and lives only in
> the delicacy with which it has moulded the changing
> lineaments, and tinged the eyelids and the hands.

This passage is a striking description of the Western subconscious with all its evocation of the occult and of delirious
vices.

Subliminal Graffiti

It is plain that the subconscious is a wicked witch's brew
of superhuman interest for all boys and girls. This *Mona Lisa*
affair raises a major aspect of Professor Key's study. *Does
the discovery of graffiti in the deodorants and aids to glamor
threaten the public of consumers, or does it merely reveal
the childish itch of the admen themselves?* For example, the
title *Gentlemen Prefer Blondes* may be both immoral and
immortal because it links hair and gold, faces and feces. For

gold and dung have always had affinities, even as the greatest perfumes include a subtle ingredient of excrement.

There is the further fetching factor of the author's name, Anita Loos. It doesn't suggest the prim Puritan altogether. Since the world of dung and excrement is quite near to the daily conscious level, are we to panic when the admen put these at the bottom of the big hamper of goodies that they proffer the affluent?

Will the graffiti hidden under the lush appeal expedite sales or merely impede the maturity quotient of the buyers? Will the graffiti lurking in the glamor crevices set up a reso-nant interval of revulsion against the consumer appeals, or will the confrontation of fur and feces in the ads merely sad-den and deepen and mature the childish consumer world? It is a strange and tricky game to mount the sweet enticing figure on a rotten ground.

To use, on the other hand, four-letter words in the libret-to of the siren's song may prove to be a metaphysical dis-covery. The poet W.B. Yeats meditated in anguish over the plight of man:

> Love has pitched his mansion in
> The place of excrement;
> For nothing can be sole or whole
> That has not been rent.

He, too, is desperate over the appearances.

Just how precarious a boundary Yeats provides can be noted in his nervous betrayal in the ambiguous words "pitch" and "rent." "Pitch" is filth and "rent" is venal. In a word, the "Love" of Yeats can no more be trusted to present a clean slate than the overeager admen with their subliminal reinforcement of glamor by graffiti. The passionately em-bracing young man asks his partner, "Why speak of love at a time like this?" The remark serves as a corollary to the moan of Yeats. But it also opens up the *Playboy* world where girls are playmates.

The Playboy's Plaything

Things have changed electrically since I published *The Mechanical Bride* in 1951. The assembly-line love goddess, abstract and austere and inhuman, has been succeeded by hula-hooping, mini-skirted, tribally anonymous jujubes. Utterly embraceable, consumable, and expendable, they expect little, for they know that the fragile ego of the playboy cannot endure the threat of any strain or commitment.

Thanks to color photography, and then to color TV, the magnetic city has become a single erogenous zone. At every turn there is an immediate encounter with extremely erotic situations which exactly correspond to the media "coverage" of violence. "Bad news" has long been the hard core of the press, indispensable for the moving of the mass of "good news" which is advertising. These forms of sex and violence are complementary and inseparable. Just what would be the fate of wars and disasters without "coverage" could be considered a meaningless question, since the coverage itself is not only an increase of the violence but an incentive to the same.

The power-starved person can easily see himself getting top coverage if he is involved in a sufficiently outrageous act of hijacking or mayhem. The older pattern of success story by achievement simply takes too long to be practical at electric speeds. Why not make the news instead of a life?

The close relation between sex and violence, between good news and bad news, helps to explain the compulsion of the admen to dunk all their products in sex by erogenizing every contour of every bottle or cigarette. Having reached this happy state where the good news is fairly popping, the admen say, as it were: "Better add a bit of the bad news now to take the hex off all that bonanza stuff." Let's remind them that LOVE, replayed in reverse, is EVOL—transposing into EVIL and VILE. LIVE spells backward into EVIL, while EROS reverses into SORE. And, we should never forget the SIN in SINCERE or the CON in CONFIDENCE.

Let's tighten up the slack sentimentality of this goo with something gutsy and grim.

As Zeus said to Narcissus:

"Watch yourself."

MARSHALL McLUHAN

1. The Mass Media's Illusion of Reality

Subliminal perception is a subject that virtually no one wants to believe exists, and—if it does exist—they much less believe that it has any practical application.

Doubtless, it would be far more comfortable to simply ignore what is going on. After all, most North Americans benefit from what is probably the fattest nation on earth, blessed with riches beyond the wildest fantasies of the Pharaohs, the Caesars, or the Khans of ancient China. But— perhaps mainly because Americans are overfed, overweight, and overindulged in a world where many people go to bed hungry each night—they should know clearly what has been done to them subliminally, regardless of the pain or discomfort that may result. North Americans, perhaps not uniquely, find it quite difficult to be self-critical, especially when the criticism is directed at their standard of living and life-style, the so-called *American way of life.*

This story is about *subliminal perception* and about *the ways we think we think.* In the concept of subliminal phenomena are included all those techniques now known to the mass media by which tens of millions of humans are daily massaged and manipulated without their conscious awareness.

Every person reading this book has been victimized and manipulated by the use of subliminal stimuli directed into his unconscious mind by the mass merchandisers of media. The techniques are in widespread use by media, advertising and public relations agencies, industrial and commercial corporations, and by the Federal government itself.

The secret has been well kept. The average citizen, as well as most social and behavioral scientists, simply do not know what is going on. Further, and most shocking, they appear not to want to know what is going on. Any investigation of the techniques of subconscious communication involves first an investigation into one's own fantasy systems, self-images, illusions, personal vanities, and secret motives. This is an investigation that might make even the toughest of us extremely uncomfortable. The inquiry, the readers will discover for themselves, can make calm, gentle, considerate individuals defensive, outraged, and aggressive.

Ecological Survival

From another view, however, if what we have self-flatteringly called our civilization is to sustain itself beyond another quarter century, it is imperative that we find out in detail what has been happening both to us and to our world at this level of unawareness.

In thirty years the world's present population will double. In one hundred years it will quadruple. Moreover, no one living in an industrialized society today is more than a few minutes away from the warhead end of a missile armed with a hydrogen bomb or biological warfare agents. The missiles may already be obsolete. Nuclear bombs can now be manufactured by any nation in the world. The technology is still expensive, but very available. These bombs, it is widely known, can be delivered in a suitcase if necessary.

It is fascinating to wonder how long this world—starving and impoverished as it is—will tolerate the incredible self-indulgence which has come to be known as the American way of life. The United States government has indicated a willingness to sacrifice the entire population of the world, if necessary, to sustain this indulgence in the face of future inevitable international crises. Vastly increased numbers of people are a certainty—like the earth's orbit around the sun —not a theory. Desperate demands for the growing shortage of world resources are already apparent. An average North American during his life-span will consume 54 times more of the world's resources than will his East Indian counterpart. According to the recent Rockefeller population study, individual American consumption will double its present level within the next quarter century at the present rate of increase.

In a world such as this one, straining from population growth and resource depletion, the ability to differentiate between illusion and reality will soon become even greater a necessity to survival. It is entirely possible that the self-delusions of the world's industrialized nations have already approached a level where any abrupt return to reality would be catastrophic to their entire way of life. But this may be getting ahead of the story.

What we *consciously* perceive about ourselves and our worlds has, of course, much to do with our behavior. The subject has been virtually exhausted, however, or at least would appear to be well on its way to exhaustion. During the past decade dozens of excellent books dealing primarily with *cognitive* or *conscious* human experience have reached the best-seller lists. This book acknowledges the role of conscious perception, but it will concentrate upon *unconscious* perception—subliminal experiences which manipulate, manage, or control human behavior, but of which humans are consciously unaware. The entire subject of human subliminality is largely unknown, even though omnipresent in the behavioral environment.

Subliminal Seduction, in addition, does not presume to tell the reader what he should see or read in verbal or pictorial stimuli. This book is concerned only with content planted within media which readers or audiences are *not supposed to see or read,* at least at the conscious level.

Subliminal Hardsell

Appearing in the July 5, 1971, edition of *Time* magazine, on the inside back cover, the Gilbey's London Dry Gin advertisement is a classic design of subliminal art (see Figure 1). Assuming the ad appeared in *Time*'s World Edition, the inside back cover space would have cost $68,450, plus another $7,000 for art and production, bringing the total to roughly $75,000. This ad could have involved 24.2 million readers, with a break-even 20-1 sales point of $1.5 million, which would buy enough gin to float the proverbial battleship—or at least a small destroyer.

Over one thousand adult male and female test subjects were asked to look at the advertisement while relaxed. The subjects were not familiar with subliminal techniques. They were requested not to analyze content, but to just let feelings come to the surface as their eyes moved over the page. Feelings, of course, are nonverbal, but the subjects were asked to try and put whatever their feelings seemed to be into words—no matter how far out or absurd these words might appear to be. The ad was neither explained nor discussed

any further after these instructions. All possible precautions
were taken to avoid pre-programming the test subjects.

Thirty-eight percent apparently saw nothing but a gin bottle and collins glass and were unable to verbalize any feelings
they might have experienced. This does not mean, of course,
they perceived nothing. They were consciously unaware of
feelings, however, and unable to verbalize on the perception.

Sixty-two percent, on the other hand, described feelings of
"satisfaction," "sensuousness," "sexuality," "romance," "stimulation," "arousal," and "excitement" and several young
women reported "horny." None of the test subjects discovered any of the subliminal details in the advertisement.
The subliminal technique used by Gilbey's remained invisible
both during the evaluation and during a lengthy discussion
afterward.

The advertisement was painted over a photograph and was
published during the summer, promising the reader cool, re-
freshing pleasure in return for his purchase of Gilbey's. The
bottle cap is removed, making the contents easily accessible
to the reader. This, at least, is the obvious, consciously transmitted message coming from the frosty bottle, ice cubes, and
water drops beneath the bottle and glass. There is, however,
far more to the gin ad than meets the conscious eye. Be
certain to view the ad, while relaxed, a few moments before
continuing.

Let your eyes concentrate momentarily upon the third
ice cube from the top. Without stretching your imagination
beyond reasonable limits, can you see an E formed in the
cube? Some interpret the letter at first as an F. But, hypo-
thetically, for the moment consider the letter an E. Do not
read further until the E is established clearly in your mind.

The second ice cube from the top is also interesting. Let
your mind relax and consider what letter might be in this
cube. This is slightly more difficult to perceive than the
E. Start at the top of the lime slice, letting your eyes move
left to the point of the slice, then down and right, following
the lime pulp to about the midpoint on the slice where a
black line (shadow) slants diagonally from the slice to the
left. You should now be on the bottom line of the second ice
cube, so follow the line to the left.

Now, briefly retrace the above instructions.

You should have outlined on the ice cube, in the silhouette
formed by the lime slice, the letter S. Should you have come

up with another alternative, please note it for future reference.

Most people—roughly 90 percent—will at this point be able to discern clearly two letters in the ice cubes: S in the second and E in the third. Again, should any other meaningful possibilities have appeared, please note them.

Now look at the forth or bottom ice cube. Hold the page at arm's length and let your eyes move from the S to the E and then to the fourth ice cube. Most readers will immediately discern the third letter.

If you haven't discovered the letter by now, locate a point in the center of the collins glass at the bottom of the fourth ice cube where a track—somewhat similar to that made by a heavy automobile tire—angles up diagonally from the bottom of the cube. The track, though it becomes blurred halfway across the cube, extends to the top left corner. Now, locate the midpoint on this diagonal track. If you are relaxed enough, you will perceive a lightly etched line cutting diagonally across the first diagonal line. Give the perception time to register—and keep relaxed. If the X does not immediately appear, try looking away momentarily, then back quickly at the fourth cube.

Unconscious Sex

You have just consciously perceived your first subliminal SEX. There will be many others. You cannot pick up a newspaper, magazine, or pamphlet, hear radio, or view television anywhere in North America without being assaulted subliminally by embeds such as those in the ice cubes. Incredulous though you might be at this point, these subliminal SEXes are today an integral part of modern American life— even though they have never been seen by many people at the conscious level.

You might consider, as well, that you instantly saw the ice cube SEX—at the unconscious level. This invisible dimension of meaning in the Gilbey's ad was not hidden on the *Time* cover. The SEX was available for anyone to see—all 24.2 million weekly *Time* readers—men, women, and children. Readers make such illusions invisible to the conscious mind through a psychological device psychologists have labeled *repression,* one of the perceptual defenses.

Keep in mind that this book is not telling you what you should see in the ad or what it should mean; it is only con-

cerned with the perception of phenomena you are neither
supposed to see nor consciously supposed to deal with in
terms of meaning. These are subliminal stimuli and they
have been regularly used in the North American mass media
for over twenty-five years without anyone getting wise to
what was going on.

But, there is much more to the Gilbey's ad. At the risk of
overextending the reader's credibility, could there possibly
be a face in the top ice cube? It is a humorous cartoon-type
face, reminiscent of the archetypal "Kilroy Was Here!" face
that decorated men's rest room walls all over the world
during World War II. Kilroy, of course, was probably the
most famous graffiti voyeur in American history. The ice
cube face appears to be peering down on the ice cube SEX
below, and—with a slight stretch of the imagination—wink-
ing one eye at the reader.

Now, drop your eyes down to the bottom ice cube again.
Look behind the X you earlier discovered in the cube. Could
there possibly be another face peering out from behind the
letter? Just to the right of the crossed lines in the X appears
what could be described as an eye. To the left, hidden behind
the heavy track diagonal, might be another eye. The nose
could be formed by one of the markings in the track.

Give your mind time, at least thirty seconds, to assimilate
consciously the outline marks of this face. It is probably that
of a woman, as on the right side of the bottom ice cube are
lines and shadows suggestive of long hair.

Once this woman peering out from behind the X is fairly
well established in your mind, try to follow her line of sight.
What does she appear to be looking at in the ad? You will
probably find her line of sight is directed somewhere around
the bottle cap which is lying casually beneath the frosty
bottle.

The bottle cap is rather conventional—removed from the
bottle by the artist to convey the idea that this symbolic Gilbey's gin is open, easily available to the reader. The *reflection*
of the bottle cap, however, has several rather unusual dimensions as it reflects out of the mirrorlike table surface.
With another only slight stretch of the imagination, the bottle
and bottle cap reflections could be interpreted as a man's legs
and partially erect genitals. At this point, you probably
should take several deep breaths in order to relax; there is
much more to come, if you'll pardon the expression. Sub-

liminals are very difficult to perceive consciously if you are the slightest bit tense or apprehensive.

The melting ice on the bottle cap could symbolize seminal fluid—the origin of all human life. The green color suggests peace and tranquility after tensions have been released. Therefore, the scene is likely after orgasm, not before. This interpretation is reinforced by the less than fully extended penis. The melting ice on the frosty bottle, of course, could also suggest seminal fluid. Who could ever have guessed Gilbey's had so much to offer these 24.2 million readers?

At this point, if you are curious and broad-minded, you might look between the reflection from the tonic glass and that of the bottle. The vertical opening between the reflection has subtle shadows on each side which could be interpreted as lips—vaginal lips, of course. At the top of the opening is a drop of water which could represent the clitoris.

If the scene were put into a story line, this still-open vagina is where the discharged penis has just been. The seminal frost all over the bottle might suggest to a primitive part of the human brain—the portion some theorists call the unconscious—that *coitus interruptus* had just occurred, or as the copy would suggest: "and keep your tonics dry!"

There appears one additional female genital symbol horizontally drawn into the tonic glass reflection. The vagina is closed, suggesting the owner might be lying down awaiting her turn.

When you add up the number of individuals symbolized subliminally in various parts of the advertisement, there are five—three women and two men, including our Kilroy-like voyeur in the top ice cube. The subliminal promise to anyone buying Gilbey's gin is simply a good old-fashioned sexual orgy which developed after "breaking out the frosty bottle."

Mental Pollution

The Gilbey's ad was tested with over a thousand subjects. Sixty-two percent of these men and women reported feelings of sexual stimulation or excitement. Male test subjects appeared to resist a conscious response to the ad content slightly more than did the women. None of the men or women tested, however, was consciously aware of the subliminal content, or ever discovered the secret until it was explained to them after their responses were recorded. The ad appears to have been purposefully designed to reach both men and women through unconscious perceptual mechanisms.

The *modus operandi* of the ad is to sell Gilbey's through a subliminal appeal to latent voyeuristic or exhibitionistic tendencies within the unconscious minds of *Time* readers. The Gilbey's orgy has also appeared on the covers of several other national publications.

The unsettling thing about all this is that the Gilbey's ad is not an isolated instance of subliminal manipulation through pornography: North America's mass media is saturated with similar trickery—some of it far more morally objectionable than the Gilbey's ad. After all, advertising is a $20 billion annual affair in the United States. Another billion dollars is spent in Canada. An enormous proportion of this expenditure today is dedicated to the research, development, and application of subliminal stimuli with strong sales or manipulative potentialities.

There are, of course, serious moral implications in the use of subliminal techniques such as this in public communication. An individual's right to decide issues, even if they involve only the purchase of a gin brand, on the basis of his own conscious determinations or free will, is a precious heritage basic to the entire concept of democratic freedoms.

Moreover, the invasion of one's privacy—there is nothing more private to an individual than his unconscious mind—is also considered a fundamental human right in Western society. Should anyone have the right, and North Americans must think this question out most carefully, to ruthlessly exploit the desires, needs, fears, or anxieties which function uncontrollably within each human being?

Health Dangers

Subliminal persuasion can be even more dangerous to mental health. In the service of commercial profit, highly skilled technicians are probing into and manipulating the most intimate, subtle, and complicated mechanism of the human nervous system—a mechanism still virtually a mystery to science.

To illustrate: 9.5 percent of the test subjects who described a sexual response to the Gilbey's ad also reported pronounced *fear reactions*. The number of test subjects was too small to use as a base for completely accurate projections, but if this 9.5 percent was projected into the 24.2 million *Time* readers, the distinct possibility arises that 2.3 million *Time* readers—assuming they had all perceived the inside back cover even momentarily—could have experienced pronounced negative feelings without knowing why they were upset.

Two typical individual fear reactions to the Gilbey's subliminals follow. They speak most eloquently for themselves. Not one word has been edited or changed. Neither of the two test subjects knew of the ad's subliminal contents when they wrote these reactions.

Test Subject A: male, age 28, high school physical education instructor.

It gave me a chilly, almost sinister feeling of watching something somewhat loathsome. My first sensation was that I was looking at something I had no business watching. I felt strange. Then I began to get a very alone feeling. It was cold, dark, and quiet. I felt as if I was looking in on "creation." This effect seemed to come from the stars in the background and the "gaseous" feeling I got from the green base. Still the predominant mood was one of uneasiness. Things did not seem to be quite right.

Test Subject B: female, age 35, high school teacher.

Coolness, remoteness, aloneness, aloofness, separateness, disengagement. These further resulted in fear, near panic, helplessness, and hopelessness.

Now it is scary! I don't even want to look at it. I want to put this "thing" as far away from me as I can get it.

It is hideous, like a monster. I feel trembling and I can feel perspiration on my hand. My rate of breathing has increased. This is so queer! I enjoyed the coolness of it initially. What has happened to me? I feel such a fear of this thing! This feeling didn't develop though, I think, until I started to write down the words. As I did so, I could sense this panic feeling building. Now I don't even want to look back at the ad to analyze it. Right now I dread the thought of doing so tomorrow night. It is as if by doing so I'll have to face something painful. I would rather look at a nest of wiggling snakes.

I still can't get rid of that terrible feeling. I feel as if "something" were going to get me. It is a childish, primitive fear. Now I am ashamed of myself.

Shocking? Indeed, it is very shocking. This highly successful commercial representation might have been designed for display on the walls of a men's toilet by some frustrated exhibitionist. But far from it. The ad was designed by skilled, highly paid technicians in the fine art of subliminal manipulation.

It is staggering to consider that this subliminally pornographic Gilbey's ad could enter the homes of 5.5 million families and be read by up to 24.2 million individuals. Incredibly, none of these readers will consciously perceive what is being done to them. Many, indeed, will even respond to the subliminal promise of a wild sexual indulgence and purchase Gilbey's gin. The truth, of course, is that of all the enemies of sexual virility, alcohol is at the top of the list.

There are several other versions of the ad which have appeared in such publications as *TV Guide* and *Reader's Digest*. But again, this is only one illustration of subliminal technique—only one among thousands.

This, in essence, is what *Subliminal Seduction* is all about. First, however, we will look into a world in which media dominate the customs and culture, the norms and the nuances. And to gain meaningful insights, we must learn to look from almost a microscopic perspective at representative bits and pieces. Media content is assembled in small bits and pieces, but presented as an avalanche of perceptual stimuli in which the bits and pieces have become invisible. To penetrate the illusions and trickery, we must take a close-up, almost molecular approach to media content analysis. This is not at all easy, as our nervous systems have been carefully trained not to perceive consciously what is going on at this level.

It is virtually impossible to comprehend subliminal perception, or even to recognize it, without having explored various theories of perception and behavior. The next two chapters will survey and summarize what is known about subliminal phenomena.

2. The Language Within a Language

Subliminal Languages Are Not Taught in Schools: The basis of modern media effectiveness is a language within a language—one that communicates to each of us at a level beneath our conscious awareness, one that reaches into the uncharted mechanism of the human unconscious. This is a language based upon the human ability to *subliminally* or *subconsciously* or *unconsciously* perceive information This is a language that today has actually produced the profit base for North American mass communication media. It is virtually impossible to pick up a newspaper or magazine, turn on a radio or television set, read a promotional pamphlet or the telephone book, or shop through a supermarket without having your subconscious purposely massaged by some monstrously clever artist, photographer, writer, or technician. As a culture, North America might well be described as one enormous, magnificent, self-service, subliminal massage parlor.

Subliminal perception is not a new phenomenon. The existence of the human unconscious has been documented over many centuries by composers, artists, poets, philosophers, and scientists. An intellectual fad exists today, especially in America, that insists nothing is significant unless it can be consciously quantified and programmed into a computer. Creative experiences and other insights into the subliminal dimensions of language and human behavior are often discarded as meaningless romanticism. Measurements are often confused with quantification. I quantify, therefore I am—reads the metaphysic of modern social science research.

Intuitive or insight logic, on the other hand, appears based upon an implicit perception at a level that cannot be defended as conscious thought. Insight conclusions are reached with limited, if any, conscious awareness of the process by

11

which the conclusion was obtained. Such conclusions are often even derogatorily described as *intuitions* or *guesses*.

The Creative Unconscious

Many of the most significant scientific discoveries have been derived from intuitive, unconscious, or insight logic—including Albert Einstein's discovery of the relativity equations, if we can accept his own autobiographical testimony as to how the concept developed.

Much, if not most, of significant human thought operates in this strange wilderness of the unconscious mind. The unconscious apparently does not simply perceive *things,* but somehow perceives *the meaning of things.* Unconscious thought processes have long been believed to be the source of man's creative ability, perhaps the source of all his innovations. Composer Richard Wagner explained that mythology, folklore, and music—especially music—are the unconscious of the storyteller, composer, or musician speaking to the unconscious of the audience, society, or culture.

Several theorists believe intuitions and the entire creative process may be grouped together with dreams and subliminal perception as *prelogical insight experiences,* as opposed to the logical processes of reason through which humans consciously and purposefully rationalize their actions and feelings.

Point One: This study proceeds upon the premise that there exists in the human brain and nervous system something (a mechanism of uncertain description) responsible for such labels as the *unconscious* or the *subconscious.* That this machinery exists can be empirically demonstrated, beyond any doubt, to be a vital aspect of human behavior in all its manifestations.

Point Two: How this machinery (subconscious, unconscious, or what have you) works is largely unknown. Science, philosophy, and technology have so far produced only theories about how this subliminal portion of the brain functions. At present we really do not comprehend—in terms of bio-neuro-chemo-etc., operations, interrelationships, and actual circuitry—how the brain functions.

The various theories of both individual and social behavior, nevertheless, are often useful—not necessarily true, nor necessarily false—only useful. Most intellectual progress and comprehension of complex phenomena cease once the

mind deludes itself into believing it has uncovered a Holy
Grail or an eternal truth. *Any meaningful analysis of reality
must consider all such so-called truths as merely tentative
expedients.*

This writer, therefore, cannot be completely certain
whether Carl Jung's theory of archetypal symbolism, or
Freud's theory of dream significance, or Arnheim's theory of
Gestalt form significance, or Adler's inferiority complex the-
orization are right or wrong. They could well be either, or
both. The defense or rejection of theory will be left to other
writers searching for new theoretical syntheses.

As subliminal perception phenomena can be dealt with
only in terms of theoretical assumptions, theories will be
applied in this book only as a source from which subliminal
phenomena can be explored. Much of this phenomena cannot be considered, explained, or even discussed without reference to theory as a tool with which to probe the unknown.

Any specialized reader, such as an artist concerned with
actually embedding subliminal stimuli in a painting, would
likely benefit from more precise explorations into the numerous theories of, say, how the human eye functions—no
one is completely certain just how or why an eye performs.
Theory is vitally important to an understanding of the highly complex world of illusions and realities in which we continue to survive. The social sciences have really produced
very little certain, hard, or real knowledge during the past
half century. Much of the present-day social sciences could
be critically described as *antisocial* and *unscientific.* So much
for this theory of theories.

This volume, therefore, has a limited objective—simply to
establish and demonstrate the existence of subliminal reception within the human body and the use of subliminal
techniques in the communication media which assault our
senses during many hours of each day. This assault from the
media has a specific ability to manage, control, and manipulate human behavior in the interests of a multibillion dollar
national economy.

The range of effects upon the human nervous system of
subliminal massaging through the media can only be touched
upon in this volume. We know, beyond any question, that
subliminal stimuli sell products. There is no question in the
author's mind that these stimuli do much more to people
than just sell them deodorants, denture adhesives, and the
like. But the question of sociopathic or psychopathic media

effects must be left to another study. It will likely be most
difficult for many readers to consider the effects of a phenomenon or technique they are still reluctant to admit exists.

Mechanical Man—A Model

Though the mass communication media at present exploit
primarily two of the human sensory inputs into the brain—
sight and hearing—some of what is known about human
sensory abilities should be briefly reviewed.

Aristotle initially explored the significance of our five basic
senses: sight, hearing, taste, feeling, and smell. His definitions
ended up in theological dogma, and severely restricted Western man's view of himself for nearly 2,000 years. During the
Middle Ages the concept of five senses was integrated into
scholastic philosophy, later to appear in such church ritual
as *extreme unction*—a ceremony, performed by a priest when
a person is near death, involving a blessing of the five senses.

Even further limiting man's view of himself were the various mechanistic schools of psychology in the twentieth century which insisted that senses be studied in isolation. For
example, many current university psychology courses evaluate *sight* as separate from *taste,* from *hearing,* etc. This
simplistic approach to man's study of his own body is often
thought amusing by Asiatic scholars, many of whom have
developed under an intellectual tradition that saw man as a
naturally integrated assemblage of sensory inputs. The inte-
grative-man notion is paramount in the traditions of Bud-
dhist, Taoist, Confucian, and Hindu thought. Only recently
in the West has an integrative, non-Aristotelian insight into
how man experiences the world and himself begun to develop as an aspect of existential philosophy, general semantics, and Zen Buddhism.

In simple practical terms, the idea can be demonstrated
by the serving of food in Asiatic, as opposed to Western,
traditions. In the East all senses are considered to be involved in dining. The way food appears, or feels, or smells
influences the flavor. Also, of course, the total dining environment—emotions, color, temperature, sound, etc.—affect the
flavor of the food. Perhaps thanks to Aristotle, and the institutions that used his studies as instruments of power, it is
often very difficult for Westerners to appreciate all that is
involved sensually even in such a simple and routine experience as dining.

Today, in the last half of the twentieth century, the concept of five senses is hopelessly anachronistic. There are generally acknowledged to exist at least thirty-seven differentiated sensory inputs into the human brain. More senses will likely be discovered and added to the list as time goes on. Of the thirty-seven senses, over two dozen are involved with touching.

If humans could be said to possess one basic sensory input that supplies the brain with information, it would involve *touching*—the sensation or experience of tactility. A human simply could not adjust and survive without touching. This could include both actual contact touching and touching by *synesthesia*, whereby touching can be experienced visually or via another sensory input; the phenomenon is frequently studied in art schools. One example of synesthesia would be a picture of a textured fabric which could stimulate the brain into a feeling of tactility or touching. Examples of synesthesia in art will be discussed later, in relation to a *Playboy* centerfold.

Now, considering there are at least thirty-seven sensory inputs, all these senses are inputting data simultaneously and constantly into the brain. A bias—temporarily favoring sight, or hearing, or whatever—may occur as a person changes concentration from, say, a newspaper to a radio broadcast, but none of the senses ever stops operating. Cooking aromas from the kitchen become an unnoticed or subliminal part of the message transmitted by a television program being viewed in the living room while dinner is being prepared.

This complex of at least thirty-seven separate sensory inputs into the brain—all operating continuously and simultaneously in a constantly changing series of biases where one sense or several become temporarily dominant—is complicated. But, the human sensory machine is even more complicated than even this suggests.

Conscious-Unconscious Perception

Data provided from studies in neurology and psychology strongly support the conclusion that all senses (including those yet undiscovered) operate on at least two perceptual levels. Information is collected at what might be called a cognitive or conscious level, a level where each human is consciously aware of what is going on. Information is also collected simultaneously and continuously at a subliminal

level, a level at which there is no consciously apparent
awareness of data entering the brain. There could be many
other levels between conscious and unconscious perception,
but for purposes of illustration, the discussion or theory will
be restricted to only those two—conscious and unconscious.

These two major perceptual input subsystems are capable
of operating quite independently of one another, often in direct opposition to one another. For example, a young man
might consciously desire a sexual experience so strongly that
he can think of nothing else. At the unconscious level, however, the young man could be terrified of sexual involvement.
These two thought processes operating simultaneously within our young man could result in substantial unhappiness,
possibly impotence.

The system that processes subliminal stimuli appears to
deal mostly with very basic emotional information content
and is thought to be the oldest part of the human brain
developed during evolution. These simple subliminal manifestations of brain activity go on even when one is unconscious, or asleep, or in a coma. Further, many theorists maintain that the conscious mind merely adapts itself to the basic
program established in the unconscious; *no significant belief
or attitude held by any individual is apparently made on the
basis of consciously perceived data.* Conscious considerations,
rationalizations, and the significance given them by an individual appear to be merely accommodations to the unconscious.

The basic attitudinal or perceptual frame of reference,
through which data are evaluated, appears to operate
through the so-called unconscious. But, and this is important
to consider, all human perception—whether conscious or unconscious—is a struggle toward meaning and significance.
The name of the perceptual game, in fact, is *meaning*—a
large measure of which our culture demands we repress or
somehow consciously avoid.

So for the moment, consider each human brain as being
simultaneously and continuously fed information by at least
thirty-seven senses operating on at least two levels of perception. As bewildering, complicated, and possibly frightening as
this appears, it has presumably been happening in our bodies
for a very long time. Also, keep in mind how rapidly this
human machine operates. Impulses flow through neurons in
the body at a speed of roughly 60 meters per second. In the
intricate complex of neurological structures within the body,

a staggering number of events can occur during, say, the time it takes a pencil to reach the floor after being dropped from the hand.

Another analogy, based upon the work of George Miller and others who study language and behavior phenomena, suggests that the words the human voice speaks are seven, plus or minus two, ahead or behind those already assembled in the brain waiting to be spoken. In other words, as these individual words are being written down, the author's brain is actually five to nine words ahead of the typewriter.

Perception, as Marshall McLuhan has expressed it, is total. Everything happens and is perceived in totality. The editing process—the small portion that becomes conscious—is somehow accomplished inside the brain, which retains the major portion of what is totally perceived in some kind of storage, over varying periods of time, completely unknown consciously to the individual.

The incredible complexity and speed of all language and behavior phenomena—and the inability of an individual to visualize this speed and complexity—make the whole subject of subliminal perception difficult to accept. This is especially true in Western cultures, which have strongly reinforced the individual's self-delusion that he can, and even must, consciously know all of what is going on around him.

The processes generally described above are largely unknown by what we presently refer to as "science," especially in terms of the complex interrelationships involved. There are only theories available which *attempt* to explain all of this—sometimes useful theories, but only theories. Modern man is still quite uncertain as to how the language and behavior mechanisms within his body actually function.

Environmental Subliminal Influences

Both our natural and man-made environments are full of influences perceived at this subliminal level; many of them remain subliminal simply because they are common, everyday aspects of our lives that go unnoticed consciously. It appears strange that so many contemporary social and behavioral scientists have carefully and systematically ignored such obvious things as the subliminal effects of, say, body language upon human relationships. This cannot be dismissed as merely an oversight.

Indeed, subliminal stimuli appear to be normal, perhaps

even necessary, to human survival and adjustment. These invisible perceptions apparently provide humans with significance in an otherwise insecure and unstable world. Subliminals could not be legislated out of existence. Perhaps some of the excessive and potentially destructive commercial applications in the press and television might be restrained, or at least exposed, discussed, argued, and studied; but, subliminal influences will be a part of human life as long as there are humans. Somehow humans must learn to live with them.

The term *subliminal perception* will be used here to describe sensory inputs into the human nervous system that circumvent or are repressed from conscious awareness—or, more simply, inputs that communicate with the unconscious. The term has, of course, popular implications which suggest brainwashing, manipulation, and other unsavory—though romantic—practices. Other, possibly more scientifically defensible names for the phenomenon are *subliminal reception, threshold regulation, unconscious perception, and subception*.

Indeed, it might well be argued that today—in a modern world dependent upon and emersed within an environment dominated by the mass media—anyone who cannot read and understand the subliminal languages of symbolic illusion is functionally illiterate.

Industrial designers include subliminal meanings in products such as automobiles, soft-drink bottles, lawn mowers, clothing, food containers, cosmetics, pharmaceutical products, homes and home furnishings, appliances, and virtually everything produced for consumers in our commercial fairyland of mass production.

The packaging industry, for example, has long since ceased to be simply the provider of bottles, tubes, and cartons into which something is safely and conveniently stored. Packagers are today merchants of symbolic images which supply significance and fictional delusions of variety and value to a multitude of competitive products. A stroll through any modern supermarket will reveal that for many of the items which we have come to view as life necessities, the packaging has cost more than the contents. Competition among consumer products has developed into a contest between competitive symbols or images rather than between material values. And the struggle for market supremacy is waged through the consumers' unconscious minds rather than through their conscious awareness.

As an example, the giant New York-headquartered International Flavor and Fragrances, Inc.—with 1971 sales of $112 million, manufacturing outlets in fourteen countries, and sales in over a hundred countries—has contributed to Masters and Johnson's Reproductive Biology Research Foundation for studies into the relationship between odor and sex. Scientists have long been aware that higher mammals communicate by secreting subliminal odorous substances. IFF is hot on the track of a subliminal aromatic released by women during ovulation. If they can synthesize a chemical capable of amplifying the odor, consider the possible effects of such a subliminal aromatic in perfumes and colognes.

Struggles to Understand the Unconscious

The first recorded mention of subliminal perception may be in the writings of Democritus (400 B.C.), who maintained "much is perceptible which is not perceived by us." Plato also dealt with the notion in his work *Timaeus*. Aristotle more specifically discussed subliminal awareness thresholds in his *Parva Naturalia* nearly two thousand years ago and appears to have been the first to suggest that consciously unperceived stimuli could affect dreams. Aristotle, 2,250 years ago, explained in his dream theory that: "Impulses occurring in the daytime, if they are not very great and powerful, pass unnoticed because of greater waking impulses. But in the time of sleep, the opposite takes place, for then small impulses seem to be great. This is clear from what happens in sleep. Men believe it is lightning and thundering when there are only faint echoes in their ears. They believe they are enjoying honey and sweet flowers, when only a drop of phlegm is slipping down their throats." Aristotle anticipated what in the early twentieth century came to be known as the *Poetzle effect*.

The philosopher Montaigne alluded to the phenomenon of subliminal perception in 1580. Leibniz, in 1698, also probed the notion that "There are numberless perceptions, little noticed, which are not sufficiently distinguished to be perceived or remembered, but which become known through certain consequences."

The work of Sigmund Freud and his colleagues, during the late nineteenth and early twentieth centuries, explored new concepts and theories of the subconscious or unconscious. Freud's dream theory formed a basis upon which one of his associates, Dr. O. Poetzle, made one of the first scientifically significant discoveries about subliminal perception. Freud described dreams as having three major characteristics: (1) they preserved sleep by converting potentially disturbing material into dream images; (2) they represented wish fulfillments; and (3) dream stimuli were symbolically transformed before emerging in the dream, especially those stimuli potentially threatening to an individual.

Poetzle discovered that a stimulus or information consciously noted by a person does not appear in subsequent dreams. Studying reactions to embedded or hidden figures in drawings, Poetzle discovered that dream content was apparently drawn from stimuli perceived at an unconscious level prior to the dream. The scientist formulated his *Law of Exclusion* around the curious observation that humans exclude consciously perceived data from dreams. He concluded that dream content was primarily composed of subliminally perceived information. Poetzle speculated that Freud's transformation concept, the third dream characteristic, was essentially a transformation of subliminally perceived material. This transformation phenomenon was later described as a *perceptual defense*—a mechanism whereby the individual protects himself from information which might have unpleasant, potentially damaging, or anxiety-producing consequences. The threatening information deposited in the unconscious must either remain buried or be transformed into something relatively harmless before admission to consciousness. Dream analysis during psychotherapy is based upon interpreting the transformed state slowly and carefully so a patient can learn to live comfortably with the troublesome memory as it emerges from the unconscious.

Poetzle's colleagues theorized that the eyes make about 100,000 fixations daily—only a small portion of the information in these fixations is consciously experienced. Somehow, subliminally perceived content is singled out and transformed for reproduction in dreams at a later point in time. This discovery suggested that subliminally induced stimuli performed with a delayed reaction "alarm clock" or "time bomb" effect upon behavior.

A conscious association can, in effect, trigger a subliminal percept buried deeply in the unconscious weeks, months, or possibly years after the subliminal percept occurred. Consider the promise such a demonstrable theory held for anyone in the business of controlling and influencing human behavior.

By 1919 a relationship was strongly established by Poetzle between *subliminal stimuli, posthypnotic suggestion,* and *compulsive neurosis.* An individual will perform acts which he has been instructed or programmed to do without any knowledge of why he is doing such a thing. The relationship between subliminal stimuli and posthypnotic suggestions is extremely important.

Unseen Manipulators

The study of subliminal perception again came to public attention in the late 1950s. Behavioral scientists had quietly experimented with Poetzle's theories for thirty years. In 1957 one American market researcher, James Vicary, demonstrated the tachistoscope, a machine for flashing on a screen invisible messages which could be seen by the subconscious. After the publication in 1958 of Vance Packard's book, *The Hidden Persuaders,* motivation researchers Ernest Dichter and Louis Cheskin were publicly admonished for their scientific contributions which had supported advertisers' attempts to manipulate mass audiences.

At the time, legislators and the public were shocked at the implications involved in subliminal or subaudial perception. Legislation was introduced—though never passed—in half a dozen state legislatures and in the U.S. Senate, to prohibit legally the use of subliminal techniques in the public communication media.

This public reaction of a dozen years ago is interesting to review. *Newsday* regarded the subliminal device as "the most alarming invention since the atomic bomb." *The New Yorker* stated, "we had reached the sad age when minds and not just houses could be broken and entered." Phyllis Battelle of the *New York Journal-American* said, "Aside from my basic horror at the idea of being prodded into acting without all my wits about me . . . I picture the invisible commercial as a direct route to incontinence." *The Saturday Review* was eloquent. In a full-page editorial they said: "The subconscious mind is the most delicate part of the most delicate apparatus in the entire universe. It is not to be smudged, sullied or twisted in order to boost the sales of popcorn or anything else. Nothing is more difficult in the modern world than to protect the privacy of the human soul." Congressman James

Wright of Texas sponsored a Federal bill to forbid any device that was "designed to advertise a product or indoctrinate the public by means of making an impression on the subconscious mind."

In a recent survey of business and community leaders, the more than 90 percent who had heard of subliminal communication techniques believed the techniques to be prohibited by statute in both the United States and Canada. Many individuals interviewed appeared revolted at even the suggestion that such techniques would be considered for use by American business. Roughly 60 percent of those who had heard of subliminals believed the whole idea of subliminal communication was absurd, science-fiction nonsense.

A check of U.S. and Canadian statutes failed to turn up any legal prohibitions against the use of subliminal or subaudial techniques in public communication. Though many such laws were introduced during 1957-58, and their introduction received wide publicity, none of these laws was ever enacted. It was, therefore, strange to discover that virtually everyone appeared to believe himself protected from manipulation through his unconscious. Even those who did not believe such manipulation possible were certain they were "protected by laws."

Mechanical Induction

The initial experiments with mechanically induced subliminal perception were based upon the tachistoscope which is simply a film projector with a high-speed shutter which flashes messages every five seconds at 1/3000th of a second. The speeds can be varied for different effects. The tachistoscope was patented through the United States patent office by Precon Process and Equipment Corporation of New Orleans, October 30, 1962, and carries patent number 3,060,795.

The tachistoscope was initially used to flash messages superimposed over motion pictures in theaters or upon film being transmitted through television. The high-speed messages were invisible to the conscious mind, but planted messages in the viewer's unconscious which were acted upon by a statistically significant number of people. During one six-week test of the machine in a theater, involving 45,699 patrons, messages were flashed on alternate days: "Hungry? Eat Popcorn," and "Drink Coca-Cola." During the six weeks, popcorn sales increased 57.7 percent and Coca-Cola sales 18.1 percent.

Audience reactions to tachistoscope-induced messages have been exhaustively studied. Though all people cannot be influenced so simply, a statistically significant number of people in any audience will obey the commands given subliminally, apparently, as long as there is no deep conflict about the command within their mind.

For example, a person who really hated a certain product, say "Clink," would not likely respond to subliminal messages commanding him to "Buy Clink." Considering the semantic possibilities available to advertisers, however, this may be small consolation. The conscious content might say "Buy Clink," which the viewer rejects at the conscious level. The subliminal message might read, "Buy Virility with Clink." What North American male could resist the promise of virility?

A recent chat with the research director of a major national food product distributor revealed that his corporation had sold his tachistoscope three years earlier. He called the instrument "obsolete" and proceeded to explain the latest twist in mechanical subliminal perception devices.

Light intensity projected beneath the level of conscious awareness brings about an audience reaction far superior to that achieved by the tachistoscope. A simple projector is connected to a rheostat and the light intensity is turned down to below the level that the conscious eye perceives. The message, nevertheless, is still perceived by the unconscious mind.

The research director explained this is far more effective than the tachistoscope, because the message is transmitted continuously rather than intermittently and cannot be detected. Tachistoscope flashes are apparent in an oscilloscope as they intermittently break up the continuous patterns. Low-intensity light is undetectable since it becomes a regular part of the continuing wave pattern. Experiments with ultraviolet photography, he explained, have also failed to detect the unseen images. Brief telephone calls during July, 1971, to New York, Chicago, and Toronto located thirteen commercial research firms which offered mechanically induced subliminal message services to advertisers, or anyone for that matter, who could pay their fee.

Frightening though it may appear, devices to mechanically induce subliminal stimuli are much more than merely marketing toys. They are being used commercially every day in North America, but they do imply a certain risk of discovery and public denouncement. There are other, nonmechanically induced, subliminal techniques just as effective.

Today in American advertising it is not what you consciously see that sells, it is what stimulates the unconscious. In the words of Marshall McLuhan, "advertising is a subliminal pill designed to massage the unconscious."

Current State of the Art

Experimental research in the late 1950s yielded data strongly emphasizing the enormous potential for the mass communication industry of subliminally induced print and electronic media content.

By the late 1960s subliminal perception had been exhaustively tested in at least eight areas of human behavior: *dreams, memory, value norm anchor points, conscious perception, verbal behavior, emotions, drives,* and *perceptual defenses.* There is, at present, no serious question that human activity can be influenced by stimulation or information of which individuals, groups, or even societies are completely unaware.

Dreams: The study of dreams has provided wide insights into subliminal phenomena. Subliminally induced content, such as that in the Gilbey's ad (Figure 1), has been recovered from dreams days or weeks after the initial exposure. Dream analysis has, for over half a century, provided a major technique of demonstrating the existence of subliminally induced information in the minds of test subjects over extended time periods. Dreams, of course, are one of the major empirical events regularly occurring through which unconscious processess can be studied.

A strong relationship has been developed between posthypnotic suggestions and subliminally induced information. The two techniques of manipulating the unconscious appear to have much in common. In fact, the hypnosis model may provide insight into the individual or social influences of subliminal media content.

Subliminal stimuli and posthypnotic suggestions are both unavailable to normal conscious perception. They both affect behavior without conscious awareness. And, they both involve a unique *trusting* relationship between subject and hypnotist or audience and media.

Like posthypnotic suggestions, subliminal stimuli may cause a symbolic transformation or modification before the information emerges in a dream. Subliminally induced dreams are relatively easy to decode when the input or stimulus is known to a researcher. In one experiment with posthypnotic suggestion a female volunteer test subject was told while under hypnosis that she would dream about committing fellatio with her employer, toward whom she professed antagonism. The instruction was then removed from her consciousness by posthypnotic amnesia—simply a suggestion she not remember the instructions upon waking. She was also given a posthypnotic instruction to report dreams which occurred that night. The next day she reported a dream in which she bit off the end of a banana which had been offered to her by the employer.

Some theorists believe that subliminal perception, like posthypnotic suggestions, is unlikely to cause anyone to do anything he might not wish to do under normal life conditions. One note of caution should nevertheless be considered. A posthypnotic suggestion might well lead a subject to follow a command he might not consciously wish to follow, but unconsciously desire very strongly to follow. Experiments have shown that some test subjects under hypnosis will throw what they believe to be acid into another person's face after a posthypnotic suggestion to do so.

Similarly, information has been recovered from the dreams of test subjects exposed to several of the illustrations in this book. The Gilbey's orgy (Figure 1) was recovered from dreams several days after exposure in the form of a kissing game at a children's party where "spin the bottle" was played. The test subject thought it rather strange that the six children in her dream were drinking Gilbey's gin.

The three subliminal wolves in the Calvert Volcano ad (see Figure 16) were recovered from a dream a week after exposure as three wolves howling outside a cabin while the test subject lay dead surrounded by his family who were drinking whiskey—the subject was uncertain of the brand.

The Con in Confidence

The apparent similarities between subliminal stimuli and posthypnotic suggestions are extremely important in terms of the *trusting* relationship necessary for the two techniques' effectiveness in planting suggestions within the unconscious.

Mass communication media's image of *trust* or confidence (often referred to as a high credibility source), which has been established by public relations, as vital to advertising and media effectiveness. Unless magazines, newspapers, or TV programs communicate an image of trust and confidence, subliminal advertising content will not effectively and predictably motivate brand preferences or purchasing activity.

A curious parallel seems to exist between media—with its high-credibility images—and the confidence man. In a prison environment, for example, the one crime not accepted by inmates is *confidence* or *bunko*. Inmates are generally indifferent to the criminal conviction responsible for their cellmates' incarceration. Murderers, thieves, rapists, and the rest live more or less compatibly with other inmates. The con man is the one notable exception and, invariably, the loneliest man in prison. Inmates know that in order to commit a bunko or con, the mark had to be first manipulated into a trusting relationship.

Similarly, in the mass communication industry, media content—news, programming, and the like—has degenerated into devices to create a high-credibility media image which can be merchandized to advertisers. Once the reader or viewer trusts or believes or identifies, subliminal advertising content —like posthypnotic suggestions—can most effectively control and modify human behavior. Media audiences should be cautioned never to forget the *con* in confidence or the *sin* in sincere.

Public-communication media have concentrated upon the development of subliminal technique directed at audio-visual sensory inputs during the past fifteen years.

Conscious perception operates within specific frequencies of both light and sound. However, outside the range consciously perceived by the eye and ear, sub-threshold frequencies exist which are capable of communication. Information transmitted at these invisible frequencies is perceived only by the unconscious portion of the human brain.

Thus, visually there is a finite limit for both speed and intensities of light that can be consciously perceived by the eye; the frequency ranges outside this limit are invisible to the eye and the conscious mind and are capable of inputting data into the unconscious. Likewise, auditory perception at the conscious level is limited to a finite range of sound, volume, and tonal frequency levels; beyond these ranges are frequencies where information can be transmitted invisibly into the unconscious.

The so-called "silent dog whistle" is an example of sound frequencies invisible to human conscious perception—though dogs consciously hear these high frequencies. People can also hear these whistles, though not via their mechanism of conscious perception. Data transmitted at these high tonal frequencies will register in the unconscious.

One of the striking things encountered in the literature of subliminal perception is the repeated emphasis upon *passive receptivity* as a means by which individuals can become aware of subliminal stimuli. Pressure or tension appears to limit an individual's sensitivity to (ability to consciously perceive) subliminals. The most effective means of making such material available to consciousness is by learning to relax completely. Tests under hypnosis, self-hypnosis, yoga meditation, as well as relaxation simply by deep breathing, indicate that often subliminals can become liminal simply through relaxation.

Indeed, relaxation appears to have an extraordinary effect upon human perception. In one case, after several minutes of deep breathing and relaxation, several obscene words in a liquor advertisement appeared out of a background. Someone in the room asked a question. Though the observer did not answer at that moment, the mere tension-creating effect of the question upon his nervous system inhibited his perception of the low-threshold stimuli. The subliminally embedded obscene words simply disappeared from conscious view in response to the question.

It appears that *once the subliminal information becomes apparent to the conscious mind, the persuasive or manipulative potential in the data is destroyed*. Insidiously, however, the more subliminal or deeply buried a stimulus, the greater the probable effect. This can be demonstrated by a simple straight line. From A to B, let us say, is the range of conscious perception either at the auditory or visual level. Line 1 to A is the range of subliminal perception.

$$\overline{1 \qquad A \qquad\qquad\qquad B}$$

The closer the stimulus is to 1, the more effective it is likely to be. Suppose the word SEX was embedded in an ad at a subliminal level just below A. They might embed the word

FUCK or SUCK at an even deeper subliminal level slightly above 1. The deeper embedded words would have the strongest impact upon the psyche.

Behavioral Effects

Verbal Behavior: Not only have the taboo four-letter words proved effective in manipulating the response of mass audiences, but other words, with taboo implications, have also been demonstrated to possess subliminal power. Words such as *shot* (shit), *whose* (whore), *pints* (penis), and *cult* (cunt), which differ by only one or two letters from certain taboo and emotional words, can evoke strong demonstrable emotional reactions of which the individual is totally unaware. The word *tastes* is very frequently used in ad copy. A slight change of one letter, and the word becomes *testes*. Twenty-six advertisements in a recent issue of *Life* magazine used the word *come* in their ad copy.

A wide range of experiments have shown that these emotionally loaded words can actually evoke physiological signs of emotional disturbance. Electroencephalograph (EEG) tests on people while they were exposed to word lists containing words with emotional implications, have produced increases in theta rhythms, variations in heart rate, and suppression of alpha rhythms—reactions similar to those of people under strong emotional stimulation.

Memory: What is generally referred to as memory takes on much greater complexity when both the conscious and unconscious memories are considered. Information within the memory, or storage area within the brain, fluctuates in and out of conscious awareness in response to complex association patterns which appear to be dampened or modulated by perceptual defense or repression mechanisms.

Humans, in effect, remember what they wish to remember, and—in one degree or another—have the ability to forget, ignore, or repress information which might produce anxiety or discomfort. Memory is tied inextricably to the acceptable wisdoms within a society or culture.

Merchandisers, by embedding subliminal *trigger* devices in media, are able to evoke a strong emotional relationship between, say, a product perceived in an advertisement weeks before and the strongest of all emotional stimuli—love (sex) and death. Most of the illustrations used in this book demonstrate subliminal technique as memory enrichment or delayed-action memory stimuli.

Memory, further, appears organized in terms of a specific item's emotional importance to an individual. Most perceptual defenses, ways each human has of avoiding anxiety-producing conscious memories, will limit conscious memory.

SEX also establishes—in our culture—the distinct subliminal possibility of rejection. Rejection fear is a deeply conditioned aspect of North American culture. We are never permitted to ignore the expectation of rejection; it is emphasized repeatedly in advertising for cosmetics, deodorants, clothing, drugs, tobacco, alcohol, and so on. Beginning with the peculiarities of our no-touch culture, where parents stop touching children at very early ages, the fear of rejection is a well-oiled main bearing in the engine of American marketing and sales promotion.

Rejection fear is especially pernicious as it operates, for the most part, beneath our conscious awareness. When the fear of rejection subliminally activates an early infantile memory of rejection—of which everyone has an abundance in our society—an unconscious oral fantasy will almost always be evoked. Feelings of rejection, it has been abundantly demonstrated, are usually dealt with by some oral indulgence —eating, smoking, drinking, etc.

Value Judgments

Value Norm Anchor Points: One very critical and disturbing consequence of subliminal manipulation has been demonstrated in dozens of experiments by changing the position (anchor point) from which an individual evaluates the world about him. Anchor points might be described as the position between two opposed concepts from which an individual evaluates loud or soft, heavy or light, good or bad, moral or immoral, rich or poor, strong or weak, sane or insane, and so on. A subliminal stimulus and a posthypnotic suggestion both have the ability to move the anchor point between virtually any two such concepts in any direction desired.

As an illustration, two university classes were shown a picture of a male model taken from a *Playboy* magazine advertisement projected upon a screen. They were asked to evaluate the ad in terms of masculine and feminine on a five-point scale.

The first class evaluated the model as it appeared in the

magazine. Over 95 percent of the students classified the model within a range of 3-4 on the scale. The students were very similar as to ages, socio-economic backgrounds, religions, etc.

Another similar group of students was shown the same *Playboy* ad, but superimposed upon the projection was a tachistoscoped word flashed invisibly at 1/3000th of a second every five seconds: MAN. The scale dramatically changed when they were requested to evaluate what they consciously thought they saw:

Masculine	1	2	3	4	5	Feminine
1st Class	1	2	66	29	2	
2nd Class	26	35	21	11	7	

Value norms are critically important to human survival and adjustment.

Humans are continuously indoctrinated by the invisible pressures of "culture" toward certain anchor points or base reference points for evaluations. For example, people within a generally common culture will tend to agree on general criteria of hot or cold, loud or soft, heavy or light, large or small, strong or weak. Compared with a Panamanian, an Eskimo would have a totally different concept of hot and cold. Teen-agers, with their rock music, have a different notion of loud and soft than do most adults. A construction engineer who operates a giant crane daily has different reference points for heavy and light than does a watchmaker.

In a single culture, however, there is strong unconscious adherence to a large assemblage of reference points. They are usually not acknowledged or discussed until someone ignores or violates them. This violation occurs often from outsiders, who are likely to be punished for their transgressions against what is "normal" in the particular group.

Small discrepancies from these reference points can be pleasant, providing diversity and innovation. Large discrepancies from the reference points tend to be very unpleasant, often evoking group-imposed suppression or controls.

Value norms involve nearly everything in our lives—from notions of temperature to complex standards of sexual or economic behavior—and most are invisible. Anchor points can be moved around, controlled if you will, by subliminal stimuli. Anchors can even be added if they do not exist, or manipulated upward or downward to serve a commercial objective.

Rock music is an example of media content which, over a number of years, drastically changed the meaning of loud and soft in order to even further isolate a rich market segment for record sales. High-volume sound is isolating, whether it emanates from hi-fi stereophonic speakers or from a boiler factory. Isolated markets are exclusive hunting grounds for marketing technicians.

It should be relatively easy, given the power of mass communication media, to reorganize verbal value systems surrounding any individual or subject. For example, a political candidate could be made to appear more honest, more trustworthy, and more sincere than his actual appearance and voice might lead one to believe. These values, one might conclude, are often illusions buried within illusions.

A long-time basic theorem of successful popular recording is the simple principle that the kids will buy almost anything certain to drive their parents up the wall. As far as anyone can find out, this has long been a fundamental principle of the record industry. Record companies, like so many other corporations dependent upon the youth market, have turned the coming-of-age problems of Americans into a solid industry which substitutes for what, in more primitive and tribal societies, would be considered a puberty ritual. Young people have always had the need to cut the cord at some point in time and become adults. This was a painful and too often traumatic experience even at the time of Socrates, as he testified in his *Dialogues*. There is no reason to believe it is any less painful today or, for that matter, more painful. It is a normal event in life; at least it was until it was proven to have staggering commercial possibilities.

A tribesman in a New Guinea aboriginal tribe, when he reaches puberty, will be sent out alone in the jungle to demonstrate his manhood. He will possibly kill an enemy in battle, shrink a head, or accomplish some other feat considered the prerogative of male adults. In our Madison Avenue-dominated society, heads are shrunk only in psychiatrists' offices. The record industry records the plaintive puberty pleadings on plastic discs which sell millions of copies.

By increasing the volume of popular music, thereby making the recordings even more unbearable to an older generation (selectively manipulating the anchor point between loud and soft between two age groups), rock music becomes even more special to the affluent youth culture. Judgments of loudness were altered by introducing tones and harmonics at subaudible levels. These subaudible sounds, especially those in the bass ranges, became audible when the volume was increased. Record producers, with their highly sophisticated electronic equipment, were like the farmer leading his jackass by a carrot dangling from a pole. They manipulated the rock market into reaching further and further for subaudible stimuli by continuing to increase volume. Volume increase expands the frequency range which can be heard at both conscious and unconscious levels.

However, there appears to be a human limitation regarding loudness. Many rock fans of five years ago, now in their early twenties, have begun to wear hearing aids. A few have already learned to read lips.

Cultural Sets

Conscious Perception: There is considerable evidence that consciousness is built around various groups of "sets," or ways of seeing, hearing, or experiencing the realities around us. Sets are usually established by cultures and subcultures. For example, many theorists have speculated that a society's basic sets or perspectives are established by *the economic means of subsistence.* An engineer will likely see a bridge across a deep canyon in far different terms than would a truck driver, social worker, or housewife who must cross the bridge to reach a market each day. A physician, moreover, would likely have a distinctively different organization of "sets" than would an automobile salesman. Some people are able to assimilate a large number of sets during their lifetime.

An example of set value systems would consist of the Soviet and the United States concepts of democracy. A citizen of either country would discuss democratic concepts with a passionate belief in the democratic *truthfulness* of his system. An outside observer, if one could be found who was uninvolved in the polemic, would find that each person's conceptualization of "democracy" was based upon an entirely different group of basic sets or perspectives. Both individuals were probably quite truthful in their concept of democracy as derived from their respective sets.

Sets are thought to be maintained by inhibitory mechanisms involved with human consciousness. This inhibitory process may be fundamental to the human's concept of reality. Another way of expressing the paradox is, *a way of seeing is also a way of not seeing*. Ways of coping with "right" or "wrong" concepts within a culture or society are established through the use of sets.

Sets can perhaps be generally defined as traditional or generally followed ways of perceiving reality at the conscious level. Subliminal conditioning by one's culture establishes these sets during early childhood. Culture has been defined as merely a unique organization of sets—sets, however, usually invisible to members of the culture.

The art of the stage magician, as well as the mass communication expert, involves circumventing these traditional ways in which the world is perceived. Various optical illusions —the famous two facing profiles outlining the shape of a goblet, for example—demonstrate the problem of sets. In the goblet illusion, the mind will likely keep switching back and forth between the two illusions—faces or goblet.

In the Gilbey's ad (Figure 1), however, the audience's established set pattern demands they see only a gin bottle and a collins glass. Indeed, at the conscious level at least, over 24 million readers presumably could have seen this page and consciously interpreted only what was within their traditional sets or culturally induced expectations. At the unconscious level, however, the real brand preference motivation trigger —an orgy with five participants—was fed into their unconsciouses. A major part of the set, of course, is the belief that the prestigious *Time* magazine would never do anything so outrageous to their readers. Such widespread belief in high-credibility information sources increases a society's vulnerability to subliminal manipulation.

Should the readers' conscious minds have been unable to channel closely into a set, the illusion could not have been used. Anyone able to think consciously outside his sets—a most difficult thing to do, usually requiring extensive training —would have stood an excellent chance of penetrating the illusion. Of the over 1,000 subjects involved in the many Gilbey's ad experiments, none ever penetrated the illusion or discovered the subliminal content on his own.

Interpretations of facial expressions have been experimentally demonstrated as modifiable by subliminal stimuli. In one such experiment, test groups were shown a sketch of an expressionless face. One group was subliminally exposed to the word *angry* subliminally tachistoscoped (at 1/3000th of a second) over the expressionless face. Another group received the word *happy* over the same face at the subliminal level. Both groups overwhelmingly interpreted the emotional content of the blank face consistent with the subliminal stimuli.

Backward masking or metacontrast is another technique which, though not purely subliminal, does affect both conscious and unconscious perception. The technique is used on television advertising and in TV programs such as "Laugh In." A quick joke sequence is spliced into the continuity ahead of a longer, slower, less funny comedy sequence. The quick sequence, though seen consciously, cannot be consciously remembered; it is masked by the later longer sequence. However, the emotional effect of the first sequence carries through the second.

Virtually everyone in North America has found himself laughing at a "Laugh In" joke without being able consciously to recall the joke. The quick splice simply establishes a carry-over mood for a longer, perhaps not so humorous sequence. Coca-Cola uses a similar approach in its rapid-interval mosaic television advertising. The technique has also been applied to poetry and literature.

Subliminal stimuli exert a significant influence upon behavior related to fantasy production. Consciously perceived sexual fantasies are common, predictable responses to subliminal materials. The fear of rejection, stimulated subliminally, has originated oral, wish-fulfillment fantasies built around some earlier rejection in the test subject's life. As *oral gratification is a basic human response to rejection threats*, the rejection theme is a persistent and successful technique used in the merchandising of cigarettes, cigars, pipe tobacco, and food.

In a series of experiments, commands were given to test subjects to perform certain acts, such as "write" or "don't write." When consciously perceived, the commands had virtually no effect upon the subjects when made against counter commands by an equally authoritative source. Subliminal commands, however, in spite of conscious counter commands, were acted upon by the test subjects.

Emotional Response

Three types of emotional experience—if they could be conveniently categorized and defined—to which the unconscious appears particularly sensitive include:

1. *Experiences that conflict with cultural taboos of long standing.* A large proportion of any society's taboos directly or indirectly involve sex and death—the beginning and the end of life.

2. *Experiences relative to personal or group neurosis or psychosis.* These would include a wide range of psychopathology—from phobic responses to serious delusions of persecution or even paranoia.

3. *Experiences acquired from recent painful or anxiety-producing situations.* These might include responses to a wide range of recent difficulties in such areas as marriage, health, employment, etc.

Much like hypnosis, subliminal stimuli have been demonstrated to arouse or initiate all three types of emotional experience as well as activate autonomic bodily functions —blood pressure, respiration, or other processes within the body which function automatically. As emotion and intellect are inextricably interrelated, emotional significance is an aspect of meaning. The ease or difficulty with which persons, words, pictures, or things are recognized depends upon their meaning or personal significance involving some aspect of emotion—fear, anger, love, hate, etc.

The stronger the emotional implication to an individual or group, the more powerful subliminal stimulation is likely to be. The more puritan or inhibited the individual or group receiving the stimuli, the more likely they are to be emotionally affected by stimuli counter to their inhibitions. The direction of emotional involvement appears relatively unimportant. At the subliminal level either love or death will ensure an emotional response and an identification with products or brands. The only emotional state mass media communicators must avoid, if they expect to be successful, is neutrality or indifference from their audience's unconscious.

Drive-Related Behavior: Memory is also related to drives or sources of motivation. Such drives as sex, aggression, hunger, thirst, territoriality, and maternity are sufficient to evoke related memories at either the conscious or unconscious level. Hunger, for example, could trigger a conscious or unconscious memory of a restaurant advertisement. This drive-memory interrelationship could also be strengthened by the subliminal emotional stimulus of sex embedded in the advertisement. The result: an intense feeling that you want to have dinner in a specific restaurant. This precise subliminal technique is part of the main course in virtually all of the nationally franchised restaurants—Howard Johnson's, Colonel Sanders' Chicken, etc.

In terms of motivating behavior, subliminal stimuli appear to work best when they can relate unconscious memory traces to consciously occurring drive systems. For example, a cigarette ad may show a couple on a walk in the country on a beautiful spring afternoon—a scene in which the reader may identify with one of the models used. Suppose that embedded in the trees or grass are the words SEX aimed at the unconscious. The SEX establishes the possibility of the reader unconsciously identifying with a model, relating drive-oriented behavior with the cigarette brand.

Audiences, however, cannot be simply avalanched with drive-related stimuli if media are going to achieve maximum effectiveness. Subjects need to be primed to accept drive-related subliminal input. This calls for a reinforcing integration of media editorial content and advertising. The notion that advertising and editorial or program content are separate is merely one of the mythologies of the mass media.

For example, the articles, fiction, and interviews of *Playboy* magazine serve as primers for the subliminal trigger within the ads. Readers are flattered into a narcotized state of self-admiration by the sex-oriented consciously perceived content, as a way to set them up for the advertising manipulation. The same general technique works in all media. Televised football games, portraying a struggle for male dominance and territory, play into viewers' dominance-aggression-oriented drive systems. Sports fans are, in effect, set up or primed by the game to absorb the Schlitz, Gillette, or Chevrolet advertisements with their subliminal commands directing brand preferences.

A newspaper also presents, via its nonadvertising, or "news" content, a subliminally perceived picture of the world which primes the reader for drive-related response to advertising content. In the absence of any strong existing habit structure or contrary drive state, subliminals will usually influence overt behavior.

In media, it is the function of content—news, articles, pictures, etc.—to reinforce existing habit structures or modes of thought. For this reason, most newspapers are extremely culture bound and must remain so to fulfill their economic functions. They must, generally, reinforce the self-image delusions and fantasies of their community of readers or cease to exist economically.

For example, in North America there is available an enormous variety of media—more on a per capita population basis than in any other continent. The problem is that people read those publications or view those programs which reinforce their predispositions. They attend to ideas with which they already agree. The function of mass communication media, then, becomes one of maintaining the prejudices of a particular audience rather than changing or expanding its attitudes, opinions, and beliefs.

Though *Ramparts* magazine and *The Wall Street Journal* can be read by anyone with the purchase price, the readership will never overlap significantly. Each publication is purchased and read because of its ability to *tell the reader what he wants to hear about the world and about himself as the center of his mythical universe.*

Underground newspapers are flourishing among the so-called youth culture. They are also making, very quietly, enormous profits for their publishers through advertising. Record companies and book publishers have found the underground press a most effective primer for ads that appeal to such drives as sex or aggression.

Perceptual Defenses: Of all the areas of human behavior that have been affected by subliminal stimuli in the mass media, perceptual defenses are perhaps the most critical for the reader to understand clearly. Indeed, most individuals do not realize their nervous systems and brains contain mechanisms which will defend them against anxiety-producing information by simply helping them not to perceive consciously the information. In other words, humans can easily—and perhaps they must in order to adjust and survive—shut out from their conscious awareness any information which might deeply trouble or shock them.

The area of perceptual defense is so important an aspect of the subliminal perception phenomenon as to justify a general discussion in an entire chapter. It was through an understanding of perceptual defense mechanisms that media and its advertisers learned to manipulate their audiences subliminally.

3. Perceptual Defenses Hide Meanings in the Service of Subliminal Manipulation

Perceptual defense mechanisms within the human brain and nervous system provide one of the most curious and significant explanations of subliminal response behavior available.

Experiments have demonstrated that humans can receive, process, and transmit information which makes no conscious appearance at any stage of its passage through their nervous system. Indeed, the *unconscious* can operate quite independently from the *conscious* mechanism in the brain. The two perceptual systems often appear to be operating in opposition to one another.

It has already been stated that perceptions that somehow threaten the individual, or that he finds difficult to consciously handle, are subject to being sidetracked from the conscious into the unconscious. Humans defend themselves in this way from perceptual damage which might result if this inhibitory mechanism did not operate.

There are several techniques we use to protect ourselves from perceptual damage:

Repression: Considered the central mechanism of perceptual defense, repression is probably the most significant technique by which humans avoid dealing with reality. This would generally involve the barring or censoring of memories, feelings, or perceptions with high anxiety-producing potential. The repression mechanism will be dealt with later in considerable detail.

Isolation: The avoidance of perceiving or recalling linkups of related information through associations or identifications which might arouse anxiety is a commonly used perceptual defense. One dramatic illustration of the technique recently observed involved a military briefing by a general who for two hours discussed nuclear strike capabilities of the Strategic Air Command. Not once did the heavily decorated officer use words or symbols which might have permitted his audience to link nuclear bombs with millions of burned and vaporized human beings. The incredible assortment of euphemisms included such technical slide-rule-associated symbols as "overpressures," "blast parameters," "temperature thresholds," and "fallout interfaces."

Regression: A common defense against anxiety occurs when an individual regresses to an earlier stage in his life where he was secure and someone else assumed responsibility for him. Regression can usually be anticipated among those going through a serious illness. Indeed, the defense is often useful to physicians and hospital staffs by helping a patient submit quietly to the necessary control and management of his illness.

Fantasy Formation: A major defense often used by both children and adults, fantasy formation can—in mass media —become part of isolation. This could and perhaps often does result in a situation where fantasy and reality are indistinguishable. Fantasies, for example, of "Bonanza's" Cartwright family applied unconsciously to the real-life intricacies of family relationships can invite disaster.

Sublimation: Sublimation is the redirection of drives and emotions into more acceptable channels. Sex drives, for example, may be redirected into more socially acceptable channels such as athletics. The creation of busy work for men enduring a space flight as a technique of maintaining a healthy emotional environment by avoiding anxiety is another illustration of sublimation.

Denial: An often utilized defense is to merely deny the existence of something disturbing, such as aggression or sexuality. Denial often offers a release from responsibility through a projection of blame onto another person.

Projection: As a perceptual defense, projection concerns the transfer to someone else of feelings or wishes that are unacceptable or anxiety-producing.

Introjection: As opposed to projection, introjection relates to the defense against disillusionment in another by accepting blame or responsibility. The aggression or hostility, for example, might be self-directed rather than aimed toward someone else.

It is often not easy to differentiate among the above perceptual defenses. They can interrelate or overlap in many different patterns. For the purposes of media study, however, repression will here constitute the major preoccupation— even though the other defenses are frequently implied within repression.

Perhaps the American Negro writer Eldridge Cleaver defined the media game well when he described the new American revolution as the blacks fighting *oppression*, while the whites are fighting *repression*. It took American blacks, according to Cleaver, a long time to comprehend the magnitude of their own repressions. They simply couldn't bring themselves to believe what was being done to them by whites was really happening. But, much worse, the white man still doesn't know what he has done to the blacks.

Consciousness Cleansing

Playboy magazine recently ran a two-page subscription advertisement (see Figure 30) which pictured a large wreath and a rather bosomy blonde, kneeling and tying a ribbon to the wreath. Of a hundred or so young male test subjects who had carefully read the 260 pages of this issue, over 95 percent recalled the ad. Over 70 percent specifically remembered the wreath, but could provide only vague ideas about the blonde's description. Over 40 percent of those who recalled the ad were not even certain she was a blonde.

It seemed strange that two pages out of 260 could have made such a strong recall impression. None of the test subjects had the slightest idea why they were able to remember the ad. Only about 5 percent had actually read the textual copy in the ad. A few of these admitted an interest in subscribing to *Playboy* by sending in the coupon. The remaining 95 percent reported they had merely glanced at the wreath and the girl before turning the page. But, they all remembered the wreath.

A careful look at the subscription ad reveals why the information was repressed. The reader need only ask what kind of flowers were used for the wreath. The first conscious perceptual defense is to see the wreath flowers as nuts—possibly walnuts. A more careful examination reveals they cannot be nuts. This wreath has been cleverly constructed of objects which resemble vaginas and the heads of erect penises. One way of assuring the repression of information into a subliminal stimulus is to make it so outrageous or threatening that no one would believe a famous, high-credibility, nationally distributed magazine would do such a thing.

Playboy is purchased by young men with a median age of 24.5. The wreath is composed of genitals which subliminally communicate with and motivate these young men to forward a subscription check. The bosomy blonde in this case was only a consciously perceived prop for the subliminal content.

All humans have this curious capacity to block out from the conscious awareness information which conflicts with their conscious value systems. The repressed information is capable of evoking feelings or desires or attention without one's conscious awareness of what is happening. Repression seems to occur when ideas involved in the communication may threaten an individual's ego.

The phenomenon can be illustrated with a small, inexpensive copy of the famous sculpture "The Three Graces" (see Figure 2). The actual sculpture—excavated near Cyrene, Lybia—is now displayed in the British Museum. It was created between 500 and 300 B.C. by a sculptor of the Greek Dionysian Cult. Millions of these reproductions have been sold to tourists throughout the Mediterranean area. They are often available in North American gift shops.

A 12-inch-high reproduction of the statue was shown to over 500 test subjects at a North American university. A brief historical description, similar to that above, was given. They were encouraged to handle the sculpture individually, look at it from all sides, and feel it before passing it on.

After each person had carefully observed and handled the statue, the work was removed from the room. Each subject was then asked three questions: "How did the statue make you feel?" "Do you recall anything about the hands?" "What does the statue mean?"

The answers were startling.

A casual examination of "The Three Graces" indicates three nude women in an affectionate embrace. Every line designed by the sculptor into the masterpiece leads the eye to one singular detail—the girl on the left has her hand lovingly upon the right breast of the girl in the center. The visual lines of the arms and robe all lead the eye toward this detail. It is impossible to look at this statue without the eye ending up on the hand covering the breast. Other details, consciously obvious when they are explained, reinforce the meaning of the statue.

The girl on the right is affectionately pressing the center

girl's head against her own. Her right breast is pressed against the outside of the hand on the breast. There are hidden body contacts of breasts against torso on the left and right figures. Hidden anatomical details play an important role in art. The mind unconsciously, apparently, assimilates and structures unseen portions of the anatomy in a search for meaning. A sculpture's deeper meaning is often communicated through what is not seen but is logically there, the perception passing only into the viewer's unconscious. This technique is often utilized in modern mass media, especially in such illustrations as the *Playboy* centerfold.

The meaning of the statue is obvious and simple. The sculpture is portraying a homosexual love relationship among three women—not at all an unacceptable notion to a Dionysian Greek. If the sculpture was considered as time-stopped at a particular instant in a process of events, implying a before and after, the three women have probably just left their bath, were drying each other with the towel, and were distracted by their mutual affection. If one were to ask what they would likely be doing ten minutes after that moment, a reasonable answer would be a three-way homosexual experience.

Of the 500 test subjects, only 9 percent answered the questions in any way which suggested they had an idea of what was going on in the sculpture. This appeared strange, as the information content of the statue is not at all subtle. An additional 33 percent were able to describe the hand-on-breast detail, but in their descriptions they did not evaluate the meaning of the detail: they simply saw it, but consciously ascribed no meaning to it. Sixty percent of the test subjects had no conscious idea whatsoever of what was meant by the sculpture.

Their answers to the three questions were all very similar. The statue made them feel there was a warm, beautiful, affectionate feeling among the three women. A number of comments suggested that a feeling of sadness was projected. Responses in regard to *meaning* were universally vague, most often repeating the answers to the first question. Whatever the statue meant at the conscious level was, apparently, beyond the test subject's ability to verbalize.

Some of the individual responses were interesting. Two dozen subjects stated they had a copy of the statue in their homes. Several had purchased them as souvenirs in Europe. One stated her brother had brought the statue home, and she had often wished "he would throw that cheap tourist junk out of the house." None of the subjects who had had contact with the statue was consciously aware of the obvious sexual implications. Another girl admitted to purchasing the statue in Athens and keeping it on her dresser for nearly a year before she noticed the hand on the breast. She admitted not ever being consciously aware of any deeper meaning implied by the affectionate caress. A large number of the subjects used the term "art," implying that art has no specific meaning. Curiously, once the label "art" was applied to the statue, the label appeared to impede—like a stone wall—any further insights into the feelings or meanings projected by the statue.

Incredible as it may appear, it is most likely that hundreds of thousands, perhaps millions of people have viewed "The Three Graces" without ever actually consciously perceiving its meaning. Only a minuscule proportion appear to have penetrated into the theme of the masterpiece, even though they absolutely had to see the hand-on-breast detail. The brain, however, does not always consciously register what the eye sees.

Knowing as Deception

The implications of the repression mechanism are fascinating in the field of art and in the field of mass communication. If humans repress the meaning of such a simple and beautiful masterpiece as "The Three Graces," how much of the reality of the world surrounding them is also repressed? These repressed perceptions appear to influence individuals through the unconscious rather than the conscious mechanism of their minds.

Consider the supposed factual news reports on an international crisis, conference, or what have you. How much information, one might well wonder, is repressed into the unconscious? The observation has been made by many theorists that what is not consciously perceived might well be consistently more important than what *is* perceived. When the information exclusion concept is turned upon the mass media, a curious paradox appears when content is interpreted in terms of what was left out instead of what was put in. This inverse approach to media analysis provides an analytical perspective that may help us understand the published content of North American newspapers.

The perceptual defense mechanism of repression, which appears to control conscious memory, may well turn out to be the key in explaining many heretofore enigmatic aspects of human behavior. Intelligence, for example, which is determined by tests that supposedly measure what we have in our memories, are based only upon abilities to consciously recall, reason, think abstractly, make relationships, apply principles, and respond quickly to timed exercises. If the totality of perception registers instantly in the human brain, then it is actually the perceptual defense repression mechanism that may determine our intelligence by regulating what is admitted from the unconscious into consciousness at any particular time in our lives.

The concept of intelligence as it relates to memory, for example, is predicated upon a major North American industry which sells tests. This industry actually establishes cultural norms by labeling children early in life as *superior*, *average*, or *slow learner*. Intelligence tests have been known to be scientifically worthless ever since the first one was invented as an experimental laboratory device: First, the entire concept of "intelligence" is hopelessly ambiguous, based purely upon the simplistic concept of conscious memory—comparable again to studying an iceberg only from what protrudes above the surface. Second, intelligence, whatever it may eventually turn out to be, is hopelessly culturebound—limited by group identifications and hidden meanings, producing over an extended period of time individuals with vaguely similar repression patterns. In other words, intelligence could more reasonably consist of what is repressed from consciousness rather than what has merely been left within consciousness. No intelligence test can cross cultures, in this sense, and any major city will include dozens of definable (and doubtless many undefinable) subcultures.

Nevertheless, the definitions we accept for "intelligence" serve administrative and social motives in behalf of various power structures. People can be almost automatically channeled in and out of various occupations or groups, even religions, in an often destructive—though economically efficient—manner. We serve our own self-flattering image by categorizing easily the *more* or *less* intelligent, usually using our concept of an average person (ourselves, of course) as the reference point.

Learning a language is the single most complex task any human could undertake in terms of innate intelligence—if there were such a thing. The vast majority of individuals in any society learn some language, many of them far more complex in syntax and meaning than culturally repressed middle-class English. The profanity-saturated language of the ghetto is far richer in information yield and subtleties of meaning than the formal one-dimensional phrases of most experimental psychologists. In fact, the Ph. D. may—with his multisyllable words, complex qualified syntax, and pedestrian linear logic—be practicing a far more limited and intellectually more primitive form of communication than does the ghetto resident with his rich and symbolically meaningful vocabulary of four-letter words.

Another way of viewing perceptual defenses was suggested in a curious approach to language studies—and what is repressed or left out of language at the conscious level—initiated by Professor E. H. Sturtevant some years ago at Yale University. Sturtevant proceeded upon the assumption that the real motive behind the evolutionary development of language could just as well have been to develop a system of symbols based upon *deception* rather than *truthful* information—in the service of survival and adjustment. In both the plant and animal worlds, deceptive communication behavior is not at all unusual. Deception, in fact, may be the norm. This does not necessarily suggest that man's lies or deceptions are consciously malicious. Indeed, man must first repress his real motives and lie to himself before he can effectively deceive others.

Many species of fish, animals, and plants have evolved complex communication systems sustaining their survival. One tropical species, the *chaetodon capistratus,* or four-eyed butterfly fish, carries a large eye on its tail which deceives larger fish as to its size and suitability for easy conquest.

In what is often discussed as the most thorough *con* job occurring in nature, one species of orchid—*crypotosylia*—depends upon a small unique fly to carry its pollen to other orchids. The orchid emits an aromatic very similar to that of the female fly while in heat, and its pistil has a texture similar to the mating surface of the female fly's body. Upon landing, the male fly thrashes about upon the orchid's garden of delight, in the process covering himself with the orchid's pollen. During the busy sex life of the male fly, a dozen orchids a day might be pollinated. Had the symbiotic relationship not developed through centuries of evolution, the orchid species would have probably disappeared.

There are hundreds of such known phenomena in nature involving some form of communication—virtually all of them interspecies survival techniques based upon some kind of deception. Man appears to be the only species of life which uses intraspecie deception as a basic mode of communication, deceiving his own kind.

Several years ago, at one of the interminable—and most usually ill-fated—conferences on international peace, speaker after speaker bemoaned the turgid history of ineffective communication between the United States and the Soviet Union. During the entire afternoon "lack of communication" and "real understanding" between the two countries was blamed for their inability to agree even on the time of day. Finally, late in the afternoon, a senior and very distinguished American diplomat took his turn on the speakers' platform. He threw away a long, prepared text, and simply said with a voice betraying his exhaustion, "Ladies and Gentlemen, we have always known exactly what the Russians want. The Russians have always known exactly what we want. The problem is that both of us frequently want the same thing. Our communications are simply designed to prevent each other from obtaining our respective objectives. They know this and we know this. Further, they know we know they know and we know they know we know. We simply understand each other perfectly."

Theories of the Unconscious

There has been an enormous literature in psychology over the past half century theorizing on the role of the unconscious in the life of each human. Nevertheless, the unconscious remained only an abstract theory until 1957, when Canadian neurosurgeon Dr. Wilder Penfield empirically demonstrated the existence of the unconscious mechanism in the human brain. During brain surgery, while their cerebral cortex (the outer layer of the brain) was being probed, Penfield's patients recalled events, scenes, sounds, aromas, and other perceptions which had been long buried and consciously forgotten. This was probably the first empirical demonstration of a specific mechanism in the brain which illustrated what theorists had been arguing about since and even before

Freud. The unconscious had become a medical or "scientific" reality, though far from a well-understood one.

Prior to Penfield's work, hypnosis was the only other empirical technique which could penetrate perceptual defenses and which clearly demonstrated the existence of the unconscious mechanism. Among many medical men hypnosis is still suspect. Virtually none of the medical schools in North America will tolerate serious discussion of hypnosis—even though most patients can be totally anesthetized by hypnosis. Other nations, such as the Soviet Union, have made substantial medical and scientific progress through the study, experimentation with, and application of hypnosis, and it is still the most easily available form of communication with the unconscious.

Theories of the unconscious suggest that it actually dominates human behavior, controlling motivations, value systems, interpersonal relationships, personal identities, and, in effect, all major and minor aspects of life which differentiate humans from animals. Conscious or cognitive perception is viewed by many as peripheral and superficial to perception at the unconscious level. Conscious functions primarily support the ego—individual and group pretensions, perspectives toward ourselves and the world we would like to see, as compared with the world as it may actually exist.

This view of man as being dominated by a mechanism within his mind of which he has no conscious knowledge is to many a frightening attack upon the ego. Anyone who incautiously probes into unconscious perceptions or motives may wind up ridiculed by an outraged, self-righteous mob. A large portion of North American psychologists today refuse to concede the existence of the unconscious—even though psychology was first established to deal with subliminal phenomena.

Are Images Real?

The popular euphemism *image* is merely a positive way of describing a stereotype. The ways in which images are pieced together by the unconscious mind is curious.

In advertising recall studies, for example, advertisements are rarely or never recalled by the conscious mind. Any ad that can be recalled by a significant number of readers is of doubtful value. The conscious mind values, differentiates, and makes judgments. Conscious ad recall can subject an ad to *critical judgment*—the last thing to which any advertiser wants to expose his product. Ads are designed to implant themselves within the unconscious where they will lie dormant uncriticized, unevaluated, and unknown to the individual until the time a purchase decision is required. The buried information then surfaces as a favorable attitudinal predisposition. This phenomenon can produce some interesting and complicated situations.

In a nationwide public relations study of seven giant chemical producers in the United States, a research organization discovered curious insights as to the images people held of corporations. Each of the seven corporations are vast industrial and commercial empires—Du Pont, Monsanto, American Cyanamid, Dow, Olin Mathieson, Allied Chemical, and Union Carbide. Even the individual presidents of any of these empires would be hard-pressed to enumerate offhand the staggering number of products produced annually by their companies.

The survey was conducted among a sample of several hundred corporate presidents and executive vice-presidents, whose companies were heavy users of chemical products and who each had long-term experience as major industrial customers for chemical products. During the more than one-hour depth interview, few of these executives recalled specifically any advertising by the giant chemical corporations. Of the few who believed they could recall either institutional or product advertising in magazines, newspapers, television, or radio, most of their recollections proved to be in error.

A large number of executives, when asked to describe the Olin Mathieson Corporation—a vast international complex of chemical companies, as a person—described OM as an elderly, thin, wizened man with a sharp face and balding head. He wore a stiff, heavy wool suit, a thin celluloid collar, and high-laced shoes. He was shrewd and untrustworthy, tight with money, and feared and hated by his subordinates. This image of Olin Mathieson was described quite frequently, often in elaborate detail, by executives from all over the United States.

This strongly negative image of OM appeared inexplicable. The researchers could not understand how an organization as large and complex as Olin Mathieson could have acquired such a consistently negative image. Its advertising revealed dignified and interesting institutional magazine ads as well as generous support for public service television programming during the preceding five years.

Finally, and quite by accident, one executive was discovered who in his youth had actually worked for Olin Mathieson. He recalled an OM senior executive of some thirty years earlier who fit the description that had developed in the research. The OM executive had been dead for over a quarter century—dead but apparently not forgotten in the unconscious memories of the executives who, because of their age and work experience, had probably had dealings with him during their youth. A recheck of the executives who described OM in this negative image revealed that none consciously recalled the actual executive. None could even identify the man's name.

The Monsanto image was also unusual for a giant conglomerate corporation. A significant proportion of executives described Monsanto as a beautiful, sexually provocative woman. She was blonde, in her late twenties, of medium height, thin, very well proportioned, cultured and well educated, and probably married to a high-ranking corporate executive. She was clothed in a low-cut, strapless evening gown of metallic appearing fabric which fitted her very tightly but was in "good taste." Several of the descriptions of the blonde were quite erotic.

The researchers began to wonder how anyone—especially these hard-nosed executive types—could see a giant corporation in sexually oriented terms. A review of Monsanto's advertising over several preceding years supplied the answer. Two years before the study Monsanto had run full-page, four-color advertisements in national magazines such as *Life, Fortune, Saturday Evening Post,* and *U.S. News and World Report.* The ads were institution-oriented toward Monsanto's plastics division. Standing gracefully in the layout of each advertisement was the beautiful blonde dressed in her strapless gown of metallic-appearing material made from a synthetic fiber developed by Monsanto. A recheck of those executives who thought of Monsanto in these erotic terms revealed that none could consciously recall ever having seen the plastics division advertising—even after it was described in detail for them.

The study was sponsored by one of the major chemical companies. In terms of corporate competitive strategies, once the client corporation understood the intimate details of his competitors' as well as his own image, he was in a position to exploit the strengths and weaknesses of these images to his advantage. There is a measure of honesty in the competitive system, however, in that each of the seven corporations can utilize similar competitive strategies based upon similar research into their public images.

Maximal Meaning in Minimal Space and Time

Words are carefully structured and lineal. In English they read from left to right, one line at a time. Different lineal patterns appear in Hebrew and Chinese. The reader has been carefully trained to consciously cope with verbal symbolism—organizing, categorizing, assimilating, and finally formulating a complex of meaning.

Lineally perceived words, as we have been trained to slowly grope our way through the jungles of syntax and paragraphs, impose severe limitations upon the quantity of words we can ingest during a given period of time. An average person reads at roughly 400 words per minute. Training in lineal techniques of rapid reading can increase the speed to, perhaps, 1,200 words per minute. Writers and editors work to achieve simple syntactical structures with verbs and nouns rich in symbolic, often archetypal, meaning to increase the information load and reader assimilation rate to maximum.

However, there is a fixed limit to what most people can handle. Western society has been oriented, through traditional language training, to handle words in this slow, pedestrian, lineal manner. Some interesting experiments are now being conducted in which people are successfully taught to read at rates as high as 10,000 words, or as much as 50 pages, per minute. Incredible as it may seem, several hundred nine-to-twelve-year-old children have already been taught to read, comprehend, and retain information from reading at what to most of us would be a bewildering speed. This new approach appears to be based upon a utilization of instantaneous perception similar to that normally used for nonverbal visual stimuli. Scholars have long known that visual perception operates through neurons connecting the eye and brain, at a speed of 60 to 100 meters per second. In other words, the eye perceives a stimulus, say a photograph, instantaneously encoding and processing the content through highly complex neural structures in the brain's cerebral cortex.

At the unconscious level, every minute detail in a photograph is recorded instantly within the brain. Conscious perception apparently works more slowly. With pictorial stimuli, conscious perception follows focal points in the picture as the eye is led from one major detail to another. If the picture has been professionally designed, the eye will cover most major details within a second or two.

The fovea, an area smaller than a pinhead located near the center of the eye's retina, appears to be the major source of consciously induced visual information. The perceived image upon the fovea rapidly jumps from point to point, operating at millisecond speeds. Once it is targeted toward a specific point, it cannot change its path of movement, or *saccade*, as the path is sometimes called. When a subject is difficult to consciously identify, the fovea fixations are longer and the fovea image will jump back to the subject again and again, moving as rapidly as 500 degrees per second.

Looking at any example of art or advertising, the movements of the image upon the fovea are relatively easy to determine. Upon first viewing the picture, the eye mechanism will move toward a specific point. This has been referred to as the primary focal point, designed by the artist as the specific location where conscious perception of the picture begins. The fovea image will then move from point to point in a succession of rapid jumps as the ad is scanned. Artists can predict how most viewers' eyes will move; the fovea image jumps toward anything novel or emotionally stimulating. In viewing commercial art, there would be great similarity in the fovea paths followed by most individuals as they scan the advertisement.

During the one or two seconds in which most print advertising is designed to be perceived, the fovea may race through a dozen or more focal points. Information perceived at these points is transmitted into consciousness. Humans are apparently aware of what they have seen via the fovea. The fovea, and its saccades across a wide variety of visual stimuli, has been studied exhaustively with the Mackworth motion picture camera—a two-camera device with one camera focused upon the magnified image of the retina and fovea, the other focused upon the scene in front of the viewer.

The fovea, however, collects only a small portion of the totally available information. Not more than 1/1000th of the visual field can be seen in hard focus at a time. Even if the fovea jumps to a hundred different focal points on a

painting—far in excess of the usual jumps made while ob-
serving an average advertisement—only 10 percent of the
total visual information would be perceived.

What appears to be happening, however, is that the total,
instantaneous perception of the picture is repressed in favor
of certain obvious details. *All the information and meaning
are recorded instantly and totally,* but the mind plays what
amounts to a trick, permitting only certain details—often
what we want to see or what we can identify with—to
filter through into conscious awareness. This could be the
mechanism by which the brain enables us to survive the
vast totality of data passing each day through our sensory inputs into storage areas within the brain. Humans simply
cannot consciously handle all this information. Consciousness,
therefore, appears to be a limiting facility of the nervous
system.

The brain's storage capacity has been estimated at some
20 billion units of information, only a small part of which
is used during the course of a lifetime. Only a small portion
of total stored data even filters through into levels of consciousness. In fact, perceptual defense mechanisms may be
vital to human survival. We repress because we must repress
or endanger sanity and survival.

Once a total page of words is perceived and recorded in
the unconscious, the problem is then one of moving the
meaning into a level of consciousness.

Total visual perception is not limited to what is perceived
via the fovea. The retina transmits the total picture perceived into the brain; this process is sometimes referred to
as peripheral vision. Though individuals can be trained to
become more consciously aware of their total perceptual
content—such as in rapid reading, memorization techniques,
or in eideticism (photographic memory) with or without
hypnosis—peripherally perceived information is generally
routed into the unconscious. Precisely how this mechanism
works is unknown, and may never be fully understood. This
brief theoretical outline, nevertheless, is generally supported
by research in both neurology and psychology.

Thus, most of the meanings applied consciously have really been interpreted by our brains from data in both the
conscious and unconscious mechanisms. Greater significance
and meaning are derived, apparently, from the unconscious
—from the enormous quantity of subliminal information

stored and available since our moment of birth, possibly even before. The argument over whether information, ideas, archetypes, or concepts are genetically inherited is still far from a settled issue.

Maximum meaning in minimum time and space is the basic theorem of the mass media in America—and not just casual meaning either, but meaning that will sell media and the advertised products of American industry through which media are sustained.

The Unconsciousness's Photographic Memory

Studies recently undertaken at the Massachusetts Institute of Technology lend strong support to the concept of total, instantaneous perception of even tens of thousands of tiny dots of information, edited within the brain, into conscious and unconscious storage. Using a new technique developed with the Bell Laboratories, subjects were tested with slides containing random dot stereograms—pictures appearing to have depth. The scientists discovered that certain individuals have seemingly incredible memory abilities.

Eidetic images are memory pictures of past events wherein total scenes appear to individuals, complete down to the smallest detail. The mental picture allows the subject to examine every detail, and may last several minutes. There is substantial evidence to suggest that eidetic images of virtually every event since birth, as we perceived it happening, are stored in the brain. The phenomenon has often been recorded during hypnotic regressions and various meditational practices. Certain individuals appear to have greater conscious access to the images than others, particularly children.

In the experiments, each individual stereogram slide presented only a random series of dots—with no specific meaning apparent. But together, one superimposed on top of the other, the slides formed a stereogram with the dots combined to form letters, words, or meaningful symbols.

The scientists exposed one of the stereogram slides to the left eye during one time interval. Later, the other stereogram was shown to the right eye of test subjects. They delayed the right eye exposure for increasing time periods. Results were staggering in their implications.

Test subjects, in order to play the game, had to remember the dots, their numbers and positions, in the first slide and then match this memory later with the second slide. The task required them to remember—either consciously or unconsciously—the exact number and position of thousands of dots.

Eidetic image stereograms, with ten thousand dots, were recalled over time periods as long as three days. Million-dot patterns were recalled for as long as four hours.

After viewing the second stereoscope slide, eidetic test subjects required about ten seconds to make their evaluations. The recognition time period is similar to that involved with much subliminal phenomena; it usually requires about ten seconds for anyone to consciously perceive subliminally embedded words in advertisements. This ten-second period seems to relate closely to an individual's state of relaxation. The recognition period, however, only involves conscious perception—an individual's conscious sensitivity to subliminal stimuli. Perception appears to be instantaneous and total, or very near to total, at the unconscious level. An individual who wants to utilize a greater part of his brain-stored information must simply learn how to move information from the unconscious into the conscious level of cognition.

Amazing individual memory feats have been recorded in history. The Shass Pollaks, Hebrew scholars, could accurately memorize which word appeared in which position on every page in each of the twelve volumes of the Babylonian Talmud. A. R. Luria described the eidetic journeys mnemonists, or memory specialists, took to reconstruct very complicated lists of materials. The Bell Lab scientists reported that one of their test subjects, a young woman, could recall pages of poetry in a known foreign language which she could copy from bottom line to the top line as fast as her hand could write.

There is no known relationship between this type of memory ability and intelligence as evaluated by the various standard tests. Popular mythology suggests, nevertheless, that anyone who can recall so prodigiously must possess a very special kind of intelligence. This does not appear to be true. In studies with hypnosis, virtually anyone who can be led into a deep trance can be regressed to some earlier point in his life and experience eidetic images in minute detail. There appears a strong implication that most humans have eidetic abilities unavailable to their conscious minds, but which appear in a hypnotic trance.

Experiments with hypnosis, the rapid reading techniques, dot stereograms, and mnemonists suggest that perhaps the

key to using the natural capacities (both conscious and unconscious) of the brain and nervous system is to circumvent
the repression or control systems which hold down perceptive
capabilities, channeling the tightly directing consciousness
along certain socially approved avenues or sets. In other
words, intelligence in all its complex manifestations appears
not to be something you either have or do not have—but
more likely to be innate in most everyone and controlled by
the degrees of repression or other perceptual defenses developed during childhood.

Indeed, what we have come to accept as measurable intelligence may actually only be a limited index of materials
which have filtered through the screen of repression into
consciousness—a small drop in an ocean of stored experience.
The socialization and education processes of Western economically developed nations may, in effect, be limiting man's
intelligence by forcing him to repress greater and greater
amounts of what he actually perceives.

The implications to mankind are enormous. If individuals
have innate neurological abilities vastly beyond their apparent conscious levels, the entire history of intellectual
evolution must be reviewed to seek out society's hidden
motives or needs to control which have solidly erected social,
educational, economic, religious, and linguistic systems which
act as barriers to human growth and self-realization.

Symbolization Abilities

Suzan Langer, the American philosopher, believed man
has a basic emotional need, instinct, or drive to make symbols—a drive comparable to hunger, thirst, sex, or survival.
Other writers have considered man's symbolizing ability
as the primary basis for his differentiation from animals, as
the only way the past can be related to the present and the
future, and as the glue which has held together cultures, religions, societies, and families. Science and technology, in a
twentieth-century context, are based upon exercises in symbol-making which have not liberated man from symbolic
quagmires but embedded him more deeply into dependence
upon symbols and what he believes they either *mean* or
don't mean.

Archetypal symbolism, specifically, refers to symbols that
have appeared in many places, at many times, with an inexplicable similarity of meaning. These archetypes are found

in religious rituals, folklore, fairy tales, mythologies, and in dreams. Carl Jung, the Swiss psychoanalyst, believed these symbols stemmed from images already present within all men in the turbulent depths of the unconscious. Jung, Levi-Strauss, and many other scholars have theorized that our so-called modern ways of thinking at the conscious level are quite different from the primitive thought processes of our early ancestors. These differences primarily consist of consciously derived information, including technologies, education or training, and complex systems of socialization.

At the unconscious level, however, man is thought to have remained essentially as he was during the Upper Paleolithic or late Stone Age. The unconscious perpetually flows into man's consciousness through visions, dreams, fantasies, and myths—providing a base of meaning from which to consciously interpret the world of reality.

Taking the concept from St. Augustine, Jung applied the word archetype to define universal symbols which sustain a constant meaning and efficiency in their applications. He maintained that archetypes were not genetically inherited, but represented a hereditary disposition of man to produce parallel images out of very similar common psychic structures. He referred to this ability of man as the *collective unconscious*. In other words, Jung theorized that the conscious mind displays incalculable differences or variation between individuals, cultures, and groups in its day-to-day functions; the unconscious, on the other hand, displays very strong similarities, expressed through the collective unconscious as symbolic archetypes.

Jung further defined archetypes as systems involving both images and emotions inherited with the brain structure. They are, in Jung's theory, the source of the most powerful instinctive prejudices, as well as support for instinctive adaptations. Freud called these archetypes *primitive fantasies*.

Archetypes have also been described as "all-embracing parables," with only partially accessible meanings. They, in any respect, are a type of symbol with a much more profound and deeper meaning and significance to human behavior.

Practical examples of archetypal symbolism used in modern advertising include such images as the genitalia (phallic and vaginal symbolism discussed later in this chapter), the moon, the family, love, water, birth, rebirth, fire, sun—the list is almost endless. Specific symbols related closely to these archetypal concepts would likely elicit similar responses among both modern and primitive man—in terms of meaning at the unconscious level.

Everything's Symbolic, Functional, or Both

Everything perceived by humans can be considered either symbolic, functional, or both. Symbolic meaning operates within the unconscious either verbally or nonverbally. Symbols involve what an object or situation *means* to us, rather than what it might *say* to us. Symbolic meanings appear to form the basis upon which perception becomes deeply meaningful. A differentiation between signs, signals, and symbols can be briefly developed here for the purpose of explaining conscious versus unconscious phenomena.

A consciously perceived flag, for example, could be termed a *sign* denoting a particular nation. At the conscious or intellectual level we identify the flag *sign* with a large and complex reality—each in our own distinctive way. A storm flag beneath the national flag might be termed a *signal*, denoting an event shortly to come. Similarly, a stoplight signals that traffic will shortly cross in front of us. Again, however, signals are perceived at the level of consciousness and are intellectualized inputs into our nervous systems. Both the sign and the signal have unconscious implications, but function primarily at the level of conscious discrimination.

The emotional meaning of the U.S. flag's stars and stripes is symbolic. A portion of the symbolic meaning is conscious, but as with the iceberg, the largest and most meaningful portion lies beneath the level of consciousness. Unconsciously, the stars and stripes could symbolize security, clan dominance, self-sacrifice, loyalty to the ideals of a parental figure, and so on. Significant symbols are culturally determined, condensed ideas which neglect the emotionally unimportant and exaggerate characteristics that are important to individuals. Symbolic indoctrination is believed to begin in early childhood. Several theorists maintain that certain archetypal symbolic meanings are inherent within the human brain.

Love and Death in American Media

Symbols, in this sense, appear throughout history and focus upon two dimensions of life common to all peoples, from New Guinea's to Manhattan's jungles. These symbolic common denominators of all the world's known cultures are organized around two polarities of life: first the origin of life, procreation, love, or—in the *Playboy* vulgarization —sex; and second, the end of life, death, and its related implications of aggression and violence. These two symbolic polarities, sex or love and death, lie deep at the root of all the world's literature, art, philosophy, science, religion, and human behavior.

"The most strictly tabooed areas of human experience in our Western culture," wrote Dr. Thass-Thienemann, "are those that reveal the negative aspect of life: the separation from the mother, the separation from the body, and the final separation from life which is death."[1]

In the mass media of communication, the preoccupation with love and death symbolism is apparent in every newspaper, magazine, and television program. Genital symbolism is universally used in the media, though rarely recognized by the audience as such. Commonly used phallic symbolism includes neckties, arrows, flagpoles, automobiles, rockets, pencils, cigars and cigarettes, candles, broomsticks, snakes, trees, cannons, pens—the list is endless. Vaginal symbols are developed from virtually any round or elliptical shape —lips, eyes, belt buckles, the oval feminine face surrounded by hair, apples, pears, oranges, cherries, balls, eggs—again, the list is extensive.

The union of male and female symbols can also be represented by a key inserted into a lock, a nut being screwed on a bolt, a beer glass foaming at the top as it is being filled from a bottle—there is no end to the possibilities.

Death symbolism in the mass media also offers limitless, though depressing, potentialities—wars, police actions, nationalistic and patriotic totems, religious guilt and fear, athletic contests (which involve the symbolic defeat or killing of one side). The instruments of dominance are symbolic of the genital origin of life—bats, balls, hockey sticks, pucks, and the like, aggressive and violent acts of a thousand different varieties against both people and their property or territories. Death symbolism in North America somehow dominates what we call news, information, education, as well as much of what is usually described as entertainment, from TV drama to the so-called funny books.

---

[1] Theodore Thass-Thieneman, *The Subconscious Language* (New York: Washington Square Press, 1968).

Americans' clumsy and self-conscious attempts to produce sex education films for use in public schools, for example, have generally been shattering failures. The symbolism underlying the meaning of this visual instruction material relates more to death than the origin of life—mechanical functions of the internal organs in simple cause-and-effect analogies (like insights into bodily functions provided by aspirin television commercials), hospitals, doctors, authority figures, guilt, shame. Curiously, this sex education material de-emphasizes the whole subject of love and emotional needs in favor of stated or implied threats against anyone who transgresses against conventional morality.

In the highly ritualized television or movie potboiler the hero can find love, sex, or what have you with the heroine only after a ritual enactment of violence and aggression, usually during which someone must die, often many. The symbolic use of sado-masochistic themes is an integral part of much North American media content—though well hidden symbolically so as to find its major appeal only at the level of the unconscious. Death, or the fear of death, underlies virtually all of the symbols of state, authority, governments, political parties, and military, commercial, and social institutions.

Archetypes

The love-death symbolism in common everyday use within the media has archetypal characteristics. The meanings of archetypal symbolism have persisted for centuries. Similar archetypal meanings appear often in primitive cultures known to have had no physical contact with each other. The phallic symbols of pre-Hispanic American cultures such as the Mayan or Toltec appeared also in medieval art, and can be found today in the pages of modern magazines such as *Playboy*.

Man apparently has an innate *need* to symbolize, a need he is almost totally unaware exists. The symbol-making function has been described as a primary human activity like loving, eating, looking, or moving about. Indeed, human symbolizing—the manufacturing and searching for symbols and the response to symbols—continues in each human from birth to death and appears to be a fundamental and automatic mind process.

A typical example of the use of archetypal symbolism appeared in an *Esquire* advertisement for Seagram's Extra Dry Gin (see Figure 3). Directed at the *Esquire* reader, median age over 40, upper-middle class, married, with nearly-grown or grown children, the ad uses an orange being peeled as the object to be derived from the phallic bottle of Seagram's. For centuries the orange has symbolized woman —young, ripe, and sexually available. Peeling the orange is symbolic of undressing the woman. The rather simple subliminal message in the ad suggests that you undress the woman or seduce her through the use of Seagram's Gin. Remember, the ad is designed to be read in a matter of one or two seconds. Few readers will read the copy. Even if they do it is most unlikely they will be able to consciously recall the ad even ten minutes after it was perceived.

The strategy is to slip the seduction symbolism into a reader's unconscious. Several weeks later, while in a liquor store, he hopefully will select Seagram's from among its competitors. The reader will never consciously recall the ad. Indeed, at the point of purchase, if questioned as to his brand preferences, he will likely provide elaborate rationalizations for his behavior. "Seagram's," he might say, "has the best taste." As the ad has been repeated dozens of times by Seagram's in national publications, presumably the theory works.

In several contemporary cultures the orange symbolism for women is still at the conscious level. Apparently in America, however, the symbolic relationship has disappeared into the unconscious. In Mexico, for example, the word *naranja* (orange) is often used idiomatically to describe prostitutes. Even in the Soviet Union the orange as a symbol of woman was used recently in a poem by Andrei Andreijevich Voznesensky titled, "Strip Tease."

On stage:
    There's a dancing girl who strips until she's bare . . .
    Do I rage? . . .
    Or do these strong tears come from the floodlight's
      glare?
    Scarf she takes off, shawl she shakes off, all the shine—
    Tinsel that she peels off like an orange rind.

Symbolic implications in advertising and mass communication are often frightening, especially in terms of North Americans' ego-centered notions of free will. As was said earlier, the human nervous system is capable of assimilating symbolic content at incredible speeds. Lineal conscious rationalization of content occurs much more slowly. The conscious mind discriminates, decides, evaluates, resists, or accepts. The unconscious, apparently, merely stores units of information, much of which influences attitudes or behavior at the conscious level in ways about which science knows virtually nothing. The mass communication industry long ago realized the resistance to advertising which develops at the conscious level. However, there is little if any resistance encountered at the unconscious level, to which marketing appeals are now directed.

The majority of national advertising and media displays are carefully pretested before being published. After publication, audience reaction to the stimuli is also carefully evaluated against retail store audits, circulation studies, audience research of a dozen varieties, and a plethora of audience-reaction measuring devices and techniques.

Archetypal Families

Magazines, television programs, and other media content are often constructed around an archetypal symbolic family concept. Father, mother, and sibling relationships appear symbolically in the most unlikely places. After all, the family has been the basic social survival defense for mankind over thousands of years. The symbolic family archetype is today present in politics, business corporations, military and civil organizations, and virtually any closely integrated group with a collective security need.

In the mass media, however, the family structure is intentionally woven into the commercial fabrics of plot and characterization to ensure audience identification.

The archetypal symbolic family is constructed around four central characters:

Father: The political leader who provides government, long-term strategies, direction, and control, and serves as spokesman for the family.

Mother: The spiritual leader who provides moral support for all members of the family. In effect, mother serves as a security blanket or crying towel for the group. Her role, in the minds of the other family members, is supportive and sustaining. As a sounding board, she listens to problems and confessions and offers moral encouragement.

Children: The archetypal family will contain two children or subordinate citizens. One will symbolically represent the *child/craftsman/artist*, supporting the technical needs of the family. The other will play the role of a *comedian* or *clown* in the family, supporting needs for humor, entertainment, and pleasure. These symbolic children can be of either sex or of any age.

The psychologically ideal family is common to every society and culture known to have existed. This idealized structure may not exist in reality, considering the high divorce rate and the intermixes of maternal-paternal dominance characteristics. But the symbolically ideal family does exist in the minds of all the world's peoples. Even the communists, who have been at war with the family archetype for half a century as they tried to replace the traditional symbolic structure with one based upon the supremacy of the state, have generally failed to upset the structure.

FAMILY	FATHER/ POLITICIAN	MOTHER/ PRIEST	CHILD/ CRAFTSMAN	CHILD/ CLOWN
Beatles (pre-Sgt. Pepper)	John	Paul	George	Ringo
Mod Squad	Captain Greer	Julie	Link	Peter
Bonanza	Ben Cartwright	Hoss	Little Joe	Candy/Hop Sing
Cosmopolitan	Psychiatrist and Male Authors	Helen Gurley Brown	Female Authors	Ads and Fashion Models
Gunsmoke	Matt	Kitty	Doc	Festus/Chester
Playboy	Hefner and Magazine as a Whole	Cover and Centerfold Surrogate	Male Authors	Cartoons, Ads, Fashion Models
Peanuts	Charlie Brown/ Linus	Lucy	Schroeder	Snoopy
Star Trek	Captain Kirk	Spock	Scott	McCoy/Sulu
Johnny Carson Show	Johnny	Ed McMahon	Guests	Doc Severinsen

The human need to project into or identify with the symbolic family structure is used by writers, directors, and other media technicians as a subliminal device to hold an audience's interest and attention and to effect identification between media content and audience.

When popular media content is analyzed for family structure, the sustaining characters drop neatly into their familial roles.

Archetypal Families in the News

The list could be endless. Once characterization in the symbolic family has been assigned, however, it is virtually impossible for the characters to change roles. The Beatles were a notable exception to this rule. In the Sgt. Pepper album they did a complete switch of familial roles—the new roles are depicted on the Sgt. Pepper album cover. The record, incidentally, dealt on one side with the fact that life is an illusion and on the other with the necessity for that illusion.

The mother/priest role, of course, can be symbolically assumed by a male actor—though there are definite rules to the game. A symbolically maternal male must assume and maintain a role of asexuality. The character Hoss in "Bonanza" would have never made out with a girl even if the show ran for another fifty years. Spock, in "Star Trek," had to endure a similar fate.

From time to time, in America particularly, strange modifications of the basic family image appear. In an archetypal symbol, *function*—not sex—is the primary basis for gender. Children can be of either sex. Maternal roles can even be portrayed by men. Paternal roles can be assigned to women. In one of the early TV family comedies, "The Nelson Family," the maternal role was designed into the character played by Ozzie Nelson. The father's role was given to Harriet. The children were, of course, portrayed as clown and craftsman.

The archetypal family does not end with fictional dramas on television or motion picture screens. It can be found in news information, it is an integral part of team-sport image development, public events, and even in politics. Is it possible that these archetypes actually exist in reality or that our perception of reality transposes people and events into archetypal meaning structures?

For example, in every manned space flight the astronauts —as they have been represented to the American public by NASA public relations and the various news media—have comprised archetypal families. In every flight there is a father/politician, mother/priest, child/craftsman, and child/ clown. In the early days when the flights were manned by one- or two-man crews, individuals in ground-support functions were designed into the family—NASA public relations officers, scientists, engineers, technicians, or newsmen. Both Chet Huntley and Walter Cronkite, and even their staffs, were drafted on occasion to fill the symbolic roles of mothers or children in various space-shot families. This phenomenon is apparently not consciously planned, but appears to evolve naturally from an unconscious awareness of audience expectations. There are some TV directors and writers, however, who will openly admit they consciously structure an archetypal family into a news situation to achieve closer audience identification.

President Nixon and his close White House associates have also been presented as an archetypal family structure through the media. The President, of course, is the father/ politician. This brings a question to mind that if you consider the United States a matriarchy—as do many cultural anthropologists—is it possible the American president will one day be compelled to play a mother/priestess role? Secretary of State William Rogers was typed into the mother/priestess archetype. In the Lyndon Johnson administration, Vice President Hubert Humphrey was pictured in the maternal role. Henry Kissinger, the Nixon administration's one-man brain trust, naturally falls into the role of child/craftsman. And, last but certainly not least—every family must have one— Vice President Spiro T. Agnew played the part of child/ clown—the hell raiser, *l'enfant terrible*, provocateur, always good for a laugh or a cry depending upon your particular persuasion.

A review of old newspapers and magazines reveals that every American president has been presented to the American public—together with his close associates—in an archetypal family role. The roles, of course, are quite likely to be fictional at the reality level. Any image must be fictional, as it is only a gross simplification of reality. The reality of any man, especially that of a successful American politician, is complex, inconsistent, and most unknowable. Images are always crystal clear, simple, consistent, open, believable, and *absolute nonsense.*

The Boston Bruins hockey team is another classic example of archetypal family planning. Over a hundred test subjects agreed, almost unanimously, on the familial roles of characters in the Bruin's cast of players. The father/politician was Phil Esposito; the mother/priestess, Don Awrey; the child/craftsman, Bobby Orr; the child/clown, Derek Sanderson.

Every well-publicized sports team in the nation has characters their fans can immediately place in the family role structure. These roles are probably created most often by the sportswriters who create the symbolic dimension of the rich and powerful sports-world industry in America.

Apply this family archetype to groups with whom you are familiar—in the neighborhood, at home, fraternally, at work, in sports, politics, even in religious groups. These family archetypes surround each of our lives almost everywhere we look. If they do not readily exist, we will create them. They are the stock-in-trade of the mass media. The danger, of course, is that people are not really like the family roles in which we place them and from which we assess their characters, abilities, moralities, etc. We select clues from dress, physique, background, and what we perceive as their image, and blend this into an already prepared mythological framework—a totally unconscious archetypal structure.

Myths, folklore, children's stories, as well as news, comics, dramas, and frequently musical lyrics are often inextricably involved with the family archetypes. When the mass media are viewed from the two principles that *conscious data are always superficial and illusionary* and *it is necessary to go beyond consciousness to gain a perspective into meaning*— it appears there is much more going on in newspapers than merely all the news that's fit to print.

Media—A Member of the Family

Consider first the complexities of the archetypal family structure which persists in all forms of media; now think of media itself—newspapers, magazines, and especially television—as actual participating members of North American families. Television is obvious in this respect. For a large proportion of the roughly 50 million U.S. families, television—the one-eyed monster resident in every well-furnished living room—controls both *time* and *space*.

Television is a major consideration as to *when the family goes to bed* (after the 11:00 P.M. news), *when the family goes to the toilet or engages in conversation* (during commercials), *when the family eats meals or snacks, what family activities will be on weekends* (relative to games, program schedules, and sport seasons), *when parents do or do not have sex* (who wouldn't be tired after a night's hard work in front of the tube's window, pushing beer and potato chips down one's throat?).

Aside from the domination of time, perhaps the most devastating part of the TV legacy is the destruction of communication among family members. With everyone perceiving precisely the same image on a television screen, there are no unique perspectives for individuals. There is, therefore, really nothing to talk about. Try discussing a program you have seen on TV with someone who saw the same program. You can cover three hours of viewing in a handful of sentences.

The dilemma was illustrated in a recent *New Yorker* cartoon. It showed a street in a neighborhood full of apartment houses. In every window of every apartment a family could be seen watching a parade on their TV set. On the street below, the parade was passing with drum majorettes, bands playing, and flags waving. The sidewalks, however, were deserted. The caption read, "Will someone please close the window so we can hear the parade?"

Had these cartoon people seen the parade from the street, each would have had a slightly different perspective. A person on one side of the street would see, hear, smell, and feel something different from what a person would experience on the other side of the street. Even two people standing next to one another would each have a unique perceptual experience—each perceiving the sights, smells, temperature, noise, etc., in differing patterns and varying intensities.

The TV camera and sound equipment substitute for human eyes and ears, but of course cannot provide a *real* multisensory experience. Sight and sound are reproduced only in one perspective or dimension. Everyone who watches the screen experiences precisely the same event. The other thirty-five or so sensory inputs will not participate in the parade, but will be preoccupied with peripheral events within the living room. In short, when you see a parade, a war, a concert, or whatever on television, you are not perceiving the event but a preprocessed and edited cameraman's, writer's, director's, sponsor's single-lensed version of the event communicated to viewers via only two sensory inputs—the eyes and ears.

Educational television experiments reveal that, indeed, many people can learn certain things perhaps better on TV than they could from a classroom with a real-life teacher. Distractions are minimized, attention is focused and concentrated, but this serves to communicate effectively only certain kinds of knowledge. Television is a superb training tool for information that is unitary, sequential, or standardized. As an educational tool, however, television is a disaster area. Education, as opposed and differentiated from training, requires subtle nuances of both teacher and audience reaction, human interpretations and discourse, multisensory experiences, unique individual responses and interpretations. Television is totally inadequate in any educational role other than that of a supplemental resource for a classroom instructor—irrespective of what people with vested interest in educational television have been telling us. In short, these experiments have established most emphatically that as a *training* device, or if you will, *brainwashing* or *conditioning* device, television has an enormous potential. Rudolph Arnheim, in his studies of art and human perception, concluded that rote mechanical learning is the very denial of meaningful experience.

Consider television, as a dominant family member throughout North America, in the role of subliminal educator over a period of, say, fifty years. Beginning almost at birth (children between the ages of two and six today perceive nearly thirty hours weekly of TV) and continuing until their mid-fifties, when over forty hours weekly is today perceived, television serves America as the greatest pacifier of them all—a total substitute for thumbsucking and toying with one's genitals. The TV machine regulates time, channelizes or unifies perceptual experience, and establishes (all subliminally) an entire range of desirable human expectations, value systems, identities, relationships, and perspectives toward the entire world. The tube has already become the primary source of information for a majority of the North American, if not the world's population. The prospects are Orwellian.

There exists no single or multiple mechanism available to

modern man which holds such a devastating potential for brainwashing, mass programming, and the destruction of individualism—with, of course, reinforcement from the other mass media. This threat is every bit as disastrous for the future of mankind and what we have come to call civilization as is pollution, overpopulation, or atomic and biological warfare.

Sensory Deprivation by Media

Indeed, media-induced sensory deprivation among millions of media audiences may already have launched at least part of modern society on the road to neurosis and psychosis. We now have an entire generation whose sense of touch has been starved. A recent survey of university students asked them to detail the role played in their lives by TV. The responses were chilling. Many wrote about incredible loneliness, isolation, and eventual alienation from their families as they struggled emotionally to survive in TV-dominated homes where almost everything was subordinated to program schedules. "No one talked or touched, either symbolically or physically, except during commercials. Then it was, Hurry! Hurry! It's starting. . . ." Communication of any sort had to be initiated and concluded within the 30- or 60-second commercial breaks.

Human relationships, the survey discovered, had not been left unscarred by television. Models for individual behavior, feelings, or actions are today found not in myths of gods and goddesses, not in the lives of our famous soldiers, scientists, artists, explorers, or intellectuals, not in the sacrifices of martyrs, saints, and heroes, but in the day-to-day stereotyped grist ground in the mills of TV production houses, much of which slips unnoticed into our unconscious and provides basic value orientations.

For over a decade the ideal two-parent family ruled the TV networks—"The Nelsons," "Father Knows Best," "I Love Lucy," and a plethora of both short- and long-lived idealized family units. More recently, the ideal family has turned out to be a one-parent family—"The Partridge Family," "My Three Sons," "Doris Day," "Nanny and the Professor," "The Courtship of Eddie's Father," and on and on. Producers believed that audience resistance had begun to develop against the program concept of two-parent utopias existing in suburbias throughout America. Actual records of divorces, family upsets, and the other shattering emotional experiences which go on among suburban American families began to make the fictional, idealized two-parent TV family just *too perfect to be credible*.

No family in the history of the world was or ever will be like these fantasy idealizations dreamed up to merchandise detergents, analgesics and other psychosomatic medicines, and the other lavishly packaged displays of household and food products. Unfortunately, these fantasy families, superbly designed products of the merchandizing imagination, are not clearly recognized as fantasies. They are unconsciously accepted as the *real* thing or as models of what the real thing should look like. There is little doubt that television's so-called entertainment provides tens of millions of viewers with an education in human values and relationships, far more pervasive and significant than the socialization or educational processes communicated in public schools.

What growing child's father could stand up under a comparison with Fred MacMurray in "My Three Sons"? Or what mother is as constantly attractive, effervescent, loving, sympathetic, reasonable, emotionally balanced, and interesting as Doris Day or Shirley Jones in their respective TV families? After all, in spite of affluence, what parent could check with their writers, see their makeup artists, or talk it over with a director before blowing their top at one of their children or their spouse?

On television, parents, or symbolic parents, are always active, involved, interesting people. They must be, or at least appear to be, for their large audiences. They have the job of selling products—and it isn't easy considering the competition on opposing networks. The real-life parent, passively stretched out before the tube for a nightly sunbath in stereotyped imagery, must appear to any child as the opposite polarity of all that is good, worthwhile, and meaningful in the night's program schedule. Is it any wonder American parents have come to be viewed by their children as emasculated slobs?

As a dominant member of the family, television not only establishes models by which other (real-life) family members will assess each other, but establishes a basis for their individual self-images, the ways in which they perceive their own beings. Self-images are, of course, reinforced by all of the other media. As a merchandising technique, the sale of identity is every bit as profitable as the sale of cosmetics and deodorants. Who are you? You can become anything or anyone you behold through the simple process of unconscious identification. Want to know how a hero behaves? Study Matt Dillon, Dr. Gannon, or McGarrett of "Hawaii Five-O." Want to be the life of the party? Take a course in Rowan and Martin or Carol Burnett. Want to be a charming, witty, and sought-after conversationalist and raconteur? Why not an advanced seminar in Merv Griffin, Dick Cavett, or Dinah Shore?

R. D. Laing, the British psychoanalyst, in his studies of schizophrenia among children, concluded that the best way to control and manipulate an individual is not to tell him what to do; that always generates resistance, hostility, and defiance. Instead, tell a person *who* and *what* they are. They will end up eating out of your hand or, in the case of the mass media, out of the sponsor's hand. Television is, of course, the most obvious director of human values and motivations among the media, but newspapers and magazines, radio, billboards, and the rest are also mutually reinforcing resources in the American struggle for identity. By the time an identity has been sorted out from the media morass, however, it has become outdated and inadequate, replaced by a new ideal identity pattern which must be discovered, pursued, and adapted, which in turn produces another. . . .

Unquestionably, this situation offers a solid foundation for any mass merchandiser, as media-advertised products are the basic ingredient of the American identity. And, the poetic irony is that the mechanism operates at a subsensory level. You can't see it, hear it, or feel it. No one even knows consciously that anything is happening.

Identity Searching Among Media Images

One brief example of the media-imposed identity delusion where media is a member of the family far more dominant and far more masculine or feminine than real-life fathers or mothers, is the phenomenon of adolescent omniscience. As a primary marketing target with billions of discretionary dollars available (unearned for the most part, but given as a media-induced tranquilizer for parental guilt over their failure as parents), young people have been repeatedly and patronizingly told they are God's own children—smarter, wiser, more sensitive, more educated, more idealistic, braver, more individualistic than all young people who have gone before them during the long history of mankind. In order to create a youth market, merchandisers first had to clearly differentiate unique qualities in the consumer's self-perception which make him different from other mere mortals.

Young people have been told *ad nauseum*—sometimes directly but usually through models and by implication—of their great unprecedented and even awesome capabilities. Usually, their omniscience is shown to be a direct product of media and the high level of saturation in media they have experienced since childhood. Media has taught them more than any other generation has known, given them greater insights into truth, qualified them to correct, discipline, and criticize their elders—who are pathetic failures, throwbacks to a stagnant, dead, and meaningless world of obsolete values.

It is even more incredible that one often hears full-grown adults talk in awe of the wisdom and omniscience of their half-grown, half-educated, half-mature children. Where—especially after what the world has endured during the past half century—would anyone come up with such unadulterated absurdity? You guessed it—media, in all its glory. Many adults, if they stopped to think about it, might still remember the wisdom of youth as it was manipulated in the Nazi, Fascist, and Communist youth movements.

Perhaps, however, in one respect these young people have been exposed to more information than any generation before them. But take a careful look at the quality of that information. They have seen war and death and violence on television and in the other media. But actually what they have seen is a carefully edited and censored version, far removed from the *real* multisensory experience of perceiving the *real* thing.

The war news on NBC has been shot by a skilled newsman, carefully trying to capture what he believes his editors, the network, and the sponsors want him to capture. If he fails to meet their expectations, he will simply be replaced. The news he writes and photographs is processed through many hands who edit, delete, and combine before the final broadcast version is prepared. A one-minute film on Vietnam appearing on the NBC News could easily have been edited out of 60 to 90 minutes of film shot and processed that day. What finally appears is a highly modified or cleaned-up version of war, reduced for perception at only the visual and auditory levels. Whatever comes through in this illusion labeled "News of the Vietnam War" has only the remotest relationship with what is really going on in Vietnam.

A similar parallel can be drawn on space flights, riots, strikes, tragedies, and disasters which are regularly featured as devices to sell media and advertising. They simply are not even remotely the real thing, but they have been passed off as such, especially among young people naturally eager for exposure to life, action, and significant events. A young man at the time of Socrates would have far greater contact with the realities of life and death than would any of the TV wet-nursed generation. War, death, famine, sickness, indeed all of life's experiences, would have been very close to his perception every time he stepped out of the front door; life at its best and worst awaited him in the streets— real life, not ersatz illusions of real life misrepresented, in the words of Coca-Cola's latest banality, as "The Real Thing!"

4. The Media Immersion—Baptism by Words and Pictures

Both conscious and unconscious motives lie behind every human communication situation. Motives are implied in every message—from a simple greeting, to a journalist's report of a news event, to an intense dramatic presentation through television or film. No form of human communication can be understood or reasonably evaluated without some consideration of both conscious and unconscious motives of the communicator.

Involvement in the transmission and reception of messages implies that each party (sender and receiver) tacitly assumes they have something to gain from the message. The message, for maximum effectiveness, must relate to motives or goal-seeking behavior at both ends of the communication. Remember, however, that motives can easily exist in a repressed state within the brain's unconscious mechanism. Many theorists maintain that most of an individual's "real" motives operate at this unconscious level. Conscious or stated motives are usually evasions, camouflage, or frequently mere rationalization serving superficial ego needs.

Motives, generally defined, involve *reasons for action or attention, goals to be pursued, or purposes to be served.* Since the conscious motive is often merely a screen for the "real" or unconscious motive, the entire subject of human motive is difficult to deal with in behavioral studies. The moment a motive is questioned, the ego becomes threatened and rises in outraged defense. This may hide the basic motive even deeper.

Any successful salesman will confirm that a basic customer strategy is to determine which purchasing motives, especially those which the prospect himself is consciously unaware, of, are most important. These unconscious but omnipresent motives rarely involve simply the quality or price of a product. They more often relate to the prospect's ego needs,

such as status, dominance, security, or recognition. If a salesman can relate his product to a prospect's unconscious
needs, he stands an excellent chance to make a sale.

The game is played in all forms of interpersonal communication. Hidden agendas, goals, objectives, purposes, desires, are implied, though rarely announced openly, in every
human situation. Most unconscious motives apparently involve how an individual sees other people seeing him. In
short, the most utilitarian motives in communication relate
to man's inexhaustible need to support and reinforce his
ego. The resultant strategies for manipulation are virtually
infinite in number.

Disguised Profit Motives

The motives implied in all forms of mass communication
are quite similar to those involved in interpersonal relationships, though perhaps in some respects they are relatively
simpler. As the mass media of communication in North
America serve primarily as a platform for advertisers, the
personal motives of communicators and their mass media
are invariably subordinated to economic motives. The name
of the game is *sell* or *communicate* (these verbs are used
synonymously in media jargon) and derive a profit. All
media are corporate enterprises in the United States. Corporate enterprises exist primarily as economic profit-making
entities. Profit is what media is all about.

This is not necessarily a questionable motive, even though
anyone who professes a profit motive too openly is likely to
find himself distrusted. Corporations function primarily in a
profit-and-loss ethic, yet in our society this ethic is carefully
camouflaged for the general public.

The media of mass communication go to great extremes,
in their public relations strategies, to disguise their primary
profit motive. The credibility of a communication source becomes highly suspect once the profit motive is emphasized.
But, profit is always there—the year-end stockholders' report which defines success or failure in terms of earnings.

Mass media must therefore appear to operate primarily in
the "public interest," publicly relegating the profit motive to
an obscure position on the hierarchy of motive if they are
to sustain effective communication with their audiences. The
illusion of public interest is reinforced by governmental, political, social, and educational institutions throughout the so-

ciety. The mass media do, indeed, often serve the public interest with distinction. There is one major catch, however: the public interest must never conflict with the long-term interest of corporate profit.

This analysis is not intended to denounce profit, corporate enterprise, or the ethics of capitalism. The benefits, as well as the disasters, these entities have bestowed upon the world are obvious. The media of mass communication will, furthermore, be controlled in every society by that society's institutions. The profit-dominated mass communication media system of Western society may, in truth, be vastly superior to the political-dominated system of communist societies—both in terms of social benefits derived and the varied perspectives presented. The point is that mass communication media must serve the motives—both apparent and hidden—of the controlling power structure within any society.

American mass media exist in a perpetual selling posture. They must sell their audiences, sell the societal institutions, and sell their advertisers. Media advertising rates are predicted upon the size and quality of respective audiences. Media cannot survive as an economic entity without maintaining the audience that will attract advertisers. Media content—writing styles, photographs, art, typography, etc.,—are the devices that control audience composition in both quality and size.

Audience size is important. *Time* magazine sells 5.6 million copies per week, providing its advertisers with over 24 million readers weekly. The "Bob Hope Chrysler Specials" on television reached audiences in excess of 70 million viewers. "Bonanza," one of the longest tenured of video families, was estimated to have a weekly international audience of 400 million viewers; it was a top-rated show in Argentina, Peru, Japan, Spain, France, and even the Soviet Union. Even newspapers, with smaller, localized audiences, fight tenaciously against competitive media to maintain reader saturation or audience dominance in their communities.

Audience quality is now as important as size, if not more so. Advertising rates in the national media are predicated upon the cost per thousand readers who are likely to purchase specific product categories.

For example, according to U.S. government statistics only 29.2 percent of all U.S. households boast annual incomes of $10,000 or more. This 29.2 percent accounts for 54 percent of the total annual personal income in the U.S. The male

head of these households is the primary audience target for
such magazines as *Esquire, Life, Look, Newsweek, New
Yorker, Playboy, Sports Illustrated, Time,* and *U.S. News
and World Report.*

Heavy Users: The Prime Target

An advertiser who is looking for prospective consumers
of men's slacks however, could not care less how large a portion of an audience consumes cigarettes. Each advertiser will
buy the medium which provides him with the largest per-
centage of people who purchase his product. Furthermore,
advertisers do not focus their expensive sales appeals upon
casual or infrequent purchasers—they shoot hard for the
heavy consumer. Of course, media must aim at very large-
sized audiences to provide the advertiser with a meaningful
number of heavy consumers in each product category.

For example, heavy users of most standard alcoholic
beverages are considered those who drink fifteen or more
drinks a week. If the advertisement can sell one of these
heavy consumers, this could be comparable to selling five
light users who consume five or fewer drinks per week. In
addition, heavy users tend to provide leadership within their
personal relationships for the products they use heavily. As
interpersonal communication from a leader within a group is
the most effective form of sales communication, ads designed
for these heavy users can serve as a catalyst for further sales.

Recall the fabled pecking order among chickens, which also curiously takes place among humans. In every group of
two or more people, there is a leader operating. Delineation
of leadership characteristics is often difficult because leaders
tend to vary in appearance and personality characteristics by
product or subject category. A man who is accepted as a
leader in beer brand preferences may well be distinctively different—both demographically and in terms of the emotional
needs he fulfills among his followers—than a person who is
accepted by the same peer group as a leader in, say, political
candidate preferences.

In one recent study a dozen men's bars were equipped
with hidden cameras. Groups of men were filmed at tables
where beer was being drunk. Once the leader was determined, the brand of beer he drank was noted. An average
of nearly seven out of ten men in each group were drinking
the beer brand preferred by the leader. This was remarkable

particularly because none of the men in these groups, including the leaders, were consciously aware of the pecking order phenomenon.

A composite portrait was synthesized of the beer leaders filmed. In a large beer advertising campaign it was used as a primary identification figure. Strangely, the leader in beer brand preference turned out to be an individual who was not particularly liked or respected by the men he led. This composite was a man few of his peers would invite into their homes. But for many reasons relative to the apparent sexual dominance of this character, he appeared to play a consciously unrecognized, though significant, role in guiding beer preference among his followers. The composite of the beer leader became a primary character in a multimillion dollar series of animated television advertisements.

Leaders generally appear to be just like their followers in respect to the product, only more so. Leadership studies in product selection suggest that the granting of leadership prerogatives by a group—at the unconscious, not the conscious level—is based upon the unconscious goals or motives each consumer hopes a particular brand selection will serve.

Cost per Thousand Users

Now to return to the basic media advertising strategy. Advertising rates are predicated upon the cost per thousand readers who are heavy product users in various product categories.

Only 6.2 percent of all adult men consume more than fifteen drinks a week. These heavy users account for 43 percent of all male alcoholic beverage consumption. Of the male readers in the *New Yorker*, 15.3 percent are heavy drinkers and they can be reached, with a black and white full-page advertisement, at a cost per thousand of $16.29. (Brand Rating Index Data).

Only 8.9 percent of *Look* readers, on the other hand, were heavy drinkers and they were reached at a cost per thousand of $25.39. *Look* had a much larger circulation than did the *New Yorker*, but on the basis of cost per thousand for heavy users, the *New Yorker* was a better buy for the general alcoholic beverage advertisers. The cost per thousand for drinkers varies, however, when the total heavy alcoholic beverage consumers are subcategorized into heavy drinkers of Scotch, bourbon, Canadian, blended, gin, vodka, rum, wine, brandy and cognac, cordials or liqueurs, beer, and ale.

In men's suits, for example, only 17.4 percent of all adult men in the United States purchase two or more suits a year. These heavy users account for 66.9 percent of all suit purchases by men. Thirty-three percent of the readers of *U.S. News* are heavy suit purchasers who can be reached through the magazine at the cost of $6.77 per thousand in a full-page black and white advertisement. Only 22.6 percent of *Life* readers, on the other hand, were heavy suit purchasers and the cost per thousand to reach them was $10.63.

Newspapers, television, magazines, direct mail advertising, and even the motion picture industry use a bewildering variety of consumer and audience research as a basis for their content design. Media survival depends entirely upon an audience's propensity to purchase the merchandise advertised.

To briefly illustrate the economic involvement of media, consider that a full-page, four-color ad in *Playboy* sells for $35,780; *Time*, $46,000; a one-minute commercial on the *Bob Hope* television show, $140,000; even a full-page ad in *The New York Times Sunday Magazine*, $7,520.

Advertising in North America is now a $20 billion annual industry ($1 billion in Canada), and is unquestionably responsible—through the movement of products and services in our economy—for a heavy portion of North American affluence.

Advertising expenditures correlate with the rate of increase in the U.S. gross national product. Should advertising be stopped suddenly, American economic affluence would almost immediately disappear, unemployment would increase, the stock market would enter into convulsions, and the country would certainly plunge into a period of economic chaos and depression. This is neither an exaggeration nor an attempt to overstate the present critical role of advertising to our way of life. Some Americans often complain bitterly about the annoyance of advertising, but in the management of markets—indispensable to their so-called way of life—media are today the basic instruments in the control and security of economic growth and affluence.

The average U.S. adult is estimated to spend thirty-two minutes per day reading a newspaper—an average of nine to ten thousand words. From sources such as magazines, books, signs, billboard, recipes, instructions, pamphlets, and so on, Americans perceive another twenty to thirty thousand words per day out of the seventy to eighty thousand to which they are exposed.

An average American adult reads eighteen to twenty thousand words per hour, so these general reading sources add roughly another hour or two of reading time.

He also spends an hour and a quarter per day listening to radio—more if he enjoys FM—and hears several thousand more professionally structured words in addition to music and lyrics.

Television is viewed by adults in the United States an average of 6.5 hours per day—throw in another seventy to eighty thousand words. The time and words involved in motion picture viewing contribute to an even heavier audio-visual load.

In the mass media, time and space are merchandised—every split second of time and every square centimeter of space. The basic reason for the existence of media is *sell*—content sells the publication or program to desirable strata of audience, providing a platform for advertising which sells products and supports the media. Time and space must be used purposively to communicate and accelerate maximum imagery levels consistent with the basic motive of media institutions—sell and make money or perish.

The Huckster Mythology

North Americans have constructed an enormous mythology about the role of advertising in media, helped of course by the media themselves. Few are willing to concede the relevance or importance in their lives of advertising. Most people simply say they make up their own minds—a very necessary illusion media must perpetuate in order to succeed in making up their minds for them. And most people sincerely do believe they are unaffected. They rarely read ads, or so they say. They claim to turn off their minds when commercials appear on television. Most have been thoroughly sold on the notion that advertising is irrelevant, completely separate from news or programs; that advertising people are rather flamboyant, foolish, and generally ineffectual; and that advertising is probably a waste of money for most clients, who merely get an ego trip out of seeing their product's name appear in print.

One executive in the office of Consumer Affairs in Washington said defensively, after reviewing some of the material presented in this book, that he "had never known an advertising man smart enough to do what they have apparently done with subliminal advertising." This rationalization is wishful thinking—$21 billion a year worth of wishful thinking.

Amazingly, Americans have elaborately hidden from themselves the embarrassing realities of an enormous industry which subtly educates them on *whose* purchases can be compared with their own, *what* is available to purchase, *why* they should replace old purchases with new, *where* they can make their next purchase most economically, *when* are the best times to purchase the incredible array of merchandise that forms the backbone of the so-called American way of life, and *how* to plan for new, more elaborate, and more expensive purchases.

A wide range of marketing studies have even revealed an inheritance characteristic in brand preferences. If a mother used a certain brand of canned milk, soap pads, detergent, sanitary napkin, and so on, the probability her daughter would continue her brand preferences (at least through part of her adult life) ranged from 40 to 80 percent on various products. Men will often continue their fathers' brand preferences for gasoline, automobiles, clothing, shoes, even wives.

In spite of advertising's mythological uselessness, retail audits and various other forms of consumer research continue to indicate unquestionable correlations between advertising appropriations, media utilization, and product sales. Like it or not, each one of us is continuously and strongly affected by advertising and the media it supports. There is literally no escape. If there is a significant difference between North Americans' response to media, it is a problem of how much they respond, not of whether or not they do.

The most carefully prepared portion of media content is advertising. The average U.S. adult is exposed to over 500 advertising messages daily, of which he consciously perceives only around 75, and may act upon perhaps a dozen or less. He blocks out from consciousness at least 85 percent of the ad messages and acts daily upon an average of 2.5 percent. The frantic competition for audiences' attention and favor is unbelievably intense and intensifying rapidly.

During the roughly *nine hours* per day of immersion in some form of commercially motivated mass communication media, the average U.S. adult consumes over 100,000 carefully edited, slanted, and skillfully composed words—words which sell, propose, and plead for his attention, his sympathy, his loyalty, and most of all—his money. This does not include stimuli that may be involved with his means of subsistence and which he must perceive and respond to during his working hours.

Visual or pictorial stimuli are even more intense than words. Through illustrations, photographs, television, and motion picture images, the visual pressure in modern society has increased at a prodigious rate during the past decade.

Media content—the articles and fiction of magazines, the news and features in newspapers, the news, dramatic, and variety programs of television—are the means by which specified types of audiences are made available to advertisers. It is virtually impossible for media to economically survive anymore by private sponsorship or by circulation income. The general audience media are vanishing—*Colliers, Saturday Evening Post, Look, Life.* Building circulation, considering the types of circulation required by advertisers, is an expensive business. Circulation income is fortunate to break even. Usually publications lose money on their wholesale cost per issue. Long ago media became subservient, both overtly and covertly, to the economics of marketing and salesmanship.

This is not intended as a casual indictment of media serving the gods of high finance, industry, commerce, or government. Indeed, media have frequently served constructive purposes within North American society. The U.S. population has materially benefited to an unbelievable degree from the effects of media. But the monster created to serve the objectives of material economic gain could ultimately turn out to have two heads—one of which may ultimately devour everyone. North American society and its life-style have evolved a tremendous dependence upon the ethics of *sell*— a dependence upon skillfully manufactured illusions and fantasies about ourselves and the world in which we live.

The Tulip Garden of Brand Differences

For centuries throughout most of Western civilization, the general criterion or definition of sanity has been *an individual's ability to discriminate between reality and illusion.* North American society appears to be moving farther and farther away from the recognition of reality. Illusions are now generated from illusions which were generated from illusions, which were. . . .

Tiptoeing through the tulip garden of commercially motivated illusion, variety and differences and entire value systems have been manufactured for us by experiential industries who relentlessly pursue our discretionary incomes. For example, there has never been any real difference among gasoline brands in the United States. Each is manufactured to strict U.S. Bureau of Standards specifications. Yet, most of us tend to seriously believe that one brand makes our car run better than another. By itself, these nonexistent differences in gasoline are probably harmless. They have actually produced an extremely effective marketing and distribution system for gasoline.

Consider also that thousands of beer drinkers, some with near religious fanaticism, believe they can clearly distinguish among major beer brands. They cannot—a fact that has been clearly proven by hundreds of national flavor tests for years. Beer manufacturers have spent a fortune in quality and flavor controls to make certain their product tastes exactly like all other dominant beers in the marketplace. Any slight flavor deviation would doom a brand to a minority market. Differences in major beer brand flavors are created by the shape and color of bottles, labels, and the proliferaion of image advertising.

In a recent national study of three major U.S. cigarette brands, trying to evaluate flavor variations in brand perception, only 1.33 percent of smokers could distinguish among the three major brands' taste—not a statistically significant number of smokers. Yet "taste" would appear to be the basic selling point for every major cigarette brand in the world.

It has been decades since any significant technical difference was designed into U.S. automobiles. They are, in fact, all the same in terms of their mechanical function at comparative price ranges. The only reason parts do not interchange is because that would destroy the exclusive replacement market created by each car sale. Once a new car is sold, the companies can anticipate selling the car again, through planned obsolescence—perhaps even twice in terms of profit derived—during the car's roughly five years of more or less dependable life.

Indeed, a Ford marketing executive in Dearborn recently

said, almost arrogantly, that automobiles have not been
marketed as a means of transportation in America for a
quarter century. Vehicles, he explained, are sold for their
image or symbolic values—female surrogates, status rein-
forcements, virility expressions, or support for a buyer's illusions of freedom and individuality. The largest and most
powerful industry in America depends for survival upon ego
images or fantasies rather than transportation realities.

Synthetic orange juice, for another example, is merchandised presently through ads which imply it is "better than its
imitators." As the TV announcer discusses the competitive
imitators, real oranges are shown visually; viewers will perceive the subliminal message that real orange juice is only
an imitation of the synthetic. Ridiculous? You can only wish
it was absurd. The TV commercials for synthetic juice are
pushing millions of dollars worth of the product into the
market monthly. Someone even managed to slip the stuff on
the last few space flights to the moon. And you, the American consumer, continue to buy and buy and buy in response
to these illusions.

The "crotch" magazines—*Playboy* and its competitors—
present masterful illusions of women who are consummate
products of skilled photo technology, lighting, and cosmetics.
There has never been, nor will there ever be, a real woman
like the centerfold picture in *Playboy*. She exists only in the
frustration-laden sexual fantasies of the immature reader.
Yet, a young man weaned upon such idealized masturbatory
fantasies may well spend his life trying to obtain a real
woman who can match the Playmate fantasy of idealized
perfection. Our Playboy is doomed to a lifetime of playing
with himself as he contemplates goddess-like centerfold
illusions. According to Freud, blindness is symbolic of castration. The sightless Oedipus was compelled to lean on a staff
for support. The staff, of course, is a phallic symbol, as is
Playboy. Imagine the pathetic plight of a real woman becoming maritally committed to a Playboy whose immaturity
and blindness to reality must be constantly nourished by
fantasy and illusion.

The media proliferation has made it almost impossible
to see what is really going on. Pressured from all sides by
competitive media screaming for attention, the average citizen blindly stumbles along, placing his trust and confidence
in his leaders somehow doing the right thing. Our modern,
"educated" citizens' support for mythology, magic, and su-

perstition—initiated and supported by media—is every bit as pervasive today as was true in the so-called primitive societies. The difference, however, is that few of us would admit that our myths are anything but reasonable, logical, scientifically proven facts of life. We study primitive religions and feel superior, medieval superstitions and feel liberated, ancient symbols of love and death and feel scientifically advanced. If modern man had the wisdom and insight to perceive himself, his institutions, and his life-styles as would an anthropologist in, say, the twenty-fifth century, he might well appear as scientifically and philosophically pathetic and superstition-ridden as the stone-age cultures now appear.

Detachment and perspective are absolutely essential for pattern recognition. The media perform a superb job of hammering relentlessly at our psyches, increasing tension to and beyond the breaking point, forcing reality into deeper and deeper depths of repression. Anthropologist Edmund Carpenter put the dilemma well: "Most journals, newspapers, TV shows, etc., merely repeat clichés, and the real clichés they repeat are their own formats. As clichés, they become environmental and hence unseen."

Biggest Bang for the Buck

The advertising industry is one of the most tight-fisted businesses in the world. Each dollar of a client's account spent must return to the client both sales and profits. If an advertiser spends 5 percent of his gross sales income on advertising, in order to break even he must realize twenty times that amount in sales from each advertisement. No one in business simply breaks even—not for long anyway.

A $35,780 full-page four-color ad in *Playboy*, to which has been added anywhere from $5,000 to $15,000 in artwork and copy, represents in round figures a $50,000 investment to an advertiser. Multiply this by 20, if his advertising budget is 5 percent of gross sales, and you have the break-even point in sales for a single *Playboy* ad—a minimal transactional value of $1 million. And, remember, this is only the break-even point; an effective advertisement might sell two or three times this break-even point.

Advertising effectiveness is exhaustively evaluated through pretesting the ad, by dozens of different market research techniques, and through retail sales audits. Direct cause-and-effect relationships between specific ads are admittedly difficult to achieve. But over a period of time, advertisers, their agencies, and the media can obtain highly accurate insights into whether the products are, so to speak, making out. Research, supporting the whole function of media in American society, is nearly a billion dollar industry in itself. Virtually every aspect of the American public's product and brand preferences, product utilization, conscious and unconscious goals or motivations underlying product selection, and response to advertising and media content are available through audience and consumer research organizations to any medium or its advertisers.

Virtually the same sales techniques are available to the producers of media content as are available to advertisers. Unless the television show, magazine, or newspaper achieves the "right" kind of audience profile, no advertiser will consider it a worthwhile investment. Media content must supply advertisers with a predictably sized audience with specific demographic as well as emotional-need characteristics. Communication success, or profit, demands every strategy conceivable in the care and feeding of audiences.

In the strenuous competition by media to have specific types of bodies included within their audience structures, anything is fair. The game is to participate as generously as possible in the roughly $20 billion advertisers' annual investment.

To assume that any medium, especially the competitively hard-pressed newspaper, is exempt from the competitive need to survive economically in this struggle for the consumer's attention is wishful thinking. Newspapers are presently at the greatest disadvantage of all media in their competition for advertising due to high production costs, limited metropolitan circulations, and high costs per thousand readers in crucial product categories. The past fifteen-year history of proxy battles, bankruptcies, mergers, and constant staff reorganizations in the newspaper field attests to the increased commercial pressures from television and other media. Therefore news and other peripheral information are, in effect, merchandised in the same behavioral sense as are underarm deodorants, cigarettes, and soft drinks.

All of the mass media are faced with the same dilemma. In competing for desirable audiences for advertisers, the editors, writers, directors, photographers, cameramen, artists, and the rest of the highly skilled media technicians continu-

ously exhaust their creativity in the development of content
material audiences will find interesting.

Our Idealized World View—of Ourselves

Perhaps the most effective general technique in the care
and feeding of media audiences is simply to *tell them what
they want to hear or what they need to hear,* at both the
conscious and unconscious levels. Audiences' idealized views
of both themselves and what they wish the world were like
are projected through the mirror of media. The reflections
absorbed by the reader projects back to him his own idealized
self-image.

This technique of self-flattery is illustrated by Marshall
McLuhan's precept—*Narcissus Narcosis*—taken from the
Greek myth of Narcissus who, on seeing his reflection in a
pool of water, was hypnotized by this vision of beauty, no-
bility, wisdom, and perfection, and fell in love with his own
image.

This is, perhaps, not an unusual aspect of human behavior.
There may be quite a little conscious Narcissus in all of us
as we preen ourselves in front of a mirror, trying to imagine
what we look like to others. Narcissus' problem, however,
was that he never found out the image he loved so passionately was his own. This major error in perception eventually
killed him. Perhaps like Narcissus, few of us see the mass
communication media as a mirror for our idealized pretensions.

How many readers saw the daily news from Vietnam, for
example, as a carefully processed and edited version of reality designed to reinforce our predispositions toward the war
and our own self-images? If you favored the war, there was
news to flatter you for your wisdom. If you opposed the war,
you were likewise accommodated. Often both sides can find
comfort in the same news story if the writer has been clever
enough. The Vietnam war news was reported to Americans
by Americans, and to other countries by their own nationals,
in ways which reflected each nation's prevailing attitude and
beliefs toward the war in terms of various national self-intere-
ests. It was a curious experience to have read the same war
story as reported in a French, British, Soviet, Mexican, and
U.S. newspaper. Even the so-called facts were often different.
The impression immediately came through that somebody

must be lying if the assumption is made that there is such a thing as objective "truth."

Lying is not necessarily the case. The media of each respective country is merely reporting an event consistent with the predispositions of the audience within that country. Of course, the views of each government and what it wants its citizens to feel about a war are also often a factor. The estimated $190 million spent annually by the Pentagon on public relations has as much to do with the structuring of war information for the American public as the Communist Party's Central Committee might have over *Izvestia* for the Soviet public—though, of course, the Pentagon's job is more difficult due to the lack of a monopoly on the media. In another example, the publication in 1972 of secret government reports increased *The New York Times'* daily circulation by 60,000 copies. The reports, of course, were valuable information to the U.S. public, but their publication also served an economic motive. It might be interesting to consider the editor's reaction to a news story which might result in a 60,000-copy decrease in circulation.

To summarize this chapter, in terms of a primary motive for the American media, the control and maintenance of an audience in behalf of the advertisers is a fundamental *raison d'être*. To accomplish this, media must reinforce existing attitudes and perspectives. Media rarely, except on a long-term basis which is highly unpredictable, brings about attitudinal change in the reader's view of himself and the world which surrounds him.

In America, media representing a multitude of views, attitudes, beliefs, and opinions are readily available. Any reader so inclined could avail himself of this rich variety of perspectives—from *The Wall Street Journal* to *Evergreen Review*, from "Bonanza" to "Sesame Street," from *The Christian Science Monitor* to the *Berkeley Barb*. The fact is, however, that virtually no one reads or selects from this rich abundance. Readers consistently seek out that medium which essentially tells them what they want to hear.

The Narcissus Narcosis phenomenon occurs on the unconscious level and includes a hypnotic effect. Audiences, like Narcissus, are unaware of what is really going on in their minds. In order for media to succeed in the care and feeding of desirable audiences, the audience is never permitted backstage. The entire field of mass communication is veiled by a self-flattering mystique. The veil is so heavy and so exquisitely decorated that even if the audience could see through it firsthand, most would probably discredit their perceptions.

Reinforced by institutionalized public relations programs, historical traditions constantly reinterpreted and updated to serve the needs of the present, and the endless catering to the audience's idealized view of itself—all of this either ignored or unconscious to the audience—constitute a basic mechanism in the subliminal utilization of the audience psyches.

5. It's What You Don't See That Sells You

The use of subliminal stimuli as a device for motivating audiences in the various media has reached a high level of technical proficiency. It is indeed remarkable that these techniques could have developed over the past decade without anyone's finding out what was going on.

The motive behind advertising is pure and singular: *sell* and *sell* and *sell*. The communicators' techniques of achieving this motive, however, are well hidden. Symbol identification and repression mechanisms, in the unconscious of the multimillion audiences, are used extensively. The possible variations appear infinite.

One ad for Bacardi rum was run in *Playboy, Time,* and *Esquire* magazines (see Figure 8). To solidly establish motive, consider what the Bacardi Corporation invested in this ad with only these three publications.

A full-page, four-color ad in *Playboy* at the time sold for $35,780; in *Time,* $55,175; and in *Esquire,* $14,300. Art and copy for a full-page national ad probably cost in the neighborhood of $10,000. This may appear like an expensive photograph but, considering the selling job demanded, it is probably cheap. It adds to a total investment by Bacardi in only the above three publications of $115,255. Estimating Bacardi advertising at 5 percent of gross sales, the ad's break-even point would be 20 times $115,225, or roughly $2,305,-000 in rum sales just on the one-time insertion with these three publications.

Not every reader of these magazines drinks rum, so the ad was aimed at a small portion of the total readership. In the United States, *Playboy* sold 4.1 million copies, with 3.35 readers per copy, or 13.7 million total readers. *Time* sold 3.9 million copies, with 4.4 readers per copy, or 17.2 million readers. *Esquire* sold 1.1 million copies, with 6.18 readers per copy, or 6.7 million total readers. The three magazines, considering only their U.S. circulations, were read monthly by 37.6 million readers. This equals the combined total populations of New York State, California, and Massachussetts.

A very large number of total readers are necessary for Bacardi to obtain a substantial, and manipulatable, proportion of the 3.4 percent of adult U.S. males who consume 82.2 percent of all rum consumed by men. Reduced to only heavy rum drinkers, defined as those drinking one or more rum drinks per week, 2.7 percent of the total U.S. male population account for 80 percent of total rum consumption.

Presumably these heavy rum drinkers, if they can be reached, will serve leadership roles at the interpersonal communication level in communicating brand preferences among the .7 percent of U.S. rum-drinking male adults who are light drinkers—those consuming less than one drink per week.

Via the three publications—*Playboy, Time* and *Esquire*—this small proportion of U.S. male adults is reached at a specific cost per thousand readers. As stated earlier, the cost per thousand (CPM) figure is the basic economic justification for all media advertising—and, therefore, content in magazines, newspapers, television, radio, billboards, and so on.

To publish a full-page black and white advertisement in *Playboy*, the cost per thousand for rum drinkers, who are 28.2 percent of their male readers, is $8.73. The CPM to reach *Playboy* heavy rum drinkers, 6.5 percent of the male readership, is $38.14.

In *Time* the cost per thousand for rum drinkers, 25.2 percent of their male readers, is $8.47. To reach heavy rum drinkers through *Time,* 5.1 percent of their male readers, costs $41.64 per thousand.

The *Esquire* CPM for male rum drinkers, 26.9 percent of their readership, is $7.80. *Esquire*'s heavy male rum drinkers are reached at $34.47 per thousand and are 6.1 percent of the magazine's readers.

The above figures are for black and white advertisements. The Bacardi ad would be more expensive as it uses a full four-color reproduction.

Now, with at least some concept of the economics involved with the Bacardi ad, the display must minimally sell $2.5 million in Bacardi rum through the three publications to break even. Examine the Bacardi ad carefully to see how this multimillion dollar transaction works.

The ad was tested with several hundred university students

who were asked which of the four rums they would prefer to buy. Over 80 percent chose number four. When asked if they understood what *ron añejo* meant, none knew the meaning or, for that matter, had ever heard the words before. No one had ever drunk *ron añejo*.

A slight preference appeared among female test subjects for the second bottle—Dark-Dry Rum. The chains around the glass curiously appeared to attract a significant number of women. But still, the overwhelming preference of the students was for *ron añejo*.

This appeared strange. The test subjects overwhelmingly preferred to buy a rum which none had ever experienced. Only about 20 percent of the subjects had ever drunk any kind of rum. There appeared no difference in the strong preference to buy *ron añejo* between those who had drunk rum and those who had not. Yet over 80 percent insisted they would prefer to buy *ron añejo*, which means simply in Spanish—aged rum.

There could be several explanations for this preference. The *añejo* bottle is slightly taller than the other three. The words "Extra Special" might establish a preference as the higher status or more expensive rum pictured. The wine-red color also might emphasize this rum over the other colors. And, the brandy glass may appear to have a higher status image than the other glasses shown.

But the name of the game is not only to establish a preference for a particular brand, but to persuade readers to buy the products. This ad is successful only if it plants a specific brand preference in a drinker's mind the next time a purchasing decision is required, which could be literally weeks after the consumer has perceived the ad and while he is consciously unaware of even having seen the ad.

So how is all this accomplished? Especially considering that even minutes after these millions of readers have momentarily viewed the Bacardi ad, very few of them could consciously recall either the ad or its content? How then could this advertisement be expected to influence a purchasing decision weeks, perhaps months, after it has been seen and consciously forgotten?

A careful investigation of the shadows in the bottom of the brandy glass tells the story. The shadows, of course, were painted in by a retouch artist. If a mirror is held above the shadows, the mirror image will read: U BUY. The unconscious mind, it has been well-established by research, is capable of reading mirror images, even upside-down mirror images.

The U BUY message is, in effect, planting what could be compared with a posthypnotic suggestion in the prospective consumer's unconscious.

True, this posthypnotic suggestion will not work on everyone—no more than would the tachistoscope or light threshold mechanical devices used to induce subliminal stimuli discussed earlier. But, there is no question that subliminal techniques of this sort will affect a statistically significant number of individuals in any large group. The 37.6 million readers who were likely, at least momentarily, to perceive the Bacardi advertisement in only these three publications, is certainly a very large group.

It is difficult to ignore the question as to how many individuals who have never before drunk alcohol will be affected by subliminal stimuli such as that in the Bacardi ad.

The Happy American Family

One of the happy families which live in various Seagram's advertisements presents another type of subliminal manipulation (see Figure 9). The cocktail party hostess ad appeared on the back cover of *Time*. This back cover, in the world edition, which sells 5.5 million copies and is read by 24.2 million people, cost $68,450. Though this layout was used in several publications, the break-even sales level for the *Time* cover alone would be around $1.5 million worth of Seagram's products sold.

Slightly over half (56.1 percent) of total *Time* readers are men—13.6 million male adults. Though the hostess ad is primarily directed at men, it also carries some interesting subliminal ideas for women.

The average age of the *Time* reader is 38 years. The average individual income is $6,501, the household income $11,071. This suggests working and somewhat independent, older, well-educated wives dominate the households of a majority of *Time* reader families.

Now, what is going on at the cocktail party and what does it mean, in terms likely to stimulate purchase preferences for Seagram's products?

Remember, advertisements are not designed to be carefully studied and analyzed. They are meant to be read—at both the conscious and unconscious levels—almost instantaneously. Designs are worked out in relation to an exposure time, for the average reader, measured in seconds. Either the ad does its job during this quick, very brief exposure, or it is a waste of time, effort, and money. Only the unconscious mind, which does not discriminate, evaluate, and make value judgments, can operate at this speed. The conscious mind, if the ad were to rely upon a cognitive thought process, would take far too long to assimilate the information and proposal. And many readers would find the conscious message objectionable on moral or other grounds.

What is the hostess, this lovely young blonde creature in her pink slack suit, doing? She is obviously listening and considering. But specifically what is she listening to and what is she considering?

She is the only woman in the room with a wedding ring apparent. Several hundred test subjects agreed the man she is talking to is not her husband. The man is speaking close to her face, confidentially, certainly something not intended to be heard by anyone else in the room. His hands in his pockets suggest he is still somewhat unsure of himself. He is, however, making some kind of a proposal, perhaps a proposition. The hostess is, apparently, considering the possibility.

The hostess's husband is likely the man standing in the upper left background wearing a light green suit. The informal suit would more closely match the informal pink hostess slacks. The man bending over and biting the sandwich is not likely the husband, as our man who is proposing might be overheard by a husband so close.

Now, where is the central male figure's wife? Our test subjects could find no woman in the room who could be identified with this man, whom we will refer to as the *lone wolf*. There are nine people apparently at the party, five men and four women (two are reflected in the mirror). The lone wolf is the odd man who is certainly not out.

Time male readers will identify with this lone wolf and female readers with the hostess. Considering the ages, experience levels, affluence, and sophistication implied by the models, who could resist projecting into such a delightfully adulterous situation?

The hostess, though she is certainly considering the possibility, has not yet made up her mind. Her mirror reflection suggests there is an invisible side to her personality, invisible at least to everyone in the room and particularly to her husband, who is not even looking. The horizontal line separating

mirror sections covers her wedding ring. Hidden from view,
her inner self is free of the restraints imposed by the symbolic
wedding band.

The hostess's inner struggle, if you can call it a struggle, is
seen by the unconscious in the drawing on the wall above
her head—the white area. In the drawing, obscure though
the figures are, appears a man looking down upon a nude
woman who stands with her hands clasped and her arms
stretched over her head, reflecting her hidden thoughts. What
married woman could resist identification with a most attractive hostess receiving the flattering attention of a handsome
male—who because of his expensive suit and ease of conversation, mark him occupationally as an executive or professional.

Peripheral symbolism in the photograph reinforces the
subliminal message. Ice tongs, the perennial castration symbol, are still on the ice bucket. Had our hostess been holding
these tongs at the time of the picture, the idea that she had
accepted the proposition would have been communicated.
The lady would have decided to put a horn into her husband.
But, she is still only considering the possibility.

The three glasses filled with drinks are curious, especially
as no one in the room is holding a drink—an odd omission in
a liquor advertisement. If gender could be assigned to the
glasses, the two with large, heavy ice cubes (two in each
glass) would likely be male. The glass with three smaller ice
cubes symbolizes the female. One male glass appears to be
moving between the male and female glass—the eternal triangle represented in ice cubes. Cool?

And how is all this exciting, adulterous, and worldly adventure brought about? Simple. The three bottles of Seagram's—phallic symbols with their caps off—are ready to
pour additional drinks and speed up the action.

All this happy intrigue has its source in Seagram's Canadian and Scotch whiskeys and in its London Dry Gin—in
effect, the source of life—and, of course, the pleasant prospect of infidelity. Once our hostess has had a drink of Seagram's, she may warm up to lone wolf's proposition.

The photographer-artist who put this ad together was a
superb technician. The production budget could have ranged
between $15,000 and $20,000. With a cast of nine models,
probably working for several days at fees ranging from $75
to $150 each per hour, the story may have required several
days for the photographer to achieve the precise results re-

quired. Considering what is at stake—at least $1.4 million in Seagram sales—the ad cost was probably a bargain.

Subliminal Gender

Ice cubes likely sell more alcohol for the distilling industry than attractive models in cheesecake poses. The inconspicuous ice cubes often hide the invisible sell—invisible, that is, to the conscious mind.

The Cinzano ad is a simple, perhaps typical demonstration of subliminal technique in ice cubes—two colors on a quarter page of *Time* at a cost per insertion in the world edition of $4,175 (see Figure 4). Study the Cinzano ad and see for yourself how it earns its keep.

As in most advertising, few readers are likely to assimilate the copy. The art usually carries all the motivational stimuli. The copy, if read, reinforces the message communicated by the artwork—an added bonus for the advertiser.

Readers of the Cinzano ad are not actually looking at an ice cube—only at an artist's representation of an ice cube. It is impossible to photograph ice under hot floodlights. And besides, ice will never look exactly like what the artist needs for the ad to do its job. A good retouch artist can complete the design within the cube, planting a variety of unidentifiable designs to gently stimulate and lead the consumer's fantasies and dreams. When presented with a *nonspecific, nondirective* design, people will often put into it meaning which reflects their unconscious motives, hang-ups, or desires. This is the underlying principle of the Rorschach inkblot test.

Within the multidimensional Cinzano ice cubes the designs can mean virtually anything the reader wishes to fantasize and project. Projections, however, quite often involve some form of sexual fantasy. In the Cinzano cubes the artist has included subtle cues which will lead the reader, at both the conscious and unconscious levels, to interpret male or female genital symbols, breasts, nude couples, animals—the possibilities are endless. Cinzano probably really doesn't care what meaning is projected into the cubes as long as it attracts the reader's attention and holds his eye on the ad as long as possible so the subliminal sell can take effect.

Once the reader's attention is focused on the cubes via his unconscious projections into the nondirective fantasy designs, hidden persuaders go to work.

Humans unconsciously, and sometimes consciously, identify symbolic representations with gender—male and female. Though some symbols are intercultural in gender, culture often determines the subliminally implied gender of a symbol. In America, for example, a boat is generally feminine, as are many automobiles and other power-oriented symbolic substitutes for sex. Designers usually imply in automobiles, furniture, appliances, and even airplanes, either male or female characteristics.

The famous Lockheed Constellation, with its three vertical stabilizers, was designed as a female image—and it turned out to be the singularly most successfully sold airliner ever turned off a production line. The competitive Douglas DC-4, with its single vertical stabilizer—strongly masculine—was a successful military transport but never was nearly as successful among the world's commercial airlines as the Connie. Lockheed executives believed the Constellation design for commercial airline travelers related to a feminine or maternal image, suggesting security. There was no aerodynamic benefit derived from either the three- or one-piece vertical stabilizer. Technically they were identical. Symbolically, however, they were vastly different. Gender can be subliminally important in every object around us in modern society.

Linguistically, gender is not consciously used anymore in English, though masculine and feminine nouns are an important part of Latin-derived languages—Spanish, French, Italian, and Portuguese. Nevertheless, even among English-speaking peoples who do not specifically use gender, sex is vitally important as we label and describe objects in our unconscious. Why not ice cubes?

Thinking in terms of male and female, which of the two Cinzano ice cubes would be female? The one on the left, of course; at least it was so designated by over 90 percent of a thousand test subjects. The elliptical-shaped chip at the top corner of the left-hand ice cube suggests something is missing—a portion of the cube's anatomy. The cube on the right is therefore masculine. Observe the top area of the right-hand cube. A phallic symbol has been painted into the surface. The long, cylindrical shape points directly at the chip in the cube at left. Hundreds of test subjects unanimously made these female-male identifications for the cubes without being able to consciously specify why they should be female and male.

Now ask, what is going on between this female and male

set of ice cubes? The drops of water or melted ice, actually painted in by an artist, suggest the cubes are melting or warming up. More drops appear beneath the female cube than beneath the male. Obviously the female is warming up faster than the male.

And how did the ice cubes get turned on? Cinzano, of course. Even considering seriously the old jokes about frigid women, or men for that matter, being "ice cubes"—much credit must be given to the American advertising industry for its success in creating a sexual affair between two pieces of ice as a subliminal device with which to merchandise a liqueur. The ad must have sold thousands of gallons of Cinzano, as it was repeated many times in a wide variety of American publications.

Whether the consumers who responded to the Cinzano appeal were any more hung up, or frigid if you will, than the general U.S. population can only be a matter of conjecture. But the ad works on the promise of turning off frigidity. Anything that can turn on a piece of ice—Cinzano included—can't be all bad.

Peer Deeply Into My Ad

The Gilbey's Black Velvet Canadian whiskey advertisement appeared in a large number of North American magazines during the winter of 1971 (see Figure 15).

The basic symbolic content is simple and obvious. The long, phallic, cylindrical shape of the black container stands close against the female, open, elliptical-rimmed vaginal symbol of the glass. This archetypal male-female symbolic design is certain to attract the reader's attention.

There is much, much more at the subliminal level. The ad is black, dark, conveying a tactile experience of smooth velvet. All smooth textures may be regarded as symbolic of remoteness and, by analogy, also cold colors. Conversely, porous textures symbolize nearness, as do warm colors. The advertisement was published during the winter months when most of North America was dark, overcast, somewhat depressing, and people were living inside their homes.

So what is subliminally promised the potential purchaser of Gilbey's Black Velvet? Look carefully into the whiskey glass.

Two figures, a man at left and a woman at right, are standing on a tropical beach as they watch a magnificent sun-

set. One of the heavy tropical clouds above the figures appears to be a sailboat cruising smoothly before the wind at
dusk as it passes the magical island. The subliminal content
is certainly remote from the winter North American environment.

The subliminal message is simple: Gilbey's will transport
you and your male or female romantic interest to a tropical
island far away from the cold, depressing, and restricting
North American winter. You can take the trip for only the
price of a fifth of Black Velvet.

The inside back cover of *Time* was purchased by Chivas
Regal Scotch to display its massive bottle with the tissue-
paper wrapper torn away (see Figure 5). The innocuous appearing ad would hardly be noticed at the conscious level by
the average *Time* reader. Virtually all readers, nevertheless,
who perceived the ad for even an instant would have its subliminal message registered deeply in their psyches, even
though only 42 percent of adult male *Time* readers are regular Scotch drinkers. This is a high level of Scotch consumption, as only 10.2 percent of the total adult male population
account for 90.8 percent of all adult male Scotch consumption in the United States.

The question, of course, is how the *Time* ad manages to
sell several million dollars' worth of Chivas Regal, one of the
most expensive Scotch whiskeys in the American market. The
copy line at the top and bottom of the page is directed at the
readers' "friends" who won't think less of them but will certainly think more of them if they serve Chivas Regal. The
question the ad subliminally poses for the readers' psyches is
simply: Who are these friends?

Market research on Scotch drinkers revealed that individuals who drink Chivas Regal rarely serve it to friends. At
best, these Scotch drinkers, even those at the very high income level of over $25,000 per year, will keep Chivas Regal
for only their very best friends, clients, or special guests
whom they are trying to impress. Chivas drinkers usually
keep less expensive brands of Scotch around the house for
general guests or casual or lower status visitors.

So who are these "friends" mentioned in the copy who will
not think less of you even if you don't serve Chivas? Man's
best friend, of course.

Perhaps the easiest way to discover man's best friend is to
turn the ad on its side with the top of the bottle to your

right. Relax and look at the paper wrapper. A light colored triangular shape directly above the base of the bottle neck forms an eye. To the left and slightly above the eye, a fold in the wrapper sticks up forming an ear. The wrapper fold at the extreme right, white-shaded, forms a nose, with a horizontal fold providing the line for a mouth. The area just above the large label, where a light appears to be glowing, would be roughly the area of the dog's neck. A dog, probably a German shepherd or collie, is the subliminal *modus operandi* of the Chivas Regal advertisement in *Time*. The ad must work extremely well, as it was frequently reprinted in other publications, such as *The New York Times*, for well over a year.

Small children upon whom this ad has been tested find the illusion absolutely delightful. It is doubtful these children will be converted to Chivas Regal drinkers, but the hidden dog does provoke their attention and laughter. The dog (especially subliminal dogs) appears to provide an unconscious stimulus for the purchase of alcohol. Traditionally in our culture the symbolic archetype of the dog has meant affection, companionship, courage, devotion, and fidelity. Faithful love and friendship are frequently mentioned as basic qualities of the dog symbolism in medieval Christian art. A white dog is a happy omen. The dog has long been believed to hold supernatural powers. Presumably these symbolic archetypal meanings are buried in the unconscious of all of us. The dog is one of the richest and most complicated of animal archetypes—especially in North America where, as people have become more and more alienated from one another, they have developed an increasing emotional dependency upon dogs, enough to support a multimillion dollar, high-profit market for the sale of dog food. An often noted characteristic of American life, commented upon by foreign visitors, is the status of American dogs who often receive more affection and loyalty than is bestowed upon people.

Animals appear to play important roles in our unconscious. The anthropomorphism (giving human attributes to animals) of animated cartoon, in children's fairy tales and folk stories, and in such things as Halloween costumes and masks is hardly mere random accident. Animal faces appear subliminally in many of the illustrations included in the book. On the frosted Gilbey's gin bottle (Figure 1) appear numerous animal faces; most seem to be dogs. A most unusual application of subliminal animal symbolism, however, was applied in the *Esquire* advertisement for Coca-Cola's Sprite (see Figure 6).

The ad was aimed at the older, affluent male readership. The bottle, opened and covered with condensation, is symbolic of the reader's erect, virile, male phallus. The cap, wet, glistening with water (semen) drops, and bent—having been removed from the bottle with great force—emphasizes the symbolization of strength and power, aggression and dominance. These more obvious symbolic constructions in the ad are sex-packed and should, by themselves, sell Sprite by the tank-carload. Coca-Cola's ad department, however, is taking no chance that the ad might not trigger a purchase motivation.

Relax again and look deeply into the almost hypnotic organization of bubbles surrounding the lime slice. Something rather strange is going on in the bubbles.

The ear, an orifice of the human body, suggests that the effervescence rising from the glass may have aphrodisiac qualities, at least at the symbolic level, especially with the two-balled earring with one ball hanging lower than the other. Something highly symbolic is, indeed, going on in the bubbles above the lime slice. Before reading further, try to psych out the ice cubes in the glass. What is Sprite trying to tell you?

The right side of the ice cube above the lime slice forms the back of an animal—a large shaggy dog with a pointed nose, or quite possibly a polar bear. The animal's legs are extended outward to the left, parallel with the top of the lime. The animal's arms (or legs, as you will) appear to be holding another figure which is human with long, feminine hair. Her face is located just above the animal's head.

The two figures, animal and human, are in what can only be described as a sexual intercourse position. The polar bear, dog, or whatever, is in sexual embrace with a nude woman.

Bestiality may be illegal throughout most of the world, but, at the symbolic level, it appears to have sold a lot of Sprite. The Coca-Cola Sprite advertisement was designed to sell around a subliminal theme of highly taboo sex.

A Symbolic Nightmare

The full-page, four-color Calvert whiskey advertisement in the October 1971 *Playboy* appears to have ushered in a new trend in subliminal manipulative technique that might well have originated in medieval witchcraft—which, of course, all of us know was pure nonsense, based upon sheer ignorance and superstition (see Figure 16).

Before proceeding, study carefully the Calvert ad for several minutes while relaxed. Try to understand how the ad makes you feel. Then briefly write out these feelings so you can check back later on how you reacted before the analysis.

The bottom of the glass contains a cone-shaped volcano from which the whiskey and ice appear to have erupted. The volcano is an ancient symbol of fertility, in that volcanic earth is the world's most fertile soil. However, the volcano and its destructive fire are also linked with the idea of evil, symbolic not only of nature's primary force (creation), but of the fire of life (destruction). The volcano represents the passions which control our energies, a sudden and frightening eruption (orgasm) preceded by an extended time of internal, enclosed, intensifying pressure.

And, what has erupted from the Calvert volcano? Life, of course, symbolized in the golden richness of Calvert Extra Blended Whiskey. Gold, the symbol of divine intelligence, all that is superior, spiritual determination, hidden or elusive treasures, and supreme insight and wisdom would naturally be the color of Calvert.

Just to the left of the volcano's erupting crater is a fish, swimming in the golden sea of Calvert whiskey. The fish has been symbolically known as the mystic ship of life, phallically penetrating the water as it swims, spiritually symbolic of the relationship between heaven and earth, the life force surging upward, and the spiritual world that lies beneath the illusionary visual world. Christ was often symbolized as a fish.

A mouse, however, appears to be riding the fish, its eyes and nose facing the rear of the fish, its tail curved up over its back across the large right ear. The large ear suggests a mouse rather than a rat. The mouse in medieval symbolism was often associated with the devil. Symbolically, the devil is looking back upon where the fish or life force has swum. To the left and above the mouse's head, in the bottom left-hand corner of the ice cube, is the sun, its rays shining down, penetrating the golden Calvert sea of life and its inhabitants.

In the cold, dead world above Calvert's ocean of life, however, is another story. Just to the left of the sun appears a skull, the brain case marked with wavy lines, the jaws open and foreboding. The skull, of course, is symbolic of man's mortality, that which survives his being once his life and body have disappeared.

To the right, frozen into the ice cube above the golden liquid, are scorpions. The scorpion for thousands of years has symbolized the period of man's existence in which he is threatened by death. In medieval Christan art the scorpion was utilized as a symbol for treachery.

Three wolf faces appear above the scorpions. One face is to the left of the bell-shaped white space at the top of the ice cube. The nose points down at a 45 degree angle toward the bottom right corner of the cube face; the two eyes—teardrop shaped—point up and out toward the animal's ears. Behind or above and to the left of the wolf is another wolf face supported by a long neck. The second wolf appears to be biting the ear or neck of the wolf in front. To the right of the white space is the third wolf's head, the two eyes staring forward on each side of a triangular nose pointing down.

The wolf has appeared in Western culture for centuries as symbolic of evil, often a power enclosed in the bowels of the earth which at the end of the world would break free and devour the sun. The wolf myth has been related to the final annihilation of the world by fire and water.

Just to the left of the top left corner of the scorpion cube is the head of a rat, its head turned sideways, the nose pointing to the right, two ears and eyes to the left of the pointed nose. Only the head is visible, suggesting the rat may be swimming in the gray fluid symbolic of the life force which fills the ice cube and is draining out from the bottom corner of the cube on top of the skull. Gray, the color of volcanic ashes, or perhaps amniotic fluid, is symbolic of the earth and vegetation, depression, inertia, and indifference which is leaking out of the ice cube onto the surface of life.

Along the glass rim, to the right of the gray cube, is a lizard. The lizard often symbolizes distrust when it appears in dreams and often typifies one who is cold-blooded, groveling, and morally contemptible. In Japanese legends the lizard has symbolized a revengeful spirit with supernatural powers.

The top ice cube in the foreground, on the left, holds a mythological menagerie. If the cube is turned upside down —remember, the unconscious can read upside down, even mirror images—the head of a shark appears, with eyes and tooth-jagged jaws pointing to the left. Symbolic of danger, death, and evil, the shark as an archetype has been around since long before man; it is one of the earth's oldest creatures.

Just below the upside-down shark, a white bird appears in the ice cube, its head pointing down at the lower left corner of the cube. Birds have frequently symbolized human souls and carriers of the dead to paradise. In particular, the white bird is an archetypal symbol for the soul of the righteous. The white bird is upside down, or dead, in the Calvert ice cube.

To the right of the dead white bird, under the upside-down shark, appears a white mask which is an ancient symbol of deception, hypocrisy, and—in dreams—betrayal and lies. In Chinese drama a white mask represents a cunning and treacherous person.

Another mask, this one a full-face mask with a grotesque expression, appears below and to the right of the white mask, in the upper corner of the ice cube side panel facing down and to the right. The upper portion, eyes and nose, are colored brown. The lower portion of the face is white.

In the upper ice cube at the rear is another fish—the head facing left in the upper left corner—which seems to have an angry expression on its face. Beneath the fish is a form that eight out of ten test subjects identified as a white bird in flight; the head faces left, with a long neck extending to the body. A curved white line across the top of the body represents a wing in flight. The bird could be a swan. A flying bird archetypally symbolizes the flight of the soul to heaven.

Just below the swan's neck appear two dark areas, almost like eyes. Below these eyes is a small white knob that could be a nose. The white area seen above as a bird now becomes the top of a head—the bird's head becoming the left ear, the beginning of the bird's wing the right ear. The mouth of what has been unanimously identified by test subjects as a grinning white cat is partially hidden behind the distorted rim of the glass as it appears through the ice cube. The white cat is an ancient Christian symbol of laziness, lust, cruelty, egoism, flattery, treachery, and witchcraft.

It appears that Calvert Extra Blended Whiskey has a greater kick in it than anyone ever suspected. The fine details in the advertisement, including dozens of embedded SEXes in a mosaic, must have required hundreds of hours of labor by the artist. Embedding technique will be discussed in the next chapter, after which the reader should carefully review the Calvert—as well as the other ads—in this chapter. The painting, if accomplished outside the advertising frame of reference, might even be considered a masterpiece. Only the painting's major symbolic devices have been commented on here. There are many more, however, which readers may discover for themselves.

In all fairness, symbol analysis is a tricky business. Jung and many other experienced analysts continuously warned sternly against glib symbolic interpretations. Symbols have highly individual meanings in specific contexts. The object of advertising is sales, however, not psychotherapy. Advertising artists must apply symbolism likely to have wide similar meanings throughout their target markets. The interpretations of Calvert's ad were reviewed for variations in meaning with a panel of individuals and general consensus obtained on meanings before any single interpretation was accepted. This, of course, represents only a reasonable conscious interpretation of meaning. We can only speculate on the interpretations at the unconscious level. This does not mean, in any respect, that each reader would attribute precisely identical meaning or significance to these complex symbols—fish, scorpion, wolf, lizard, etc.

The interpretations presented here were reviewed against several major authoritative sources on symbolic meanings. Should any reader have a more lively, or more deeply involving conscious interpretation for any of the symbolism discussed in this book, he is urged to utilize his own meaning hypothesis for an explanation of the ad's effectiveness.

In the Calvert ad, it is absolutely certain that not more than one percent, if that many, of the over 20 million people who saw the ad consciously recognized the symbolic content. Indeed, one percent is a very high estimate for conscious cognition for any ad's symbolism. A medieval mentality would probably have recognized, at the conscious level, most of the symbolism instantly. Modern man, however, has been subjected to a very long, intensive socialization process during which he has learned to repress his conscious response to symbolic content. The Calvert ad symbolism, nevertheless, will register instantly within the unconscious of virtually everyone who perceives the ad anywhere in the Western culture—and very likely in Eastern cultures as well.

In attempting to penetrate meaning parameters in any symbolic media, the first step is to recognize the individual symbols and their meanings in the specific context. The second step is to synthesize the individual meanings into a whole to obtain a thematic meaning.

When the individual symbols are lumped together into one composite message, the Calvert ad communicated a fascinating concept into the unconscious psyches of many millions of readers—young and old, rich and poor, drinkers and non-drinkers. The thematic meaning of the Calvert ad is birth, life, and death—birth from the volcano, life in the golden sea of Calvert whiskey, and death through betrayal and degradation within the hard frozen ice cubes. Earlier a theory was developed that symbols are organized around the two polarities of human existence—the *origin* and the *end* of life. Most advertising focuses upon the origin of life, love, or—in the vulgar *Playboy* fantasy—sex. The Calvert ad covers the entire symbolic spectrum and, apparently, has successfully merchandised the product. The ad was published numerous times in several national media, including *Life* magazine with 7.5 million copies and 21 million readers.

That this advertisement was successful in selling whiskey is beyond question. The four-color page space rate in *Playboy* alone is nearly $40,000. No one fools around indiscriminately with $40,000, except possibly people in government. No businessman could tolerate unsuccessful advertising expenditures for a moment.

One question, then, remains to be considered in relation to the successful Calvert advertisement. *What does the ad do to the psyches of the over 40 million people who presumably perceived the colorful menagerie of death just in* Playboy *and* Life *magazines—especially those readers who have not yet taken a drink?*

Though directed only at the 4.5 percent of all adult men who consume four or more drinks of blended whiskey a week (heavy users), who account for 71.8 percent of all blended whiskey consumed by men, the ad was also perceived by millions of other people who do not drink, or at least did not drink until then. The Calvert Distilling Company has, one can be quite certain, pretest data on the advertisements. Perhaps a congressional investigating committee should ask for all the data it has collected on the social effects of such advertising.

According to the theory, either sex or death symbolism should work as a device by which to circumvent consciously discriminating perception. Throughout his history, man's major preoccupation has been with death, not sex. True, the population increase might be at least partially attributable to sex symbolism. However, man has worshipped death in his steady and brilliant development of weapons, elaborate rituals, and magnificent religious institutions, in the names of a hundred gods—burial temples from Egyptian pyramids to Hollywood's Forest Lawn Cemetery. Death has certainly provided mankind with a major preoccupation through thousands of years of history, during which he worked diligently to find ways in which his fear of death could be repressed, suppressed, or at least hidden temporarily from his constant conscious awareness.

New research now going on in the advertising industry is investigating the subliminal manipulability of man through death symbolism. So far, relatively few death-oriented ads have appeared in American media. Sex has worked well for a very long time, but may be approaching a saturation point where its effectiveness has begun to decrease. Many research directors feel the SEX embeds may be losing their sell.

Death in the Cocktail Hour

The Barcardi on-the-rocks ads, which has appeared in *Playboy* as well as several other national media, may be one of the early examples of this new trend in American advertising toward death symbolism as a *modus operandi* for sales (see Figure 17).

The cocktail glass is covered with the conventional SEX subliminal mosaic. In the ice cubes, at the top, are masks, a cat face, a fish, a rabbit, and other animals. These symbols are located above the liquid in the ice cubes—the usual symbolic menagerie, most of which is death-associated. You might test your own skill by finding and identifying the various symbols utilized. The bat, part of the Bacardi trademark, has a curious archetypal significance. The bat is symbolic of black magic, darkness, madness, and, in dreams, peril and torment. A bat flying about a house (the bat on the Bacardi label is flying) is a death warning, the wings archetypally signifying the power of darkness.

The primary symbolic device, subliminally perceived in the Bacardi ad, appears at first glance to be an ice cube in the center bottom of the glass. Look more carefully. The ice cube is a golden skull with a flattened nose, large eye sockets, and jagged teeth.

Gold, in Western culture, traditionally symbolizes great

happiness and prosperity; the skull symbolizes death, mortality, and transitoriness. The thematic implication in both the color and skull symbolism implies that one might richly enjoy dying if well fortified with Bacardi rum or, quite possibly, Bacardi will serve to protect the drinker from a fear of death. If a rational, though symbolic, argument will sell rum, this one should really make the grade more dramatically than sex ever did.

e is a narrow range of reflected light between A and ...
h affects only the unconscious and cannot usually be seen
...e conscious mind. Within this range, emotionally loaded
...s can ... readil ... advertis ... ... or ... electronics.

6. Sex is Alive and Embedded in Practically Everything

Embedding refers generally to the practice of hiding emotionally loaded words or pictures in the backgrounds of ads. Embedded words and picture illusions are part of most advertising throughout North America today. These subliminal stimuli, though invisible to conscious perception, are perceived instantly at the unconscious level by virtually everyone who perceives them even for an instant!

Most national advertising includes embedding. Retail or local ad layouts may not have the facilities, as their artists and writers either do not know about subliminal techniques or they lack the skill and craftsmanship required to do the work well. Every major advertising agency has at least one embedding technician in its art department. The technique is taught in most commercial art schools.

Playboy magazine displays monthly some of the most skillful examples of subliminally embedded art. All other major national publications with advertising, as well as television, also use the technique.

SEX is the most frequently embedded word in the American advertising industry. Multidimensional printing techniques permit advertising artists to plant taboo emotional words dozens of times in a single layout. Words such as fuck, cunt, ass, whore, prick, and death are also used frequently as subliminal triggers to motivate purchasing behavior.

Embedding can be accomplished by an artist, who paints the illusion in over ice cubes and other props or designs in the layout. Photographically, embedding is even easier to accomplish. Consider the apparent limits to human perception of light reflection:

1   A   conscious perception   B

There is a narrow range of reflected light between A and 1 which affects only the unconscious and cannot usually be seen by the conscious mind. Within this range, emotionally loaded words can be inserted into an advertisement for communication with a reader's unconscious. Recall from the earlier theoretical discussion that humans can be assumed to have at least two sensory input systems, one incoding data at the conscious level and a second operating at a level below conscious awareness.

A photographer takes a photograph of a model and props. They are photographed at say 1/150th of a second. A double exposure can then be made at 1/1000th of a second in which only the word SEX is photographed as a faint impression across some portion of the original picture. The word SEX can be interwoven into a mosaic such as in the *Playboy* centerfold where virtually every square inch of the model's body is mosaiced with SEXes.

Another embedding technique involves painting the SEX mosaic on the photoengraving plate with asphaltum and briefly immersing the plate in acid where the words are lightly etched across the plate. This is probably the technique used on centerfolds.

Some readers will see the embedded SEXes instantly. Most readers will require several weeks to learn how to relax their perception to the point where embeds become immediately apparent. A few readers will, unfortunately, never be able to expand their conscious awareness to the point where they will become consciously sensitive to subliminal stimuli.

Once any individual learns to relax and focus attention, however, a whole new world of perception awaits him, even though much of what he will perceive in the mass media may be profoundly disturbing. A basic fact of human existence is that humans perceive just about what they want to perceive—at least at the conscious level. Mass merchandisers have known this a long time. The general public is incredibly ignorant of perceptual phenomena—and perhaps it has been kept that way on purpose.

It is entirely possible, for example, for an individual to project SEXes into clouds, or anywhere else for that matter. It is also entirely possible for a skilled artist to embed SEXes into advertisements or into virtually anything. The author was recently interviewed by a textile manufacturer who was looking for a way to embed SEXes into pantyhose, ties, shirts, and even window curtains. Merchandisers' illusions depend upon consumers who cannot be certain whether the SEXes are their own creation or that of the merchandiser.

The author's photograph on the dust jacket of this book was taken against a background of drapes. A careful, relaxed study of these drapes will reveal a mosaic of SEXes woven into the fabric. The effect of this subliminal stimuli may well have been to manipulate the reader into purchasing *Subliminal Seduction.*

As long as consumers are uncertain, should they detect subliminal stimuli they will logically assume they are imagining things and pass the notion off without a second conscious thought. People in North America have been culturally trained to believe in the inherent honesty of their governmental and commercial institutions. They find it very difficult, if not impossible, to believe anyone would do anything as outrageous as these subliminals. They will usually seek out someone else, someone more logically guilty of misleading them, upon whom to heap their anger over the betrayal. They will be helped in this, of course, by the merchandisers and the culture controlled by merchandisers. Marshall McLuhan expressed this behavioral pattern well when he commented that his critics have blamed him for starting the fire when he only turned in the alarm.

The Discovery Shock

As an individual becomes aware of subliminal phenomena, the shock may cause him some initial physical or emotional discomfort—possibly even concern over his sanity. Most insanity in our culture has a common definitional denominator in that the insane see, hear, and experience things that are not participated in by the so-called sane. It can be most unsettling when you cannot make others sensitive or consciously aware of subliminal stimuli you see quite clearly. Consensus or peer group support for perception is culturally very important to an individual's security or sense of well-being. Humans tend to repress information they perceive which is not immediately reinforced by their peers, as it threatens their self-image as a sane, or socially acceptable, individual within their society.

As mentioned before, some individuals are so defensively up tight, they could never see embeds or even the much more obvious symbolism, Should these few be forced to concede the existence of subliminally affective symbolic patterns, they would probably refuse to concede their significance. "OK," they will conclude, "the tricks or illusions are there. We admit it. But there is no evidence to prove they do anything to people."

The whole thing is a very neat, very tight, and very powerful puzzle which has been the subject of much philosophical debate during at least the 2,000 recorded years of our intellectual history. It seems almost macabre that mass merchandisers were the first to make a practical application of what had always appeared to be obscure, hairsplitting, and merely theoretical nonsense indulged in only by philosophers. Many individuals today maintain the great thinkers in our intellectual heritage were men who contributed little but confusion to the world, in which they indulged themselves with seemingly endless and worthless arguments. Today we even use the term *philosophical* to describe an argument we consider to be worthless nonsense.

Even though college students are hardly representative of North America's population, fewer than one out of ten students were unable to penetrate subliminal illusions after several weeks of study and discussion. Many, who at first were horrified at the possibility that such machinations were going on, over a period of time began to find subliminals on their own. Perhaps self-discovery techniques are really the best way to communicate information. Never, however, underestimate the phenomenon of perceptual defenses—the excluding of perceived data from conscious awareness, often described as a basic mechanism of culture. Consumer orientation, of course, is a powerful and pervasive form of cultural conditioning.

A cultural anthropologist living in a primitive culture—say in a Brazilian or New Guinea jungle or perhaps in the Arctic —appears to the people among whom he lives as very troubled, possibly insane. He cannot fulfill social, economic, cultural, religious, sexual, and other similar expectations in the primitive society. His behavior is odd and inexplicable in the extreme to everyone around him. His symbolic programming would appear to primitive peoples much as someone labeled a psychotic or schizophrenic would appear in a modern North American society. The anthropologist, in order to do his work, must live in a society which considers him emotionally disturbed. Margaret Mead, Claude Levi-Strauss, Bronislaw Malinowski, and many other anthropologists have commented upon this bewildering and sometimes traumatic experience—that precise moment when the full realization struck them that the society in which they were living looked upon them as totally mad. They perceived things going on around them that no one else perceived. The primitives, in turn, perceived things that were completely invisible to the anthropologists.

The experience often results in what some researchers have called a psychic rebirth—a totally new cultural perspective for the anthropologist or scientist, a position from which he can deal with cultures, even his own, without becoming emotionally dependent or committed to the various mythologies.

It may speak well for the tolerance, patience, and simple humanity often found among primitive peoples that more anthropologists have not abruptly ended their careers as objects of public execution, long-term penal imprisonment, or perhaps even lifelong incarceration in the primitive society's counterpart of our mental institutions. Should an anthropologist from a primitive society attempt to live in and study our twentieth-century world, he would be removed from public view, taken into protective custody, or, if he defensively reacted quite normally to the aggressions and hostilities within modern North America, he could end up being punished as a homicidal maniac.

Several dentists and physicians have compared the technique of bringing the embedded words into the conscious mind with reading an X-ray film. Apparently a similar technique is learned and used by doctors as they probe vague, obscure shadows in a film which—when sensitively transposed into information—can reveal dimensions of meaning invisible to a casual observer. The physicians are taught that tension or distraction while reading an X ray can block their perception of what they are seeing, very possibly resulting in their consciously missing the vital shadow. Many physicians have commented that every so often they have experienced discomfort after reading an X ray and not finding what they had reason to suspect should have appeared. Several hours or even days later they have taken another look and almost immediately seen the detail they had previously missed. This could well be an example of the unconscious mechanism in action.

Medical students spend months learning to read X-ray film. They are trained to relax and concentrate their attention upon one small area of the X-ray film at a time. As medical students, they may spend several years learning to probe the one-dimensional photographs which represent the multidimensional realities of the body expressed in countless subtle variations of black to white shadows—many invisible to untrained conscious perceptual capabilities. Though many physicians squirm uncomfortably at mention of the unconscious, it is quite possible they have been trained to make themselves consciously sensitive to the delicate powers of perceptual discrimination available through the unconscious.

Sex in Time, Saves . . .

Attempting to trace the origin of the SEX embedding technique is comparable to searching for the proverbial needle in a haystack full of *Playboy* models. Freud's pioneer work on the concept of a subconscious occurred within this century. The notion, however, that there is a hidden power or something within the mind, spirit, soul, or what have you which guides men's destinies, has been discussed by metaphysicians and epistemological philosophers for many centuries. Indeed, as was mentioned earlier, Democritus in 400 B.C. described what post-Freudians would probably call the subconscious or unconscious.

There is a temptation to look for some secret society which through countless generations handed down the mystic secret of embedded SEXes. Master artists and craftsmen, perhaps, whispered the secret to their most favored apprentices as they struggled for their last breath on their deathbed. The apprentices might have sworn not to betray the power of embedded SEXes until they had, in turn, trained another to carry on the tradition.

Canadian artist John Hock once mentioned during a discussion of word embeds that he had used the embedding technique several years before on a painting. After completing an abstraction of curved forms, on an impulse he painted into the background the word fuck (see Figure 22). He disguised the word in background shadows. During the two years the painting hung in his living room no one ever discovered the four-letter word embedded in the background— not even his wife.

Hock commented, however, that people who visited the house were fascinated by the painting. Often, visitors could not seem to take their eyes off the canvas. The embedded word, he explained, "appeared to give a magic quality to the painting."

John Hock insisted he had never been aware of another artist embedding words, had never read or heard of the technique before his experiment with the "fuck." In his own words, he was "just fooling around."

It is entirely possible that Titian, Rembrandt, Picasso, and others also discovered simply by accident that embedded words produced a strange effect upon art patrons. Examples of word-embedding are abundant in the so-called fine arts. Several Fine Art students who were studying subliminal techniques secretly embedded words, pictures, and symbols in their classroom painting and sculpture, with startling effect. Their work was consistently graded *A* by their art professor when subliminals were included. One student, enthusiastic but a little guilty over her discovery, tried to explain to her professor what she had done—which was to embed the word "cunt" in an abstract sculpture. The professor refused to believe that such a technique could possibly affect anyone who "really understood art." The professor vehemently criticized the student for having an overactive imagination. Fortunately, the student had already received her *A* on the sculpture.

Another possible explanation for some of the embedded words which appear so often in heretofore inexplicable places is that they are involuntary acts of an artist of which he was totally unaware at the conscious level. During an art-therapy class conducted recently in a mid-Western therapeutic clinic, a young woman was assigned to paint a portrait of herself. The self-portrait showed her with a long-sleeved, high-necked gown—every portion of her body covered except face and hands. Her legs were covered with high boots. The young woman had a chronic and severe history of deeply rooted sexual inhibition.

During the discussion, while her self-projected image was under analysis by the entire group, another member noticed the woman had lightly painted the word "sex" across one of her booted feet. The word was almost imperceptible, but nevertheless represented purposeful behavior by the young woman. Once it was pointed out, the entire class was able to see the "sex."

The young woman went into hysterics after the detail was discovered. She indignantly maintained later she had painted "sex" on the boot without being aware of what she had done. There is not even an outside chance, however, that major

U.S. media and their advertising agencies have included verbal embeds inadvertently or without full knowledge of what they were doing. These multimillion dollar businesses are not "just fooling around," nor are they indulging their creative departments with on-the-job psychotherapy.

One very large New York advertising agency research director, when confronted with the verbal embeds in a cigarette layout produced by his company, made a strange rationalization for the subliminal trigger words. He reported, with a straight face, that much of his agency's artwork was done by independent contract art producers. These are art production houses which service many of the nation's top ad agencies.

The research director solemnly theorized that somewhere in New York, perhaps working obscurely in the basement of a production house, was a Commie-hippie revolutionist who was putting into American advertising all of these dirty things which, when exposed to an outraged public, would destroy "the great institution of free-enterprise marketing." In other words, he considered the whole thing a communist plot engineered by secret agents working from within.

Love—American Style

Horsman Dolls purchased a full-page, four-color advertisement in *The New York Times Sunday Magazine* on December 12, 1971, just before Christmas (see Figure 10). The ad cost about $7,500 for space alone, and reached about 1.6 million families—roughly one-third of whom live in New York City, one-third outside the city but within a hundred mile radius, and one-third distributed throughout the United States; 44.3 percent of *The New York Times* reader families have children under eleven years old, and half of them can be assumed female. These families are also well heeled: 64 percent have incomes over $10,000 per year, 20 percent over $20,000. They are well educated: 48 percent of male and 29 percent of female readers are college graduates. Some 57 percent of male readers are in managerial-professional occupations. An exhaustive array of data and information were available to the Horsman Doll Company, enabling it to utilize sophisticated planning in the design of its doll advertising campaign.

Dolls are expensive, especially nationally advertised dolls. They are not purchased by children. As with all toy adver-

tising, the main target is adults, though some advertisers will
channel the appeal through children who will be urged to
subtly pressure and manipulate their parents into the purchase.

"Love—American Style" shows a sweet child, possibly five
years old, her hair and expensive dress obviously from an
upper-income family, affectionately holding her doll while
she lovingly talks to it, probably in baby talk as though the
doll were an actual child. The child's eyes are closed (she is
blind to reality) while she playacts the doll is a real child.
The doll appears to be staring at the child's ear and the hands
are about to touch the child's neck. It is particularly curious
to observe the use of erogenous zones in children's toy advertising and their relationship to hands, mouths, eyes, and
other points of body contact.

This is much the same relationship that held between the
mother and the child only a few years earlier. Their lips are
close. The doll either has been or soon will be kissed about
the mouth and cheeks by the child. Judging from the child's
open mouth and wet lips, the kiss will be a sloppy one. The
child's left hand, unseen, is very likely positioned under the
doll's fanny. A parent might sense a twinge of pleasure and
excitement at seeing this charming, loving child at play with
her baby doll. The scene might, in itself, evoke strong enough
identifications between mother or father and the child with
her doll to stimulate a purchase. Horsman, however, is taking
no chances.

Embedded on the back of the child's right hand, halfway
down from the forefinger knuckle, is a mosaic of SEXes.
There is also a SEX mosaic on the inside of the doll's right
hand (erogenous zone). On the child's right cheek, just right
of the ear, is a large SEX. In the child's hair—from a midpoint in the part go straight down to the light area in her
hair—another large SEX, in fact a mosaic. There are dozens
of the ubiquitous SEXes throughout the photograph. Bear in
mind that, as with all the reproductions in this book, the
reduced size and, in most cases, the absence of color make
the finding of subliminal material more difficult than in the
original ad. But for those who care to look for it, most of
the material is discernible.

Perhaps the most interesting embed, however, is on the
sleeve of the doll's left arm. From the top of the bare wrist,
where the dress sleeve meets the skin, count up the arm four
of the horizontal pink stripes. At the top edge of the sleeve,

on the fourth stripe, appears a large letter K. The K is clear, heavy, and obvious. The other letters tend to be shadows or only partial clues; however, the mind at the unconscious level will fill in the taboo four-letter word with assistance from the photographer-artist.

Just in front of the K, and slightly below, is a capital C. Between the second and third horizontal pink stripes is a U. And, drawn across the top of the first stripe is a large F. In the illustration, a blow-up of the area is shown and the letters F U C K unmistakably appear.

Love, indeed, American Style?

chance of over 24.8 million individuals monthly. One of the
21.8 million, the magazine reaches roughly 4.2 million
men monthly, few of whom actually purchase the maga-

7. The Playboy Syndrome: Who's Playing With Whom or What or Whose?

Each square inch of each page in a national magazine must
do a specific job. The inside editorial content pages must
hold readers, laying a psychological foundation for the advertising pages which must sell products. As little as possible
is left to chance. Each page layout is purposeful. Each page
must serve the corporate motives of the publisher. Some
pages, nevertheless, are more important than others.

For many national magazines, the cover—literally an advertisement or the *packaging* for the magazine—is the most
critical page in the book. The cover must sell the magazine.
The cover's job, similar to the paid advertising inside, is likely
to be performed in the mind of potential purchasers in a
matter of seconds, even split seconds, as they compare one
magazine with its competitors on a newsstand. Once the purchase is made, however, the cover no longer has any real
significance.

Playboy magazine, for example, sells 6.5 million copies
monthly, 76 percent of which are merchandised via newsstand sales. The cover is a point-of-sale advertising piece; an
ineffective *Playboy* cover could reduce newsstand sales as
much as 5 percent. Many competing magazines are less expensive. Many decorate their covers with stronger, more
lurid and libidinal attentions. *Playboy* covers, considering
they could display an infinite range of content from overt
sex scenes to intimate anatomical details, are strangely modest and subdued. They depend upon a subliminal sell.

The question is, how does the cover sell *Playboy* when no
obvious hard-sell sales technique ever appears?

There are two *Playboy* audiences: the magazine *purchasers* for whom the cover is primarily designed, 6.5 million; and the magazine *reader* for whom the content and
advertising are designed—3.35 readers per copy, of which
2.7 are men and .65 are women. This constitutes a reading

audience of over 21.8 million individuals monthly. Out of the total 21.8 million, the magazine reaches roughly 4.2 million women monthly, few of whom actually purchase the magazine but read their husbands' or boyfriends' copies.

The average *Playboy* male reader is 25.4 years old, 73.6 percent are between 18 and 34 years old, 60.4 percent are married, 52.5 percent attended college, 50.3 percent have household incomes of $10,000 or over, 26.8 percent make $15,000 or over, 31 percent are in professional or managerial occupations, and 51.9 percent have one or more children.

Forty-five percent drink gin; 48.6 percent, vodka; 28.2 percent, rum; 42 percent, bourbon; 35.8 percent, American wine; 22.5 percent, imported wine; 23.1 percent, cordials and liqueurs; and 22.4 percent, brandy and cognac. Readers will, of course, overlap in their alcoholic preferences.

An enormous quantity of information on the purchasing habits for clothes, automobiles, tobacco, entertainment, toiletries, travel, personal finance, and every other conceivable market describes the *Playboy* reader to editors, writers, advertisers, and the other technicians involved in selling and producing the publication and its advertisements. The data are as detailed as modern research techniques and the most advanced systems of electronic data processing can provide. Minute details are examined with precise care, validity checks run, and in-depth interpretations formulated as complex and detailed as those which physicists might apply to analyzing the intricacies of a new model hydrogen bomb.

For several examples of the prodigious data available on the *Playboy* reader: 25.2 percent of these young men consume more than seven drinks per week of distilled spirits, 18.1 percent more than ten drinks per week, and 12.1 percent more than fifteen drinks; 17 percent own three or more cars; 54.4 percent purchased their principal car new; only one percent own a high-priced foreign car, but 5 percent own low-priced foreign cars; 17.9 percent expect to purchase a new car next year; 23.8 percent purchased two or more suits last year; 12.8 percent purchased seven or more pairs of slacks; 17.3 percent purchased seven or more dress shirts; 18.3 percent seven or more sport shirts; 16.3 percent four or more pairs of shoes; and 15.5 percent sixteen or more pairs of regular stockings; 20.8 percent are heavy smokers (one pack or more daily); 21.1 percent own stocks and 24.8 percent expect to buy stocks and bonds during the next year; 8.3 percent own mutual funds and 15.5 percent expect to buy mutual funds during the next two years; 20.5 percent purchased life insurance last year while 10.5 percent expect to purchase life insurance next year; and on and on and on.

Exhaustive quantities of such data are also available for every major newspaper, magazine, television program, and radio station audience in North America. The media of mass communication know, as precisely as it is possible to know, *who* their audiences are demographically, and *what* these audiences' emotional as well as purchasing needs involve. The game is predicated upon capturing—through content—as affluent a slice of a particular audience with specified need characteristics as possible.

Centerfolds Sell Magazines

As mentioned, the *Playboy* cover is probably the single most important page in any issue of the magazine, at least in terms of maintaining and increasing circulation. Photographers are reported to have received $8,000 to $10,000 for their camera click which winds up on a *Playboy* cover. In comparison, a centerfold photographer reportedly may receive only $5,000 for his photograph. One might well wonder why any photograph could conceivably be worth this small king's ransom.

The objective of this very expensive artwork is the *Playboy* reader—a young, married male from an upper-middle-class background, with some college experience. His emotional needs, however, are quite complex. It is upon these emotional needs that photographers, editors, and writers must base their communications and successfully merchandise the magazine and its advertised products. These technicians know their reader far better than he knows himself. Indeed, if the reader had the insights into his own unconscious needs that are readily available to media technicians, he would likely throw the magazine down in horror.

Ostensibly, the image reflected by *Playboy* is that of a self-assured young man who is a giant among his peers. He is pursued relentlessly by exotic, beautiful, sex-crazed—though subservient—young women. He drives a high-powered sports car, dresses in the latest fashion, and dines in only the best of restaurants. His friends are famous, celebrated, and sought-after people. He lives in a decorator-designed bachelor pad with thousands of dollars in stereo hi-fi equipment and a private bar stocked with only the finest of liqueurs and imported vintages. He is surrounded by abstract art, expensive imported furniture, and an enormous circular bed while he sleeps. This is the *Playboy* image, designed with loving— money-loving—care and projected into the susceptible minds of 21.8 million readers monthly.

But what is the reality behind this romantic image?

At this point the reader might reflect for a few moments over one of the *Playboy* covers. Looking at the February 1970 cover (see Figure 11), an art critic might ask two simple questions, just as he might while viewing a Rembrandt, Hieronymus Bosch, or Van Gogh painting.

Time and Space in Art

Considering that a picture is time stopped at a particular instant, most pictures will imply a *before*—measured in seconds, minutes, hours, days, weeks, or even months—and an *after,* measured in the same terms. Simply expressed, the question is: *What is going on in the picture?* The time dimension is usually communicated to a viewer at an unconscious level. Few people are consciously aware of the basic time dimension which exists in virtually all art forms. They are not supposed to be. Quite often the artist will rely upon a viewer's inability to consciously perceive this time dimension in order to evoke a deep emotional feeling of identification within the viewer's unconscious.

The second question is: *What does the picture mean?* As the meaning is the servant of motive, the question involves the artist's objective. A painter's primary motive may be to communicate a deep feeling or sensation. There could also be a conscious or unconscious motive to sell the painting for a high price. In the case of a *Playboy* cover, the primary motive is relatively simple—the cover must sell the magazine. In order to do this effectively, it must relate to emotional needs, both at the conscious and unconscious levels, within the mind of the specific prospective purchaser and must stimulate him to purchase the particular issue. Evaluate any relationship in the picture between people and people, people and things, and things and things.

With this in mind, study for a moment the February 1970 cover. Ask yourself the two questions, what is going on and what does it mean? Your answer should explain, in some way, how the reader is moved to purchase the magazine via the cover message.

These two questions were asked, in precisely this way, to over 500 university student test subjects, a large proportion of whom were regular *Playboy* readers. Not one single student was able to answer the questions. They apparently blocked out of their consciousness all of the information communicated by the cover. Even after two weeks of constant probing they were still unable to explain the cover. This was strange, as each had an extended time period in which to study, think out, and discuss with friends what they all perceived from the photograph. Seeing is believing, as the old, trite, and very foolish platitude goes—that is, if you can consciously see anything.

Remember, however, no one considering the purchase of *Playboy* is consciously aware of the cover. Whatever the information content in the cover, it must be perceived instantly by the purchaser—but certainly not at a level of consciousness which would convey an understanding of the cover's meaning.

In order not to oversimplify the problem, keep in mind that among the 6.5 million who receive the magazine each month, a certain proportion are regulars who will buy the magazine irrespective of its cover. Another proportion are irregulars who have already purchased occasional issues. Then there are *the first-time purchasers*. The *Playboy* editors are aware of these exact proportions. The name of the game, however, is to increase sales, considering that each month there is a certain attrition. The new circulation input must exceed the attrition rate from the preceding month. The cover, therefore, is most specifically designed for the new or occasional purchasers who are likely to be younger than the average readers—far younger, at the emotional development level, than anyone would suspect.

A second group, 150 students, was shown the February 1970 *Playboy* and asked each morning for two weeks what was going on in the cover. No one was able to answer, until one of the students, when asked pointedly what the model was holding in her arms, finally replied, "It's a b-b-b-b-baby."

The student, as it turned out, was not a stutterer. It was, in his own words, as though he had to force his conscious mind to verbalize the word-symbol "baby." The moment he said the word baby, however, there was a gasp from the entire group. Once cued, they perceived almost immediately what was going on.

The model on the February cover is in a nursing posture.

Notice the curvature of the left shoulder and arm, the tenderness with which the arms support the magazines, the right hand caressing above the left shoulder, the expression of nursing tranquillity—implying, of course, the sexual pleasure a mother receives from her nursing infant.

The model is, indeed, nursing a baby held traditionally in her left arm. In one study of 560 Madonna and Child paintings produced over the past 300 years, 490 of the Christ Childs were held in the left arm. A physiological explanation for nursing on the left side has been that the heartbeat, which pacifies the baby, can be heard more strongly on the left than on the right.

The second question, What does all of this mean? puts us into the heart of the matter. What is a nursing mother doing on the cover of *Playboy?* Very simply, she is nursing the *Playboy* reader, giving him preference over her other two children, *Cosmopolitan* and *Vogue* magazines (see Chapter 8, The Castrating Cosmovogue). Her other children are girls (siblings) with whom the *Playboy* must compete for mother's breast.

The model's eye contact, however, is not directed at the rabbit ears on the magazine cover. She is looking in adoration at the printed word "Playboy."

Clipped by Bunny Ears

The symbol on the nursing cover, consciously interpreted as the rabbit ear trademark of *Playboy* magazine, is not being nursed. The left nipple of the model is below where the silhouette rabbit's head would be located. In fact, the rabbit is positioned between the word Playboy and the breast—in effect, symbolically interfering with the Playboy's access to the mother's breast. So what does this presumed rabbit trademark—one of the most protected trademarks in American business—*mean?* The Playboy has competed successfully against the two female siblings for his mother's breast. But there still appears to be a barrier between our Playboy and the object of his desire—namely, that damned *Playboy* logo.

To test the trademark for its meaning, the rabbit ears as they appeared on the February cover were masked off from all other features and photographed separately. They were shown to several hundred test subjects who had not seen them in the context of the cover. When asked to identify the symbol, the several hundred people came up with only five possible definitions for the symbol: *leaves, victory sign, peace sign, scarf or apache tie,* and *scissors or shears.*

This rabbit logo is probably one of the most carefully copyright-protected, publicized, and near-worshiped symbols or totems in America. It identifies a vast publishing, merchandising, hotel, and night club empire. But, again, what does the trademark *mean?* Presumably, the meaning would be related to young men who identify with the symbol. Consider the five possibilities. Only *shears or scissors* appears to have possible direct identification with the sexual needs or inhibitions of this young American male readership.

There is an interesting symbolic history connected with archetypal virility symbols. The hare or rabbit, of course, is popularly known as a symbol of virility, masculinity, and promiscuity. The symbolic rabbit has been around since prehistoric times, when it presumably had a similar meaning. The bull would constitute another, though more aggressively masculine virility symbol. Both rabbits and bulls have been found in the religious drawings on cave walls, pottery, painting, and sculpture of early civilizations.

Virility symbols overtly suggest one meaning, but also imply the opposite meaning at the unconscious level—*castration.* This is a basic characteristic of symbols whether in word or pictorial form. For example, by saying someone "won" a game, there is the unspoken implication of the opposite—that someone else "lost."

The bull, as a symbol of masculinity, male animalism, and virility is an interesting case in point. The bullfight is essentially a castration ritual. *La corrida de toros* (the run of the bulls) has nothing to do with a fight between a man and an animal. The fight is only within the man against his fear. The fear of death is not the greatest fear a man must overcome. The fear of castration, especially significant in the Latin world, is omnipresent and terrifying. Bullfighters are invariably gored in the groin. They are not risking their lives in the arena, but their masculinity before the crowds of sexually excited *aficionados.* The bull, with his threatening horns, has a dual symbolic meaning—*virility,* and its opposite, *castration.* The rabbit symbol of virility, with its scissorlike ears, communicates a similar duality of symbolic meaning.

Hundreds of animated rabbit cartoons have been produced by Hollywood which portray the rabbit as a clever, though physically weak, character who puts down or castrates cartoon animals of greater strength and power, often in an overtly sexual struggle for dominance or territory. One Bugs Bunny cartoon was titled *"The Barber of Seville."* The energetic Bugs played the title role, dashing about cutting off other animated characters' ties, in a symbolic castration ritual. The tie is one of the most obvious of modern phallic symbols about which much more will be said later.

Small wonder that in 1964 *The Society of Typographic Arts* chose the *Playboy* rabbit logo from among 1,600 entries as one of the fourteen most outstanding corporate trademarks in the United States.

If the *Playboy* trademark can be considered in its dual role as both virility and castration symbol, the logo's symbolic significance deepens considerably. Looking again at the February 1970 cover, who might threaten a young child with castration, at the nursing age—his father or mother? Or, expressed in another way, who is always between the male infant and the exclusive love of his mother? Dad, of course.

Fathers have been trapped in a competitive archetypal situation between their sons and their wives for thousands of years in human evolution—perhaps since the earliest development of the family unit. To the infant male, Mother always loves him best, even though Father is always between him and the object of his primary affection. The child must also compete for Mother's love against brothers and sisters, and sisters always seem to have an edge.

In terms of the February cover, the Playboy's primary need is to get past the threatening paternal castration symbol that is keeping him from his mother's breast. The cover is telling the young reader, in effect, his vicarious participation in this issue of *Playboy* will help him become a man more desirable than his father in the eyes of his mother.

The "Fold Here" lines appear to have no significance except as camouflage for the deeper symbolic meaning. The lines consciously suggest a mechanistic meaning to the cover and serve to lead conscious perception away from the subliminally meaningful nursing situation.

After testing this particular cover with over 650 university students, no meaningful or supportable alternate interpretation appeared.

Mother Loves Playboy *Best*

This analysis of the symbolic techniques of modern commercial communication media is certainly not merely a critique of *Playboy* magazine. Indeed, examples from *Playboy* are used because they do it so extremely well. *Playboy* pioneered in developing reliable techniques for the manipulation of their audience's unconscious. And besides, *Playboy* is good fun—especially if you can read what is going on subliminally beneath the surface.

There is a rich abundance of theoretical material on the use and misuse of the unconscious mind in human affairs. Some of these theories will be explored in subsequent analyses.

Because the implications within the February 1970 *Playboy* cover were, to say the least, unsettling, a large number of other covers were analyzed similarly, using several hundred college students. From the roughly thirty *Playboy* covers studied, 70 percent had some obvious representation of mother. These seven out of ten contained scenes with a mother figure dealing with a small infant—the small child being the object with whom the prospective *Playboy* purchaser would identify. Most surprisingly, four out of the seven of these maternally oriented covers involved infants in nursing situations. One might well wonder what infants and nursing mothers are doing on the cover of the world's most famous sex magazine. This must say something about our man-about-town—the *Playboy* reader.

Considering that *Playboy* circulation has increased a phenomenal 15.4 percent average each year over the past eleven years, the covers must have been somewhat successful in helping to merchandise the magazine. The patterns evident in these covers at the subliminal level offer some interesting, indeed fascinating, insights into the emotional needs and reality of the millions of young men who each month purchase the publication. This *Playboy* reader of the Western world begins to appear much different than his widely publicized image suggests at first glance.

Now study the June 1967 cover and make your own evaluation in answer to the two basic questions—What is going on and what does it mean?—in terms which would provide some insight into how these covers help sell the magazine (see Figure 7).

The June 1967 cover offers the reader an opportunity to identify with the ubiquitous rabbit symbol of virility, cleverness, and promiscuity. Our Playboy is wearing what appears to be a beach robe, though it could be a bath or lounging robe. He seems to be thoughtfully studying an attractive young woman lying on her side.

As the Playboy's eyes are covered with sunglasses, we cannot see his eyes; therefore, we cannot be certain what is going on in his mind. Usually in art, whenever the eyes are covered by shadows or sunglasses the meaning communicated is that the person's thoughts are hidden. Certainly the woman —the object of his hidden eyes and thoughts—cannot know what he is thinking.

On the other hand, the girl has her glasses lifted. Her eyes are visible and the Playboy knows what she is thinking as she looks at him in adoration. Now, what is going on in her mind—as projected into the perception of the reader's unconscious?

Once again, what is she doing and what is her relationship with the Playboy? Obviously she is lying on her side upon a soft surface, presumably sand, though other possibilities such as a soft, messed-up bed are possible. But what kind of a pose is this? What would a woman be reasonably preparing to do in this position? The reader is urged to consult the nearest mother.

Virtually any mother will confirm this is a comfortable and pleasant position for nursing, assumed usually at the beginning of a nursing period so the mother can pleasurably watch her child suckling at the breast.

But something is amiss in the scene. An object again lies between the Playboy and his mother's breast—the hat. Whose hat, a man's or a woman's? The hat could admittedly be a woman's beach hat. But this hat in the left-hand picture has two balls—hardly symbolic of womanhood; so the hat is symbolic of a man. Who is he—brother, friend, uncle, cousin, or—you guessed it—Father!

Reading from left to right, the almost identical photographs present a sequence. What happens as the eye moves from left to right? The pictures are identical except for one detail. One of the balls is missing in the right-hand picture— a symbolic castration of dear old Dad, who once again got between the Playboy and his mother's breast.

It is, of course, extremely important, when attempting to comprehend the functional implications of symbolic material, to carefully consider every potential meaning. Alternate explanations should be constantly reviewed and compared. The reader can attempt to develop his own alternate interpretation should he find those presented here unacceptable. Whatever it means, in the mass media it must mean *something;* and at the prices paid for these covers—and the prodigious stake in circulation involved—the meaning probably has something to do with selling. These interpretations were tested against hundreds of subjects and were overwhelmingly sustained—not immediately in many cases, and not without considerable agony among many of the test subjects.

It might be trite to remark that many men seek mates who will assume maternal dominance over their sexuality. In one recent study a large number of young wives' wedding pictures were compared with photographs of the young husbands' mothers twenty years earlier. The striking physical resemblances were awesome. This tendency, though present in all men (even though some deal with it by finding mates as completely different in appearance as possible from their mothers), is undoubtedly stronger in some men than in others. The *Playboy* reader would appear to have an abundance of this mother-worshiping tendency.

All Tied Up

Look at the March 1967 *Playboy* cover (see Figure 12). If the long tie is a phallic symbol, what does the bow tie symbolize? The bow tie is also a symbolic phallic symbol, but one that has been tied up securely. If a mother and father were to purchase ties for their small son, which would each of them purchase? The mother would likely purchase a bow and the father the long tie.

The necktie has a long-established symbolic role in our society and in our unconscious. The necktie serves no functional purpose whatsoever, but is socially mandatory in many areas of life. So what do neckties *mean?* The traditional formal male attire—the tuxedo—demands that a man wear a bow tie. His sexuality or masculinity is securely inhibited. Perhaps this is symbolically necessary as the female's formal attire traditionally permits her to display her body. On formal occasions she is licensed to wear sexually provocative gowns. As long as the male wears his bow tie, however, she is at least symbolically safe.

But on the March cover the model is in the process of untying the bow tie, symbolically turning loose the Playboy's phallic masculinity. Her expression rather clearly suggests, however, that the untying will not be permanent. The Playboy will be untied sexually by mother only while he indulges his fantasies inside this issue of *Playboy*. Once he has used the magazine for his sexual and masturbatory fantasies, mother will once again tie him up neatly and gently. The magazine symbolically becomes again a momentary escape from the ever-present fear of paternal castration.

The cover model, or representation of the reader's mother, wears the symbol of paternal castration in her hair and on her cuff links, an ever-present threat to the Playboy child. But she appears to be dealing with this threat to her beloved child with self-assurance and a relaxed dominance. As she caressingly unties the *Playboy*'s sexuality, her expression suggests she knows he will never really get away from her.

When the symbolic significance of neckties is thought out, it is difficult to comprehend how any man could seriously select a bow tie for himself. Think of the men you have personally known who consistently wore bow ties. Did these men have distinctive behavioral patterns, such as strong maternal attachments? Consider, moreover, the effect upon audiences when rock singer Tom Jones unties his bow tie during a song usually halfway through his weekly TV show.

Subliminal Virginity

Playboy magazine is constructed around the centerfold, which represents the very essence of the publication. The ephemeral virginity of this exalted creature, who is monthly undressed as the hungry reader unfolds the page, is a monument to the fantasy of female perfection. This, indeed, is a woman of whom mother would approve. In fact, she may even look a little like mother did at the age of eighteen.

A large majority of reader test subjects said they would not consider the models in *Playboy* as potential subjects for mating or marriage—for fun and games, but not for serious involvement. With one notable exception, they are only fantasy playthings for the reader, only to be used sexually or as status symbols before other men.

The one exception was the centerfold or Playmate of the

Month. A large proportion of readers tested could consider her a possible mate or wife. A number of young men admitted they could not use the centerfold as a masturbatory stimulus, as some inhibition they described as "guilt" got in the way of their fantasy.

A majority (57 percent) of the readers tested believed the centerfold girl to be a virgin, though all agreed that, if so, it wouldn't be for long. When asked whether she would cease being a virgin in days, weeks, months, or years, 83 percent opted for weeks. Almost unanimously, they agreed she would be a serious, entrapping affair, not a casual fling as would the other girls pictured in the magazine.

When a dozen *Playboy* centerfold stories and pictures are spread out on a table, some fascinating patterns begin to emerge. The girl is invariably presented as a sweet young thing from some small town, or small community in a large city. Her *good* family background is always emphasized. She is often studying social work or some other serious subject involving the welfare of society, at UCLA, NYU, or Ohio State University. She is upper-middle class. Though not a fanatic, she holds religious beliefs in great respect, understands the injustices of society but is not involved deeply in any protest movement, loves her father and respects her mother, is well liked by her employers and friends, dislikes hippies and other way-outs, and appreciates the finer things in life and—most important—has no ambition to compete with men for a place in the sun. Even in a recent centerfold where the model was presented as a hippie, a careful reading of the text revealed that she could only have been an ersatz hippie; she had friends and acquaintances in the movement, while she respectably lived on the fringes with no personal involvement.

In short, the Playmate of the Month is a square. After looking through dozens of the centerfold stories and pictures, one cannot help but wonder what this sweet young thing is doing naked in the middle of a magazine read by nearly 22 million people monthly.

The centerfold is the nucleus of *Playboy*. Looking at the magazine as a family structure, the centerfold girl is the only girl in the magazine whom the mother symbol on the cover might approve of as a daughter-in-law. The centerfold section is never run adjacent to any other sex-object photographic art. In each issue there are two sex-object sections —one in front of the centerfold and one after the centerfold.

But each of these two sections are kept well segregated from the centerfold story, so as not to contaminate the image of perfection. Once a model has appeared in the centerfold, even though she may later appear in the magazine, she has been dethroned or symbolically deposed of her virginity. In reprinting her photograph, she is condemned to a nonvirginal image in the reader's fantasies.

Though a large number of test subjects evaluated the centerfold model as a virgin, virtually no one considered her a virgin when she appeared in later issues. At least the women pictured in *Playboy* centerfolds eventually mature into women. The readers, however, must go on endlessly to a new idealized centerfold fantasy virgin, identifiable with their mothers, month after month after month.

Several hundred *Playboy* purchasers were observed as they removed the magazine from various newsstands. After contemplating the cover, the first inside page they viewed was the centerfold. *Playboy* opens naturally to the centerfold because of the heavier paper stock.

They leaf through—60 percent starting from the front and 40 percent from the back—pretending to be seriously looking for something in the printed pages. It is as though they were sneaking up from the front or the rear as it were, upon the hapless girl in the centerfold. The moment the centerfold is reached, their eyes focus and their faces take on a look of surprise. "My God, look what I found in the middle of this magazine," they seem to say.

The whole ritual drama is an exquisite pantomime, performed over and over, millions of times each month throughout the world. A see-through mirror was installed in a campus magazine store where observers could evaluate the overt behavior of magazine purchasers as they reviewed the merchandise and carried it finally to the cashier. A pattern of behavior appeared very consistently among over 70 percent of the *Playboy* purchasers. The young man enters the store and begins casually scanning the various magazines. The expressions of moral indignation, callous indifference, or contemptuousness appear too frequently in response to what he sees on the racks to be real. Some kind of a ritual is being enacted as the young men work their way slowly, often *very* slowly, toward the part of the display where *Playboy* awaits them.

When the purchaser finally reaches *Playboy*, he picks the magazine up with studied indifference, thumbing through until he reaches the centerfold—without reading anything, but feigning serious interest in the editorial content. When he unfolds the centerfold, the muscles of his jaws are tight. He maintains, however, a certain quasi-blasé smile upon his closed lips. Frequently, his eyes furtively move from side to side to see if anyone is watching.

The centerfold appears to be one of his primary reasons for purchasing the magazine. The overt decision to purchase or replace the magazine on the rack seems to occur after a quick, average ten seconds, exploration of the Playmate of the Month. If he decides he identifies with the Playmate, he turns to head directly for the cashier. But he doesn't simply carry the magazine in one hand. He carefully folds it, with the cover inside the fold, and places it casually under one arm. He glances around the room again, then walks boldly up to the cashier, opens it quickly, and quickly closes it the moment the cashier has rung up the price. As he proudly walks out of the store, the folded magazine is again under his arm, invisible to the world about him. With the cover folded over, he could be carrying the *Atlantic Monthly, Harpers,* or the *National Review.*

Even to a casual observer, the entire ritual appears as an incredible expression of guilt. One might well ask why anyone today should feel guilty about simply buying a magazine in our so-called modern and open society.

No One-Night Stand

Take a more careful look at these centerfolds.

A majority of young male readers perceived the centerfold girl as virginal or sexually inexperienced—though available to the "right man." The Playmate was not perceived as an object for a "casual" affair as were the other female models in the front and back of *Playboy.* She was described as a girl who might be a possible wife or future mother of the reader's children—an idealized image, perhaps more closely related symbolically to the reader's illusion of his sister than to his usual masturbatory stimuli.

Nowhere in the world is there a woman like the centerfold illusion of idealized perfection, faithfulness, understanding, and sympathy with the reader's hang-ups. But she is a serious, marrying ideal, not a mere one-night stand. She demands of the reader the primary loyalty which has heretofore been reserved only for Mother. Notice that the *Playboy* rabbit logo (father symbol) never appears on a centerfold display. The centerfold is maternally approved—Father has nothing to do with it. Father would probably approve of the sex objects at the front and rear of the magazine. To sons, especially sons who regularly read *Playboy*, all fathers are "dirty old men." The father image designed into the magazine's articles, stories, cartoons, and features is almost unbearably consistent.

The Playmate illusion is a carefully structured product of cosmetics, lighting, camera technique, scene design, and a teen-age physique in the idealized standards of American society. One might almost anticipate the model's jumping out of the centerfold, grabbing the nearest baton, and leading a Fourth of July parade down Main Street. She is untouched by the wear and tear of real life experiences. Nevertheless, this Playmate bears no resemblance whatsoever to a real live woman.

One curious technical feature of each centerfold is a synesthetic illusion of tactile experience. Test subjects identified the touch of the centerfold paper—a high-grade, varnished stock, heavier and with a finer finish than that used in the rest of the magazine—with human skin. A large number of test subjects identified the skin texture as that covering the stomach, a few identified it with skin from the shoulder area. An older respondent associated the centerfold texture with Duke Ellington's "Satin Doll." The synesthesia effect of eliciting a sensory experience—touch, smell, or sound—through visual perception is frequently used in advertising and promotional art. Cologne and perfume ads often communicate an aromatic sensation to readers merely through visual stimuli.

Consider what is invested in these centerfolds. Each centerfold includes at least three full pages of black and white and three full pages of color copy and art. At the going rate for full pages of advertising in black and white, these three pages would sell for $75,600. The centerfold picture occupies three full color pages, which would sell for a total of $107,340. The centerfold production budget has been estimated by the magazine as roughly $25,000—including $5,000 for the photographer and $5,000 for the model, who also receives a contract for future exploitation, publicity, and other services to the corporation. In total, the six-page centerfold in *Playboy* would be worth over $200,000. This is a big investment to dedicate simply to a photograph of a

nude girl, unless that nude girl can be made to relate symbolically to millions of readers and serve as a stimulus for
them to continue purchasing the magazine.

Jungian psychologists suggest that the type of symbols
utilized in the *Playboy* centerfold—both relative to the
model's physical position as well as to the props which surround her—are archetypal, present in the unconscious of
humans "since the beginning." Many theorists suggest that
some information is inherited in the human psyche. Who
knows what explanation for this phenomenon will finally
develop. There is already an enormous literature in mythology and psychology which attempts to theorize on how
archetypal symbols work. The fact is, no one really knows
for sure. The symbols are frequently evident in dreams, even
the dreams of young children. And, as many advertising
research specialists will testify, the symbolic archetypes are
fully capable of motivating sales among consumers.

A Playmate's Occupational Hazards

A new subliminal technique appeared in the February
1972 *Playboy* centerfold (see Figure 23). The curvaceous
photo-retouched blonde model is in a kneeling position against
a pink background of sheets and blanket. An interlaced
mosaic of embedded SEXes covers the hair, body and facial
skin, and the bedclothes. The model's erotically expectant
facial expression—and her kneeling position supported on
her elbows—rather obviously demonstrate her symbolic offering to the demanding eye of the *Playboy* reader. The
centerfold offers a masturbatory fantasy in the so-called
dog position. This, of course, is only what the reader perceives at the conscious level. There is much more. It's the
unconsciously perceived stimuli, not the conscious perceptions, that sell and sell and sell.

If the satin border of the blanket is carefully studied, embedded SEXes of various-sized letters appear. The embeds are staggered along the border from the bottom of the
page up to where the border disappears behind the airbrush-
retouched model's fanny. This dense concentration of embedded SEXes can be easily seen under a good light, if the
viewers can relax and concentrate their attention on the
area. Several deep breaths as an aid to relaxation will assist
in making the subliminal material available to conscious
perception. As the embeds become visible, notice the SEXes

are larger and heavier letters than those used in the embedded mosaic which cover the body and bedclothes. It is as though the centerfold artist were trying to tell the reader something. Hold the centerfold section up to a strong light and study the area along the satin border. This may well be one of the world's first examples of see-through subliminal pornography, communicated to the over 22 million people fortunate enough to have thumbed through the February 1972 issue of *Playboy*.

Perhaps strangely, if one thinks in the simplistic terms of logical reasoning, the *Playboy* readers were not supposed to consciously see the large erect penis protruding into the model's vagina. The centerfold section is an advertisement for the magazine. As with most advertising, if the reader is consciously aware of the technique which is designed to affect his purchasing behavior, he may resist the purchase. Anything consciously perceived can be evaluated, criticized, discussed, argued, and possibly rejected, whereas unconsciously perceived information meets no resistance or qualification by the intellect. Subliminal data are merely stored in the brain with identifications (recall the Poetzle effect) which will trigger a delayed, alarm-clock reaction capable of motivating behavior.

Should the centerfold have been consciously perceived as pornography by the highly conventional, fantasy-controlled *Playboy* readers, in all likelihood they would have immediately cancelled their subscriptions or demanded their dollar returned. The centerfold image is consistently the only "nice girl" fantasy in the publication.

Miss February's subliminal adventure into pornography was most cleverly constructed. The black-and-white photograph on the reverse side of the satin blanket border was painstakingly posed and retouched to accommodate the see-through effect. The model's knee, which has been carefully airbrushed so the outline sharply contrasts against the background, forms the head of the erect penis. The grass shading has been reversed. Instead of the gray shade it should have been, a column of white grass (as though it were reflecting sunlight) appears directly under the knee.

Recall how the centerfold works as a sales stimulus for the magazine. The propective purchaser, attracted by the cover, removes *Playboy* from the display rack. He opens the magazine to the centerfold—the book will not easily open to any other page. Opening the fold-out page to check out the monthly offering, the Playboy makes his purchase decision.

With the February centerfold, merely opening the fold-over page makes the erect penis on the reverse side visible to the unconscious. It would be interesting to obtain the monthly sales records of Playboy for both before and after the February centerfold, to calculate the practical dollar and cents rewards from subliminal manipulation.

The see-through technique has apparently been used only rarely in *Playboy* centerfolds. In the November 1970 issue, on the reverse, black-and-white side of the fold-out page a picture of Hugh Hefner's DC-9 jet airplane appears. Seen through the colored Playmate portrait, the airplane appears as a phallic shape nestling inside the womb of the prostrate model. The October 1972 issue of *Ouí*, a *Playboy* subsidiary, also featured see-through pornography in the centerfold. When it is held up to a light, a drawing of Marlon Brando appears to be committing cunnilingus between the legs of the centerfold model.

Though this see-through technique has a staggering potential as an advertising device, it does not appear to have been widely applied as yet. If the basic or primary human sensory input is tactility, and if a tactile sensory response can be initiated by see-through light as in television—or as in the February *Playboy* centerfold—in a synesthesia effect, a most powerful subliminal technique is available for the programming and conditioning of human response. It is extremely curious that anything as obvious—and as well-known over a long period of time—has not been exhaustively studied by social and behavioral scientists, who appear to have carefully avoided any contact with the subject.

The Real Thing

Perhaps the ultimate solution for the *Playboy* or sex-queen-nourished adult-adolescent is a device currently being marketed in men's magazine advertisements: a life-sized plastic female doll complete with wigs, nightgowns, miniskirts, and tight sweaters. The ads specify that the plastic model is anatomically complete, with a skin texture *"more real than the real thing."* The dolls are described as "friends who will make a delightful companion both for parties and in bed." The advantages of a synthetic woman are obvious. She does not have to be fed expensive steaks or dressed lavishly, or considered as a human being. Should the Playboy become annoyed or impatient with her, he can, if he wishes, throw her into a closet. The world of illusion may indeed have certain advantages over real life. There is no fear of rejection involved in a love affair with a fantasy or a plastic doll.

The entire basic concept of *Playboy* was built upon North American, upper-middle class, young men's unresolved Oedipal conflicts.

8. The Castrating Cosmovogue

The subliminal dimension of women's magazines is based upon what men think a desirable woman should feel, look, smell, taste, think, and sound like. Vast quantities of consumer research by the media have been concentrated upon the incredible assortment of clothes, cosmetics, jewelry, medicinals, antiseptics, and other products which are designed to play a role in woman's eternal pursuit of man and her own identity.

In attempting to decipher the subliminal themes communicated by women's publications, we must first ask: *What do women really want? What are their goals?* What basic emotional needs must the magazine fulfill in order to communicate effectively with their tens of millions of female readers? To achieve the sustained loyalty of a large audience, it is absolutely necessary for the media to satisfy these needs in some way.

Female audiences are as diverse as their male counterparts. Adolescent girls have different needs than do young mature women. Those who are married confront different emotional problems of adjustment than do those who are single. There are vast differences between the younger married with small children and the older married with grown or nearly grown children. Most successful women's magazines specialize in a particular *demographic* and *emotional-need* profile. The advertiser's demands for specific audience spectrums—which can produce *low cost per thousand* readers in fashions, cosmetics, jewelry, and the myriad female accessories—have virtually eliminated the general-circulation publications such as *Colliers, The Saturday Evening Post, Life,* and others. The CPM for general audiences is much lower on television than in general magazines.

Cosmopolitan magazine is a good case in point—a highly specialized women's magazine. The reader's median age is 37.6, individual annual income $4,359, and household income

$9,496. The majority of *Cosmo* readers are unmarried, live in large metropolitan areas, and work at secretarial or clerical occupations. *Cosmo* reaches 951,000 homes and each copy is read by 3.69 readers—3.5 million readers total. Roughly 80 percent of the readers are women and 20 percent are men, most of whom obtain their copies through women. Since 80 percent of each edition is sold via newsstands, like *Playboy,* the *Cosmo* cover is a critical merchandising tool for the publication.

The Cosmo's *Playboy*

The *Cosmo* reader image—as self-projected via Narcissus Narcosis by the ads, articles, stories, and illustrations—is that of a sophisticated woman of the world who is independent, makes her own decisions, is by her own choice unmarried, and dominates handsome men who constantly surround her and plead for her love and affection. In several strange dimensions the *Cosmo* reader's self-image parallels that of *Playboy* readers.

Cosmo models photographed for the illustrations or advertisements—with whom the reader identifies—are between 23 and 29 years old, considerably younger than the average reader. These are idealized ages into which the 37.6-year-old reader can project her fantasy self. In other words, the stories, articles, features, illustrations, and advertisements are telling the reader what she wants to hear about herself and projecting her idealized self-image.

Like all media in North America, *Cosmopolitan* integrates editorial and advertising images into a unified, complementary, and mutually reinforcing whole—predicated upon a world of fantasy projection. The idealized content image engineered by *Cosmo* editors projects women who make from $5,000 to $10,000 per year. *Cosmo* audiences can fantasy themselves into income brackets higher than their actual average income of $4,359. But there is a limit imposed by reasonable life expectations. If the *Cosmo* content image were not carefully engineered—and models or characters in the stories increased their image income to, say, $25,000 per year as in *Vogue* magazine—the image would be far beyond the reasonable life-style expectations of the reader. They would reject the high-income image because they cannot identify this far beyond their realities. Similarly, no reader would wish to identify with an image at her actual income level. She knows what it is like to live at that level, and it is probably similar to that of her friends and acquaintances. No romantic fantasies here, and likewise no reader identification.

Reader identification images in *Cosmo* are either never-marrieds or divorcees. They live in large cities like San Francisco, New York, or Chicago. They are from small towns, often in the Midwest, like Ashtabula, Ohio. They have migrated to the big city to find a career, romance, love, and marriage—in that order. The image eventually finds what she is looking for, unlike the reality of the reader who never quite makes it. The fantasy content-image characters in stories and articles maintain apartments—often with other women—in which a man could feel at home. They are, per-haps like the readers in *real* life, continually painting or decorating their bachelor-girl apartments—virtually a life-long avocation in which the apartment is never finished, even though substantial purchases toward the end are continually made from *Cosmo*-advertised products. Should the apartment ever be finished, they would have symbolically resigned them-selves to eternal bachelorhood.

The idealized Cosmo image is a woman who dabbles in psychiatrists and analysts of several different persuasions. She attends a wide variety of social and entertainment events, always escorted by a handsome male. The idealized readers are financially comfortable, but careful and judicious about money—even though they are prone to excessive extrava-gance from time to time to combat depression at the end of a love affair. Taxi rides, for example, are usually considered an infrequent and special event—when they are paying the fare—a small indulgence to compensate for some emotional conflict.

Capture, Not Liberation

Probing more deeply into *Cosmo* content, however, pro-vides a conflicting image of the reader. In order to sublimi-nally identify the reader with the magazine content, there is constant reference—in indirect and unobvious ways—to the reader's loneliness, depression, and despair over not having found marriage, children, and a home. Characters in the content often go for a drive, go shopping, or take a vacation to get away from themselves, eternally looking for clothes, cosmetics, or situations in which they can find their dream

man. A content undercurrent mirrors the readers' real fear
that time is running out, with their dreams unrealized. Marriage, for the characters in the content, is presented as a
desirable (under *certain conditions*—quite impossible conditions actually) though remote possibility. *Cosmo* actually appears to be preparing their readers for a life of not being
married, rather than holding forth a bright promise of marital bliss.

Most marital situations portrayed in *Cosmo* are unpleasant relationships between maladjusted individuals. The married woman's image is a negative reference throughout,
unless she happens to be a long-tenured single girl who has
just made it to the altar. Married women are shown as
spoiled, ungrateful, and unaccomplished women who exploit
and manipulate their hard-working and sacrificing husbands.
They don't realize how really well off they are. The proposition forcefully appears that if the reader were only in their
shoes, she would know exactly what to do with the
opportunity.

Though *Cosmo* ostensibly appears to recommend change
in the status of women and freedom from moral tradition
and restraint, the content repeatedly puts down women's
liberation—the last thing these readers are looking for—
together with hippies and rebels of all descriptions. These
readers want to be captured, not liberated. Often repeated
Cosmo lines are, "No hippies, no long hair, no pot, no pro-
tectors." The idealized *Cosmo* image of desirable young people is often summed up as, "shiny-nosed kids, glossy-haired,
middle-of-the-knee-trench-coat-kids, clean-cut, Coke drinkers
clutching slim volumes of poetry to Peter Pan blouses."

Superficially the *Cosmo* reader appears in the forefront of
revolutionaries demanding a change in American life-styles,
accepting adultery and free love, and demanding the aboli-
tion of social, moral, and religious restraints. Underneath, at
the subliminal level, *Cosmo* acknowledges the reader's need
to leave change alone because it is threatening, even frightening. *Cosmo* provides an illusion of change for the reader
—a revolution she can participate in simply through the
regular purchase of the magazine. Vicarious participation
through *Cosmo* allows her to feel she is a part of the new
rebellion without ever being compelled to fire a shot.

Strangely, perhaps, a careful reading of the editorial content consistently reveals that the reader really does not have
a "fabulous" time at parties. Parties are portrayed as painful

events, full of uncertainty and loneliness. A cruel way of putting it is that *Cosmo* is slanted toward the reader who considers herself a social loser. Constant references allude to the "lonesome city," "post-dawn emptiness," "creeping depression." Stories and articles carefully avoid any overt communication to the reader that their female characters are socially unacceptable or unwanted. If a character or author comments, "She never eats lunch," a qualifier is always added: "Not because she wasn't invited."

The *Cosmo* reader, as reflected in the idealized image of the regular columns, thinks of art exhibits, movies, and plays not as art, but as a date, a preliminary step toward the nirvana which will end loneliness—a man and hopefully marriage.

It is not just *a man* that is projected as a primary goal between the *Cosmo* covers. He is a very special man. Female models, both in the ads and illustrations, are often posed with their hands cupped together, or in some other protective symbolic shielding of their genital areas, communicating the idea of selectivity toward anyone to whom they expose their sexuality. The *Cosmo* reader's fantasy man is submissive and subordinate, often quite effeminate.

Oedipus Meets Electra

In the ads, stories, and illustrations, men are almost always dominated by women. The initiative is never in the man's hands. The woman controls, the man is controlled. The male image suggests a man in need of a mother. The subordinate male image presented by *Cosmo* permits the reader to assume a fantasy mothering role—"pet him," "wait on him," "bring him in out of the rain." The repetitive theme is "You feed them, house them, and listen to their troubles." The Electra complex is as much a part of *Cosmopolitan* as the Oedipus complex is of *Playboy*. Oedipus, of course, was an ancient Greek king who married his own mother, though inadvertently. The gods punished him with blindness.

However, though the male image reflects an immature little boy who needs mothering, it is also presented as a potential bastard who is responsible for all women's problems. The often-repeated idea, "You don't like to throw anything out, even to make room for his belongings," implies female dominance (it's her apartment) and a temporary liaison. Though the lion and other symbols of strong sexual in-

dulgence are used consistently in *Cosmo,* the male image
projected in both copy and illustrations is often that of a
homosexual or at least a very effeminate male. Male asser-
tions of masculinity are threatening to the *Cosmo* reader. So,
in the world of *Cosmo* illusions, the woman must dominate
and control. She often assumes the male role.

The *Cosmo* male image communicated is that of a swinger
superficially, even though a somewhat effeminate one. Underneath, however, he turns out to be a highly conventional
square. The male-female images are fascinating. Frequent articles reiterate this female projection of an idealized
male with strong latent homosexual characteristics. A typical
article was titled, "She-Man, Today's Erotic Hero." The
"She-Man" wore feminine clothes, behaved submissively, and
carried a pouch (purse). The "She-Man" was a "better lover,
not ashamed or fearful of that part of himself which borders
on or overlaps being feminine." The *Cosmo* male image,
"loves woman as a man who envies them."

The female authors and story characters often express the
feeling, "The more I love him, the more masculine I become."
Probing into these image projections which manipulate the
Cosmo reader, it is not at all difficult to conclude that *Cosmopolitan* is subtly—and sometimes not so subtly—advocat-
ing female homosexuality rather than heterosexuality. *Cosmo*
consistently presents a poorly camouflaged image of hostility
toward the male, perhaps justified in that, "They hurt wom-
en."

On the other hand, there appears the definite possibility
that these women enjoy being hurt. *Cosmo* has repeatedly
published material on the Sacher-Masoch phenomenon.
Masochism and related emotional syndromes are frequently
mentioned. The entire "love" concept presented in *Cosmo* is
involved with male cruelty. The reader's bruises must be
salved.

"Most American men," *Cosmo* elaborates, "are perma-
nently out to lunch. Most American women let them get
away with it." Rejection and jealousy are always responsible
for overeating, depression, bitchiness, and virtually any other
symptom a woman might complain of—there are many. The
ideal *Cosmo* male image who is jealous of women, "sounds
like Edith Piaf telling a story like Johnny Cash." The masculine male, on the other hand, is projected as a heavy who
must "break a million hearts with minimal emotional and
financial strain."

Symbolic Delivery

Though certainly not simple—no woman, or man for that matter, is simple—the basic emotional need in the readers exploited by *Cosmo* is singular. The March 1970 cover illustrates why the magazine has been so successful (see Figure 27). When the prospective *Cosmo* purchaser perceived the cover on a newsstand, in comparison with competing publications, all she consciously perceived was an attractive young woman model in a knit bikini.

The cover model, like most *Cosmo* cover models, has small breasts and a boyish figure, suggesting independence in body as well as in mind. When the cover is opened, the fold-out reveals a man resting his head on the model's knee. A simple two-page cover scene that appears, at least overtly, attractive, though consciously unexciting at least to a woman. There is no ostentatious fashion display, no overt sexual theme, and the man's body is discreetly cut off (castrated) above the waist. How, then, does this cover help sell nearly a million copies of *Cosmopolitan* to average readers who are unmarried and in their late thirties? Remember, to sell or communicate effectively, the cover content must appeal to basic motives or goals in both the conscious and unconscious minds of this specialized female audience.

What do the regular readers of *Cosmo* really want out of life? As the cover is viewed on the newsstand, the model's right arm forms a phallic symbol, with the sunglasses representing the symbolic testicles. The gold bracelet symbolically emphasizes the phallic head. Most jewelry serves archetypal symbolic needs relative to the origin of life, or in the vulgarized modern conception—sex.

The model's phallic right arm leads the eye toward the elliptical face surrounded by hair—a vaginal symbol. Within the general female genital symbol formed by the face are reinforcing genital symbols—the nose and eyes are phallic representations, and the mouth outlined in lipstick presents a symbolic vagina in a state of passion or arousal. The female face on the cover symbolizes a union of male and female genitals as the unconscious integrates symbolically the eyes, nose, and mouth.

The model's sunglasses and arm, together with her face with its reinforcing genital symbolism, also means at the unconscious level a sexual union. Subliminal or symbolic sex is the *modus operandi* of the *Cosmopolitan* cover, which is a primary point-of-sale advertising stimulus for the publication. But there is even more to the symbolic encounter.

Though she is clothed in a brief, modern bikini—suggesting the liberated American woman—a gold chain is tied about her waist. She is, even though liberated, still chained to her basic womanhood.

What every woman, especially the single *Cosmo* reader, really wants becomes subliminally evident when the prospective purchaser removes the March issue from the rack and opens out the cover. The young, rather effeminate man with his head resting on the model's thigh has his arms crossed. There are two situations where a man's arms are likely to be in this position. Arms are crossed on a cadaver, as they are difficult parts of the anatomy to handle because of *rigor mortis*. But the *Cosmo* male cover model is certainly not dead, even at the symbolic level, though his sexuality has been cropped off the fold-out. The other natural situation where a male would find his arms in this position is at birth. The fetus develops with arms folded over the chest. Symbolically, the arms in a folded situation can represent either the beginning of life—sex—or the end of life—death.

The background shape under the female's extended arm symbolizes the uterine passage. The cover model is in the process of symbolically giving birth to a male child.

The cover, ostensibly only a picture of a female and male model, includes symbolically the entire basic human drama of *coitus, conception,* and *birth*. This subliminal message—presumably successful, as the theme is often repeated on *Cosmo* covers—communicates with the magazine's readers through their unconscious; it relates their emotional needs to the publication—in effect, manipulating them via their emotional hang-ups to purchase the magazine and its advertised contents as a means to resolve their frustrations. Remember, these readers are middle-aged unmarried women. This is a promise, of course, which is rarely fulfilled, possibly leading the reader to even greater frustration.

Advertisers do not generally aim their messages at all members of a media audience. They define their specific markets demographically as well as in terms of emotional needs or psychographics. The actual market sought out by an advertisement may be a very small proportion of total audience available. The selective audience strategies are illustrated in the *Cosmo* Army Nurse Corps advertisement (see Figure 13).

Prospective Army nurses must be college graduates, 18 to 28 years old, unmarried, and must have majored in nursing or a related subject while in college. The demographics of these potential Army nurses are relatively simple, though finding the qualified candidates among the 3.5 million *Cosmo* readers may be like looking for a needle in a haystack.

The emotional-need characteristics of potential Army nurses restrict the target group's size even more than do the demographics. What type of woman is likely to find an Army nursing career attractive? Study the model in the ad. Photographers' models can be obtained in all shapes, colors, sizes, and dimensions. The nurse model was carefully selected. Her face is boyish, if not masculine. Her hair lacks the usual feminine length or style. She wears no makeup. This, of course, was structured on purpose for the photograph. It would have been quite easy to send this attractive young woman to a beauty salon before the posing session. She is posed with a background of tropical plants, suggesting overseas assignment. The model might have been posed in a glamorous gown at an officers' club party or on a moonlit tropical beach; most women would look at military service as a temporary employment while they husband-searched. This motive, of course, would not serve the interests of the Army Nurse Corps. They seek a woman who can find long-term emotional satisfaction from military service, a woman unlikely to leave the Army, marry, and have children.

So, instead of a glamorous evening gown, the model is posed in masculine work clothes. She is even wearing a man's T-shirt. Her name, Mikesell, is about as strongly masculine a name as could have been found in the Manhattan telephone directory. Her body is flat-chested and masculine. Though it is entirely possible for a woman to appear sexually attractive to a man in her army fatigues—Mary Martin did it rather nicely in *South Pacific*—this photographer has been careful to void any suggestion of femininity in the nurse-model.

To emphasize the dominant masculine image of the career nurse, a pair of scissors—the tradition-honored symbol of male castration—protrudes as the symbolic testes of a hidden phallic symbol from her breast pocket. An additional phallic symbol—designed to, so to speak, nail the lid down on her masculinity—appears in her right hand unnoticed by the conscious mind.

The caption in the upper right reads, "Officer. Nurse. Woman." The power designation of an "Officer" comes first, and is presumably the major motivation of the desirable candidate for an Army nurse career. "Nurse," is the second qualification, though the power prerogatives of the nursing profession may be an occupational attraction to women with strong power drives. The last emotional need qualification of women desirable by the Army is "Woman." The generalized needs of women are apparently subordinated by the Army to power and occupational needs.

As similar ads are used repeatedly as recruiting devices— and because the ads' success can be easily calculated by the number of coupons that are sent in by prospective candidates—the ad was probably most successful in locating the precise type of woman desired by the U.S. Army. A woman lacking these desirable emotional characteristics could not in any way identify herself with the model. Most women *Cosmo* readers would never even notice the ad as they thumbed through the publication.

The Dominant and the Dominated

The ability of advertisers to locate prospective consumers with definable emotional needs and demographic characteristics is a well-developed art and science of communication. Emotional predispositions, often unknown to the consumers themselves, are exploited with precision.

The "Tweed Again" ad is a classic example of a subliminal story told to a certain type of woman almost instantaneously as she perceives the page (see Figure 28). The Tweed ad appeared in *Cosmo,* so recall the demographic description of the *Cosmo* reader.

What is going on in the photograph? One could easily predict that sex of some description is going on, even though no actual person is apparent. The scene is an old, wealthy, traditional home, suggested by the inlaid floor and antique chair. Only an idealized husband-wife relationship could occur in this setting. Even though the consumer at whom the ad is directed would likely be unmarried, this kind of marriage would form her idealized fantasy of marriage.

The man is an "older man" because of the old-style pocket watch, a watch like father used to carry. The woman is younger, or sees herself as younger, because of the youthful slippers. She is over thirty, perhaps over forty, as she would have to be that old for her father to have carried the heavy, hand-wound, pocket watch.

Earlier, the man had been dressed to ride a horse—attested to by the boots and whip. As the boots are polished and immaculate, he never got out of the house. Whatever sexual urge overcame him, he took his boots off in a hurry, even before she removed her slippers—the slipper laces are on top of the boot. The woman was presumably overwhelmed by his passion as she dropped the red rose he had brought her—a symbol of love and passion. She removed her blouse before her hairpins, or he did it for her. Women invariably remove their hairpins before their clothing when they undress themselves. Indeed, they must have been in a hurry to *"Tweed Again."*

The boots and whip suggest that the submissive female target of the ad has a strong need for male, perhaps paternal, domination. A dominant woman would likely find the ad annoying without ever consciously knowing the reason. The perfume Tweed was presumably responsible for this sexual fantasy interlude. As the name Tweed is strongly masculine, older, dominant—like father was or like a daughter wishes father was—the woman responding to the ad can fantasy herself covered with Tweed as she anoints her body with the expensive and heavy aromatic.

Perhaps obviously, only certain types of submissive women with strong needs to be dominated are the primary market aimed at by the manufacturer and his advertising agency. Tweed perfume would have a limited market among the dominant woman's liberation enthusiasts. Again, these Tweed women desire capture, not liberation. It would probably be most inaccurate to define women into two such simple groups such as dominant and submissive. All such dichotomous definitions are simplistic nonsense anyway. Each woman, like each man, reflects both of these tendencies simultaneously. Human emotional characteristics differ by degrees of more or less rather than either/or. Emotional predispositions can also vary with time and place. A woman might be sexually dominant and socially submissive, or vice versa, or the tendency could change in degree relative to the comparable tendencies of a particular man with whom she might identify. Likewise, either tendency could be stronger or weaker at different periods in her life.

It is very important, especially in a field such as mass communication, never to oversimplify the conditions which motivate the highly complex and mostly invisible human animal.

Hostess with the Mostest

While *Cosmopolitan* is the magazine for the woman who wishes to be captured, *Vogue* readers are not searching for liberation either. They believe they already have it—liberation and freedom coupled with the power of decision, social dominance, control over their peers, and endless amusement. *Vogue* is designed for the woman who has made it and made it big, or who very soon expects to be *there*.

Vogue readers are *alphas*, in Huxlian terms, married to, about to be married to, or planning to be married to other *alphas*. Her self-image is that of a woman who parties, dines, travels, and shops with the "right" people, goes where the "right" people go, and builds her image to complement and attract the "right" people. She is quite a woman.

One well-known divorced bachelor-about-town who, like most divorced bachelors, was always searching for his next wife, commented that whenever he met a new candidate—regardless of her other attractions—he would run like hell for the nearest exit if he found *Vogue* lying about her apartment. *Vogue* readers have great expectations, ambitions, and drives, but they must find a man to do the actual work. God help him.

Vogue's demographics are revealing. With a relatively small circulation of 550,000 copies, the readers are quite well off—not as well off, perhaps, as their idealized image might propose as it looks back at them every month from the cover, the ads, and the illustrations by America's leading photographers of women. But compared with the average North American housewife, *Vogue* readers are certainly not hardship cases.

While only 10 percent of U.S. families make over $15,000 annually, 63 percent of *Vogue* reader families are in this stratum; 34 percent of the readers make over $25,000. The average *Vogue* family makes over $25,000, compared with the $8,000 average for all U.S. families.

The average age of *Vogue* readers is in the early thirties and 72 percent are married—if not happily at least comfortably. Some, the younger ones with high upward-mobility husbands, work. The majority, however, are married to men with managerial or executive responsibilities who are quite likely to be older than their wives. Men usually hit their high earning peak in the mid to late forties.

A significant proportion of *Vogue* readers will be in their second marriage, their husbands in their second, third, or fourth marriage. The more money you make in America, the more marriages you are likely to have during your lifetime. In this high socio-economic level, men on their repetitive trips to the altar marry younger and younger women. The higher the man's income, the larger the age differential is likely to be. It is quite possible that many *Vogue* readers were once loyal to *Cosmopolitan* magazine, but they would be only those who made out, succeeded, hit the jackpot.

The place of children in the life of the *Vogue* reader is curious. Two-thirds of *Vogue* families have no children under 18. This can mean two things: most of the readers are well over 40 (which does not seem to be the case), or they live in a marriage in which children do not play an important role as a source of security and fulfillment. As, apparently, most *Vogue* readers do not have children of their own, they are likely to be involved with the children from their husband's former marriage—a delicate problem.

The *Vogue* reader is well educated—78 percent attended college, 41 percent graduated. Of their husbands, 83 percent attended college, 64 percent graduated; in their occupations (which really determine life-style, fashions, clubs, travel, sports, and amusements) 35 percent are professionals and 32 percent are executives, proprietors, managers, or officials.

Children play a minor role in *Vogue* compared, for example, with the *Ladies' Home Journal* which emphasizes an upper-middle-class family image complete with children, grandchildren, and middle-aged female insecurities.

Ninety-seven percent of *Vogue* readers belong to one or more clubs. They entertain frequently with dinner parties, buffets, and luncheons, and they are entertained equally as often with a total average of 6.4 engagements monthly.

These women are involved in a social life related to, and in support of, their husband's business or profession. In virtually all known societies, familial social life is closely tied to economic means of subsistence. Parties and quiet dinners are given and attended by people who are to be impressed, entertained, and solicited—usually for economic reasons. In such a socio-economic situation, clothes, menus, vacations, and friends who are celebrated or distinguished—all the status-oriented trappings of the affluent—are vital to social acceptance and success.

Narcissus's Horoscope

Vogue content reflects probably the highest female aspirational idealization or self-image fantasy in the American mass media. The reader's power and dominance needs, as well as her insecurities, are reflected on every page. The *Vogue* horoscope (an indispensable feature for American female readers) is heavy with business advice and leadership encouragement: "The courage and dash you felt earlier will be curbed." "Your leadership will be less effectual." "Ideas you develop will come to the attention of those who can promote them." "You might enter a new profession." "Go over to the side of the winners." "Take the initiative now."

Contrast the businesslike *Vogue* horoscope with the bubbling gossip-laced, emotion-oriented advice lushly spilling out of Libra, Capricorn, or Aquarius each month in *Cosmopolitan:* "You're hung up on his money problems." "New moon is maybe marriage time—he loves me, loves me not." "The sun shines on a new self-confidence." "The 2nd and 3rd are meaningful love days." "Friends are vying for your company." "A shamelessly seductive perfume bought on the 3rd might turn that not-for-you man off, the real man on." "On the 10th and 11th, you luxuriate in your femininity and on the 19th he finally responds to your love (even talks marriage)."

Horoscopes are, of course, the most absurd kind of nonsense—fun perhaps, but nevertheless nonsense. They are usually written with considerable skill, and they disclose a great deal about the respective reader's fantasy aspirations and idealized goals in life. Horoscopes, like most regular departments and features in magazines, are mainly used to sustain regular readership. Once a woman finds support for her fantasy image in a popular publication, she will likely end by carrying a copy of the publication with her into the grave.

Two in One

The *Vogue* reader is, of course, a complex sensitive human being who somehow must adjust within her life-style, which —in spite of her indulgences—must be extremely difficult, insecure, and threatening at times. A group of sixty advanced media students were asked to select a page from one issue of *Vogue* which symbolized the major psychological dilemma, tension, emotional need, paradox, or problem in the life of the *Vogue* reader. Out of the 144 pages available in the November 1971 issue, over forty of the students selected a color fashion photograph by famed photographer Irving Penn (see Figure 20). Strangely enough, though, none of the students was certain just why he had selected the Penn photograph. They all nevertheless *felt* the composition somehow typified the *Vogue* reader. Not one of the test subjects could consciously describe any unique, specific content characteristic about the page, but they agreed the picture said something important about the reader. The following analysis resulted, providing at least some insight into what goes on in *Vogue*.

Within a very old volume on magic and witchcraft a drawing was found of the Hindu deity Ardanari Iswara, one of the many representations of the hermaphrodite goddess, with symbolic coiling snakes and lotus petals. It is reasonable to assume that photographer Irving Penn knew of this representation of the archetypal hermaphrodite before he took the picture for *Vogue*. Compare the drawing with Penn's fashion photograph.

In the *Vogue* illustration one model appears much more masculine than the other. The two models' feet are positioned across and above their knees. If either model crossed her bent knee with her opposite foot, she would be in the Yoga lotus position. The two models are symbolically united in the ancient lotus position. In the Hindu myth of hermaphrodite, a being—half male and half female—was born out of a lotus blossom.

The masculine model in the light sweater is presented without a breast line or curvature. Her belt appears to be a riding stirrup. Compare the belt with the hermaphrodite symbol which covers the genitals of the figure in the Hindu drawing. The hermaphrodite symbol often appears in jewelry. The device was used on the cover of Jacqueline Susann's novel *The Love Machine* and given a contemporary name, *ankh*, which disguised the real symbolic significance of the design. This symbol of the hermaphrodite has been known for at least 2,000 years in European as well as Asian cultures.

The silver bracelet on the light-sweatered model's right arm is symbolic of the coiled snake on the right arm of the hermaphrodite in the drawing. The model's open right hand, with fingers separated, points phallically toward her genital area; the circular earring, which also appears on the hermaphrodite's right ear, completes, at least symbolically, the male half of the fashion photograph's hermaphrodite theme.

The dark-sweatered model appears more feminine than her companion. A breast line appears in her sweater. The watchband on her left wrist is simply a ringed bracelet, quite similar to that shown on the left wrist (the female side) of the Hindu hermaphrodite. Instead of holding the five-petaled lotus flower in her hand, however, the feminine half of the *Vogue* hermaphrodite wears it as a leather necklace around her throat.

What, then, does hermaphroditic symbolism by one of the world's leading fashion photographers have to do with the well-heeled, well-educated, well-married *Vogue* reader? One conclusion might be that *Vogue* is attempting to communicate with lesbians or to promote the daughters of Sappho among their readership. This is most unlikely. Overt lesbians are estimated at 2 to 3 percent of American women. *Vogue* is not foolish enough to use the expensive talents of Irving Penn for so small a segment of readers. Lesbians, in addition, are likely to find *Vogue* offensive because of its emphasis upon feminine values and female dependence.

Another possible conclusion is that all humans contain biological as well as emotional and personality characteristics of their opposite sex. The hermaphrodite myth is common to all cultures, though biologically a hermaphrodite has never really existed, nor could one exist. Human biological sex differentiation, as it has evolved, must go either male or female. Anthropologists have pursued the hermaphrodite in primitive as well as modern societies in every corner of the world without success. A true biological hermaphrodite human, with the sexually functioning genitals of both sexes, has never been discovered except in mythology.

Men, of course, all carry female hormones, as women all carry male hormones. The *Vogue* symbolic hermaphrodite is related to this duality of emotional need which exists to some degree within every woman.

Many ancient deities were represented as androgynous or hermaphroditic—Egyptian, Hindu, Mexican, Greek, Chinese, Persian, Palestinian, Australian, and others. Hermaphroditic mythology is usually connected with birth or procreation—the uniting of man and woman into a single being, the primal life force. Plato explained man's creation from an hermaphroditic union of the sexes, permitting mortals to identify with a concept which, in Greek mythology, had been exclusively reserved for the more primitive deities. Marriage ceremonies are usually hermaphroditic in their symbolism—the uniting of male and female. The hermaphrodite has also symbolized intellectual activity not directly connected with sexuality. Many anthropologists believe all cultures looked upon their first god as androgynous.

The *Vogue* illustration was tested by a group of female *Vogue* readers, who unanimously reported the photo involved them emotionally, was interesting and exciting—and a few actually said they might purchase the exercise costumes. None mentioned Yoga or provided any conscious rationalization for their attraction to and identification with the illustration. The symbolistic design was, of course, not designed by photographer Penn to be read at the conscious level.

The ad appears to be actually a paste-up. The two models are so similar in facial lines, hands, feet, and hair that they seem to be the same woman, costumed to appear different at the conscious level, but communicating at the unconscious level the idea that masculine and feminine characteristics are combined and integrated within every woman.

For the Man Who Has Everything

The *Vogue* cover, an advertisement or point-of-sale merchandising piece, is usually quite revealing in terms of the prospective reader's fantasy life—how she would like to see herself being seen by other people (see Figure 29). A subliminal consistency appears on these covers that suggests the editors and photographers know precisely what they are doing.

The November 1971 *Vogue* cover presents a self-assured, poised, dominant image to the reader. There is a curious thing about the eyes: from whichever angle the cover is viewed, the eyes seem to be looking directly at the reader. Who is this attractive woman in her—a dangerous guess—early thirties? And how is the reader supposed to develop an instantaneous, unconscious identification with the model which will initiate a purchase of the magazine?

The cover model is unmarried. In place of the wedding band, however, she wears a massive diamond and emerald ring. This ring is not likely to be found on the jewelry counter at Woolworth. The value would be from $5,000 to $10,000 at Van Cleef and Arpels. As this model does not communicate the idea of a professionally employed woman, she is likely unemployed, at least in the usual kinds of occupations. The ring, therefore, was a gift—reasonably a man's gift—and, necessarily, a very well-off man's gift.

The dress is ivory crepe and also expensive, with a Canadian fox neckpiece over her left shoulder—a casual, even modest way to handle a small fortune in fur. The gown and fur are Saks Fifth Avenue. One might wonder how this unemployed woman could afford a gown which cost hundreds, if not over a thousand dollars.

The model appears self-assured. She knows *who she is* and *where she is going*—and it's not to a movie or a Howard Johnson's restaurant. She has likely decided or actually proposed that she and her escort will spend the evening at an expensive restaurant or supper club. She is so self-confident *she doesn't even have to smile.* Her thin, pale, almost sexless lips and light facial makeup have not been painted into the lascivious invitation to sex as they would be in *Cosmopolitan* or *Playboy*. She comes across with a strong *"I don't give a damn! We are operating on my terms!"* attitude toward her male companion or toward what the reader would unconsciously identify as her male companion. The model's phallic forefinger symbolizes masculinity—control and dominance.

Embedded across the model's hair, forehead, cheeks, throat, arms, and hands are numerous SEXes. She is certainly involved with SEX, even if only at the subliminal level, but the sex is just a means of achieving an end. The dimpled curve to the left of her lips, the only thing that gives her any emotional expression, is the top curve of a large capital S; the E and X appear in smaller letters under her lower lip.

In short, this cover model is portraying a very well-kept mistress to someone who can afford the most expensive best. Her impenetrable self-assurance suggests she has already received preferred stock in DuPont and General Motors as gifts. Presumably this image sells magazines, as it appears frequently on *Vogue* covers in a variety of forms. The *well-kept mistress* would have to be a major fantasy projection of married, respectable, *Vogue* readers. *Vogue* sells fantasies, which sell magazines, advertising space and ultimately advertised products.

9. Video's Victimized Voyeur

(It's What He Can't See That Turns Him On)

Television to the creative director, cameraman, or writer is a low-definition medium. Compare the final detail, degrees of shadow and light, and the intricacies of color gradation available to an artist preparing display materials for the hard-surfaced, varnished paper in slick national magazines with the rough, gross outline forms, color unreliability, and the rough-textured appearance communicated through the video tube. But in spite of the low-definition limitation, television must motivate sales or manipulate human behavior in a way competitive to the other media or it would soon disappear from national prominence.

Television, like all the mass audience media in North America, survives only because it sells. Vast audiences of 50 to 70 million individuals are not uncommon—all perceiving precisely the same audio-visual stimuli at the same instant. Enough of these people respond to TV commercials faithfully and dependably during the days or weeks following their exposure, to justify network advertising time charges ranging from $25,000 to $150,000 per minute. Television has developed into the master salesman of all time.

This is difficult to believe—especially after absorbing an evening of what appears to be total absurdity as men and women discuss their constipation, bad breath, body odors, smelly feet, insomnia, backaches, indigestion, and an incredible assortment of psychosomatic ailments before millions of viewers. The women on television commercials appear as neurotic morons whose main life interest involves their never-quite-white laundry, their never-quite-comfortable girdles and brassieres, their relentless search for a kitchen free of stains, germs, odors, and unsightly linoleum scratches, and—the greatest banality of them all—the struggle to obtain *really* soft toilet tissue. America's cultured preoccupation with soft stools is testified to by laxative, as well as toilet paper, advertising.

156

The men portrayed in all the commercials are, for the most part, pictured as overweight, inept losers. They look to their wives and children for guidance, to various father and mother figures who help them resolve life and death decisions over the purchase of shirts, ties, denture adhesives, headache remedies, automotive accessories, dog food, and hemorrhoid relief products.

It might be very revealing to take a one-hour film of TV commercials spliced together into an aboriginal society and ask what we patronizingly call primitive men to describe the kind of people who live in the tribe portrayed in the commercials. It might be very difficult to sell a Stone-Age culture a concept of civilization based upon television advertising. Should the communists take to the proselytizing warpath again, such a one-hour film would have tremendous impact among the hungry, the impoverished, the dispossessed, and the exploited peoples of the world.

It might be fun to also indulge in a brief critique of the television programs which carry the hard sell. These programs are designed primarily as platforms for advertisements. Like editorial material in newspapers and magazines, the TV programs merely set up the right size and quality of an audience that will appeal to particular advertisers as a market. The program "All in the Family," for example, does not exist to enlighten audiences with insights into a low-intelligence bigot's daily life. *The program exists only to sell the advertisers' products.* Oddly enough, surveys have revealed that a substantial portion of the regular audience identify *with*—not *against*—Archie Bunker. Despite the image advertising, the program is not aimed only at the liberal, intellectual elite. As any time salesman from ABC will affirm, Archie *sells*—and that's what it is all about. "All in the Family" is strongly supportive of its sponsor's products.

A number of extremely successful programs have been cancelled—even though they had enormous audiences—because the program was so good no one in the audience could remember the sponsor's name. The prizewinning television show "Medic," starring Richard Boone, went the route of a show just too damned good; it so overpowered the commercials that products just didn't move off the shelves.

Zenith of Media Creativity

This chapter will concentrate upon the commercials, the epitome of television arts and crafts. More money, time, skill, and talent are expended upon TV commercials than upon any regular program content. The commercials are technically masterpieces of persuasive manipulation. Placed in the appropriate program setting, they sell billions of dollars in merchandise each year in North America. During 1971, 63 million dollars was paid just to the actors and acresses who modeled or performed in these commercials.

The audiences for whom the commercials have been most exactingly produced almost universally consciously reject the apparent sales pitches. They pass it off with an, "Oh, what the hell!" accepting the imposition upon their time and intelligence as a small price to pay for the ego indulgence obtained from dramatic programs. Survey after survey reveals that audiences seem to be universally contemptuous of TV commercials. As costs for a one-minute commercial average around $50,000 and can go as high as $200,000 (well worth the price if it sells products at a high enough rate), this appears to be a paradox. Television commercials are the most carefully produced material in the entire field of mass communication. In a 60-second commercial, every single second —even fractions of a second—of both audio and visual content has been precision engineered to accomplish a specific end—sell the product. And television commercials work; they sell unbelievable quantities of products, and the theory suggests that they are most effective with people who believe themselves to be the most indifferent to their appeals.

The old American proverb says *if you want to con someone, you must first get him to trust you, or at least feel superior to you* (these two ideas are related), and get him to let down his guard. The proverb explains a great deal about television commercials. If we assume that people are not stupid, they must react to TV commercials with a feeling of superiority that permits them to believe they are in control. As long as this illusion of volition persists, they would consciously have nothing to fear from the commercials. People are prone to trust anything over which they believe they have control. We are told repeatedly by the media that we do not have to hear or see commercials; we can close our minds— even leave the room or turn off the set. Since we do not *have to,* of course all of us do listen to and watch an incredible number of televised commercial messages during the course of a year. We may consciously shut out a few, but hundreds, perhaps even thousands of others, will get through.

TV commercials appear foolish, clumsy, and ineffectual *on purpose.* They are made to appear this way at the conscious level in order to be consciously ridiculed and rejected. The target aimed at in the human mind is the subliminal or unconscious. The real message, the one that sells, is planted securely in the viewer's unconscious.

Every year for nearly a quarter century the New York Advertising Association has awarded prizes to outstanding ad campaigns. These are usually won by arty, interesting, and maturely expressed sales messages aimed at the viewer's conscious mind. None of the award winners has ever been among those ads generally acknowledged to have been the best sellers. Usually the most effective advertising—in terms of sales, not public relations for the advertising industry—are the drug commercials with their animated mechanical men and women, the detergent commercials with their galloping or flying knights and tornados, and the cosmetic commercials with their heaving bosoms and wet-licked lips. Most ad men will confirm that over the years the seemingly *worst* commercials have sold the *best.* An effective TV commercial is purposefully designed to insult the viewer's conscious intelligence, thereby penetrating his defenses.

After watching a 30- or 60-second commercial, the illusion that comes through is usually that the content has been casually assembled in a quick and often unpolished way. Nothing could be less true. If the same meticulous attention were given a 90-minute Hollywood feature film that is given a one-minute commercial, the film would take years to complete and the national budget to finance. A single 30-second commercial can easily require a week or more to film, not counting the extensive time often required for lab work on special effects. A single 10-second segment of a TV commercial may be shot and reshot twenty times to get it just right. Each movement, position, action and reaction are carefully studied and calculated for audience affects at both conscious and unconscious levels.

Backgrounds into Subliminal Foregrounds

Backgrounds and frame peripheries are very important as locations for either symbolic or verbal subliminal embeds. In the now famous Alka-Seltzer commercial, "Try it, you'll like it!" no one ever notices the bald waiter standing behind the dissatisfied customer who is complaining, "So I tried it. I almost died!" Viewers only begin to consciously perceive the bald waiter after the third or fourth viewing of the commercial.

The consciously unseen waiter is a very important part of the commercial. He stands stooped and defenseless as the customer complains to the TV audience. Then, throwing his napkin over his shoulder, he turns and disappears into the kitchen. Even after four viewings of the commercial, only about one-third of the audience is consciously aware of the waiter, but all have seen him subliminally the first time they were exposed. If the waiter is taken out of the commercial, the customer's complaints are not funny. The unqualified complaints would tend to annoy the audience, many of whom have undoubtedly been in the same unpleasant position in restaurants. The bald waiter makes the customer's anger a personal issue between an individual waiter and a customer, not hostility which extends to restaurants or waiters in general.

Similar subliminal background techniques have been used for years by motion picture directors, though generally not as precision-defined and applied as in TV commercials. John Huston, in *The African Queen*, used cleverly constructed backgrounds to subliminally convey feelings, moods, and information to the audience. In one scene, after a difficult struggle with the river, Humphrey Bogart and Katharine Hepburn encounter a swarm of mosquitoes which nearly smother them. When finally free of the mosquitoes, the two are exhausted. The *African Queen* drifts beside the river bank. Dialogue between the two brilliant actors is mundane, almost devoid of meaning; their expressions are grim, their sentences one-word and abrupt. If you only hear the dialogue, the idea comes through that they are exhausted, but you do not get the overwhelming sense of defeat, failure, and futility that director Huston and his two stars somehow communicate in the audio-visual context of the scene. Part of the secret to the emotional impact of this scene is attributable to a bush of bougainvillea—dying, half dead, its leaves partly yellow, the red flowers wilted and drooping. The audience never consciously sees the bush; their conscious attention is focused upon the two actors' faces. The dying bougainvillea, of course, is symbolic of death, and there is no doubt that the subliminally perceived bush reinforces the dialogue and action, setting for the audience a great depth of mood throughout the important scene.

In another *African Queen* scene, Bogart and Hepburn have just dramatically survived a dangerous rapid. For the first time in the story, the two characters forget their past—Bogart, the drunken Canadian river bum, a loser through and through; Hepburn, the frigid, up-tight, Methodist missionary lady, hiding her sexual inhibitions among an assortment of biblical platitudes. The two characters embrace in their relief at having survived the rapids. Suddenly, however, they both remember who they really are. They push each other away, both bewildered and frustrated. Bogart throws himself onto the bottom of the boat next to the boiler. His frustrated rage is inconsolable. He grasps the handle of the boiler door, opens it to reveal a fire glowing with intensity and heat (symbolic womb), picks up a large phallic appearing piece of wood, throws it aggressively into the boiler's flames, then slams shut the boiler door—a symbolic expression of impotence. This bit of business, with genital symbolism, presents a superb climax to the scene. No one except a small group of technicians ever paid any conscious attention to the symbolic meaning of this typical Huston device—though millions of people who have seen and enjoyed the movie responded predictably with their emotions. These techniques have been in use for years by such directors as Arthur Penn, Fellini, Huston, Hitchcock, and others, many of whom can command a half-a-million-dollar fee for a single film.

In a feature-length film, a director might use only a handful of symbolic devices during the 90 to 120 minutes. The TV commercial is, by comparison, tightly compressed. With only 30 or 60 seconds to use, even every half second must be loaded with emotional power that will sell the product. A one-minute commercial on the Bob Hope show sells for around $140,000. At the 20-to-1 ratio, considering advertising as 5 percent of gross sales income, the one minute must sell almost $2.8 million (560 Chrysler automobiles at $5,000 each) to merely break even—and remember, breaking even is not what it is all about. Most TV commercial directors, judging from their work, appear to be astute and disciplined students of cinematographic art forms, and then some.

Best Taste in Beer

As an example, in a 60-second TV commercial for Labatt's beer—a best-selling Canadian beer—an eight-second sequence was reshot at least a dozen times (see Figure 26). The commercial content involved a variety of scenes with young actors appearing to be at various kinds of outdoor activities. One eight-second scene within a 60-second commercial, portrays an attractive young model seated in the grass at a picnic. Her companion, standing next to her, has been drinking from a bottle of Labatt's. The relationship between her head and his genital area was strongly established in only two or three seconds. The young man, after finishing the beer, bends over and places the bottle in the grass in front of the girl—a simple and apparently innocuous movement.

After the sequence was recorded on video tape, however, and played back a frame at a time, some curious things were seen to happen during the brief eight seconds.

In the first still, the model's face is expectant, her mouth sensuous, half open, her tongue is visible. She is looking slightly upward to the level of the standing male's genital area. It is difficult to consciously identify this loving look with a mere bottle of beer: there has to be something more.

In the second still, motion was stopped at the instant the beer bottle passed before the model's face in its downward movement. The picture, with the model's mouth open to receive the phallic bottle, is self-explanatory. After several experimental rehearsals of this scene by the author and his students, it was discovered there is absolutely no way the open mouth and the passing bottle could coordinate in these positions by random chance. The timing had to be split second; the knowledge of what was really going on had to be precise and highly detailed. A *fellatio* scene was embedded subliminally into the Labatt's commercial, to put it simply and directly.

When the illusion is run at full broadcast speed, the entire action takes only eight seconds. The mouth and bottle business are unnoticed by the viewer at the conscious level. The commercial was run half a dozen times for fifty test subjects —after they had seen the still shots from the video tape— and even then no one could consciously perceive what was going on. Remember, the tachistoscope can put information in the unconscious at 1/3000th of a second. Illusions, such as the Labatt picnic, operate much more slowly, though still invisible to conscious perception. One of the actors in the commercial was shown the stills. He responded with astonishment, "So that's why the damned scene took all day to shoot."

Much like the other print examples of subliminal technique, these techniques are effective mainly because so few people have any conscious idea of how their perception actually works. We cannot seem to fully grasp the great speed at which information can be processed in our own nervous systems, the delicate sensitivity and capacity of our sensory equipment (the thirty-seven or more sensory inputs), and the bewildering reality that all these senses operate simultaneously and continuously. Obviously, the media technicians, in their intense preoccupation with the mechanics of sensory manipulation, are utilizing this general ignorance in their own and their clients' interests.

With television's audio and video, the number of possible ways to trick the eye and ear are enormous. So many possibilities exist, in fact, that equipment is not available which can thoroughly analyze even a single TV commercial, let alone continuously monitor television in the public interest. Subliminals are relatively easy to plant in either sound or visual media. It is often impossible to consciously locate them. Subaudible effects can be planted at low-volume intensities, at various speed harmonics, or at either high or low frequencies—all of which are unheard by conscious perception.

Madison Avenue account executives actually brag about planting subs which, they claim, no one will be able to find. One executive at a major international agency told of burying the words, "Buy———! Buy———!" continuously behind ten seconds of applause at the end of a 60-second TV commercial. Tests showed the instructions worked superbly on a sample of the market he was attempting to influence. He maintained that there was absolutely no way for anyone to prove the subs were actually there.

An executive from another major agency in New York told about their experience with a new analgesic (headache potion) account. Their research department had come up with some interesting data on the relationship between heartbeats and suggestibility. The human heart beats at 72 pulses per minute. Music or voice timed to this rhythm has an increased ability to affect human behavior. Several experimental commercials were prepared using 72 beats per minute as pacing for drumbeats, music, and voice. The test effects were amazing, according to the executive. The commercials were tested in a special theater with a random audience of housewives and husbands.

Had the analgesic commercial been broadcast to the roughly 30 million people watching the NBC evening news, 5 million would have developed headaches within three hours of viewing it. Frightening? But why not? Many scientists have long believed that the major effect of aspirin and its related compounds is in the power of suggestion that the drug will work rather than in the actual drug ingredients. If you can remove a headache by suggestion—as you can quite easily under hypnosis—you can certainly bring one about by suggestion.

The Clean Ones

In her hopeless attempt to find fulfillment and sexual satisfaction through cleansing products, the American housewife is confronted with an incredible array of get-clean devices—all of which imply that her home must be the filthiest place on earth. If she hadn't been carefully taught to believe that dirt was all about her, threatening her, suffocating her, she would not need all of these products offered to her countless times each day.

Soap commercials are pumped through North American video tubes by the dozens each day of the year, year after year. What they may be doing to the psyches of the millions of women—and their helpless children trapped into attendance during the afternoons, when they are usually broadcast—is largely unknown.

The commercial's plot is invariably simplistic and, one might easily assume at the conscious level, designed to excite and entertain the feebleminded. As was pointed out, this is carefully calculated banality in its most pervasive art form. But the facts are overwhelming to anyone familiar with the copy-testing research of Colgate:Palmolive, Lever Brothers, or Proctor and Gamble. These commercials *sell* in one of the world's most competitive markets—and they sell and they sell and they sell.

To increase soap sales, the giant international marketing

organizations diversified their products first. Soaps, detergents, or whatever, were packaged and sold for highly specialized purposes. The basic product was the same, the diversification psychological rather than real. No matter how you package it, process it, color it, or make it smell—it's still just soap. The second step was consumer diversification. Soaps were no longer just sold to anyone who needed to wash. Specialized soaps were developed and sold to younger women, older women, housewives, working wives, college graduates, high school dropouts, and so on. The American soap consumer has been divided and subdivided through the most sophisticated demographic and psychographic technology. Some brands are even designed for families where men do the shopping, others where the wives and husbands shop together, and finally some for the housewife who shops alone. The soap companies have meticulously studied the kinds of dirt likely to be dealt with in an enormous range of occupations and life-styles, as well as chemical composition of water in hundreds of various areas of North America to which soap ingredients and marketing practices are adapted. A significant life experience is being merchandised under the guise of soap or detergent. The never-ending promise is psychological- or emotional-need fulfillment, but at an enormous price to the consumer, in emotional as well as in financial terms.

North Americans' phobic behavior about cleanliness has been noted by millions of people outside the country as American tourists have charged about the world with their phallic spray cans full of disinfectants and deodorants, their antiseptic washes and rinses, and their horror over possible contamination or infections from clothing, food, or other items they may be compelled to touch during the course of their daily existence. Much humor, especially in Europe, has been aimed at their carrying abroad rolls of 100 percent American toilet paper. Of course, as many Europeans will readily acknowledge, infection and food poisoning are real possibilities which they live with each day. But Americans appear to have extended their phobia about germs and cleanliness to absurd extremes—extremes which may very possibly increase the likelihood of infections rather than provide a protection. The sale of colognes and other aromatic preparations with which to disguise body and breath odors is also curious. If Americans are so clean, one might reasonably ask, then why are they so concerned over how they smell?

Is it any wonder that in reaction to the soap and pharmaceutical company sponsored phobia of cleanliness, many young rebels have reacted by appearing as slovenly, smelly, and as dirty as they can possibly costume themselves? They might well be trying, perhaps futilely, to tell their parents something—possible even trying to break the stranglehold on their lives obtained by the unconscious massaging that goes on in soap commercials and advertising.

Cleaned-Up Sex

Consider, for example, the long-range effects of subliminally connecting *sex* and *cleanliness*. When the exaggerated kind of American detergent-processed artificial cleanliness is subconsciously programmed to sexual stimuli, the results may well be a rejection of odors, for example, which have somehow aided humans in emotional survival and adjustment, as well as reproduction, over thousands of years of evolution. It may well turn out to have been quite destructive to replace these odors with perfumed, aromatic substitutes. Perhaps we are reaching the point where any natural human odor, secretion, or bodily fluid will have to be sprayed or processed and disguised completely by some advertised product in order for us to feel ourselves either socially or sexually acceptable. It might be fascinating to research into how long a North American could presently endure life without a soap, aromatic, or deodorant product of some sort.

In virtually all TV commercials, the director-photographer-writer's preoccupation with genital and erogenous areas of the human body is apparent. Regardless of the product or brand—patent medicine, cosmetics, soaps, toothpaste, toilet paper—male and female models appear to have been cast primarily because of erotic lip, mouth, and tongue appearances during speech. After reviewing hundreds of commercials at slow speeds, the most impressive thing about them is their erotic-oral implications—kissing, fingers and other objects protruding into the mouth, pointed visible tongues, sensuous and precision-curved lips symbolizing the female vagina, lip thickness or heaviness, and sensuousness in eyes, facial shadows, lip expressions, and exposure of the erogenous zone on the neck beneath the ear. With TV's low-definition problem, the camera must work in close; most of the sensuous detail is lost in a long shot. The mouth, almost universally, seems to be the primary focal point.

Other often-used erotically stimulating portions of the anatomy include hair (used with all its rich archetypal erotic significance), and eyes (heavily made up to emphasize their elliptical shape and surrounded by eyelash hair and dark lids) painted in various genital colors—red, purple, or blue. TV commercial images are very often constructed around simple basic forms—triangles, circles, oblong shapes—all oriented toward some erotic suggestion. Models appear sexually excited, even orgasmic, over a triangular piece of dirty laundry that has been successfully cleaned and whitened (the triangle balancing upon the point of one angle is archetypally symbolic of man), a phallic-shaped cylindrical hair-spray can (watch carefully how the models hold and use these spray cans and the directions in which the cans always seem to point), or the round opening in the bottom of a sink drain as the foamy dishwater is sucked deeply down inside the solid round drainpipe.

The SEXes, of course, are discreetly embedded in clothing, hair, flowers, trees, in anything with lines into which can be drawn or planted in obscure folds the subliminal triggers. The television model's body language is also very important, as each carefully rehearsed precise movement can communicate subliminally—the direction of eye contact toward another body, touching, finger and hand contacts and directions, relationships with objects or people, and movements toward or from genital and erogenous areas.

Affection Substitutes in Humans

An interesting example of the body contact type of TV commercial appears in the Mattel doll ads (see Figure 21). The Mattel Company has created an entire family of expensive dolls that each Christmas drains millions of dollars from the pocketbooks of parents throughout North America. Mattel's TV advertising is aimed in two directions: at the children and at mothers likely to be watching the programs designed ostensibly for children (many so-called children's programs have more adult viewers than children). The kids from age three up must be induced to put the heat on their parents to make purchases. Children under twelve purchase very little on their own, but if handled properly by advertising they can drive their parents up a wall for denying their little darlings those nationally advertised products which are the birthright of every American child.

The scenes from Mattel commercials are revealing when
the motion is stopped. As you watch the actual commercial,
you see a child playing with a lovely doll—fondling, caressing, kissing. Somehow, though, the message doesn't come
through at the conscious level. Again, our minds just won't
cope with the reality of what is going on. Stopping the video-
tape at key action points presents another view of The Baby
Tender Love Syndrome.

The large number of oral, anal, and genital touching contacts between the child and the doll are startling, especially
when they are viewed in stop motion. One conclusion is immediately apparent: Mattel and its research department
know exactly what they are doing—which buttons to push
that will turn on purchase motivation lights all over America.
Sex is a basic drive, of course, within all humans—most psychologists maintain that it is *the* basic drive. Libido, or sexual
development, begins at birth. Infants delight in playing with
their genitalia—a normal, natural, even healthy way to pass
the day if you are a small child. It might even be fun if you
are an adult. But the American culture, possibly more than
any other ethnic group in the world, prohibits genital play.
Countless Americans have been told as infants, "Don't touch
that dirty thing!"

Touching, just touching (not necessarily genital touching),
is also forbidden at an early age in the North American culture. Mothers stop touching their sons and fathers their
daughters at a much earlier point in time than is true in the
tribal or more economically under-developed societies.
American children are often embarrassed to touch other
children—even of the opposite sex. Sex guilt and homosexual
fear start early in the American culture.

Some anthropologists attribute this no-touch cultural policy to Oedipal conflict or incest fears which are present to
some degree in all known cultures. It is often amusing to
watch Americans avoid physical contact with each other,
contact of a sort that would only be a demonstration of
friendship or affection in another culture. Touching makes
Americans most uncomfortable, even when it comes from
their intimate friends. This is sad, especially because we have
now discovered that tactile sensory experiences are extremely
important to mental health.

Many psychologists maintain that touching, or touch-
related sensory inputs, constitute the primary human sensory
experience—far more critical to human survival and adjust-

ment than sight or hearing. Masters' and Johnson's discovery that 80 percent of their patients who are sexually inadequate could be turned on through a simple three-week training course in touching and interpersonal communication is culturally revealing—as was their informed estimate that 50 percent of North American marriages were sexually disfunctional. Other American scientists estimate sexually disfunctional marriages as high as 75 percent. Americans appear literally starved for tactile experience. This sensory deprivation seems to be culture-bound, beginning at a very early age.

From its commercials, Mattel has apparently researched the tactility problem in the American culture most carefully. In Baby Tender Love, they are offering the child a human surrogate which can be touched, kissed, fondled (even genitally caressed) with parental approval and encouragement. Recall the life-sized, anatomically complete plastic dolls being advertised in men's magazines. It might be important to question where all the love lavished upon dogs, cats, horses, dolls, and other objects which serve as human surrogates could be leading American culture. Why can't Americans love people?

What parent could be so cruel as to deny his child the socially approved touching experience available simply through the purchase of Mattel's Baby Tender Love? Regardless of price, the reward of deep emotional fulfillment promised the child would be worth every penny. These touching experiences were very likely denied the child's parents. It is almost reasonable to assume they would jump at the opportunity to provide their children with a synthetic substitute for emotional fulfillment which they were denied as children. The game is pathetic, but highly profitable for the toy manufacturer. And the game will be most strongly defended by those who are the most victimized.

During recent years many individuals in government and educational fields have voiced concern about children's advertising. Various investigations have generally failed to reveal anything other than what is superficially obvious: advertisers are making a hell of a lot of money out of manipulating kids manipulating their parents. But the actual mechanics of how it is done and the social effects—most importantly the long-range social effects—still remain a mystery to everyone but the manufacturers, their advertising agencies, and the motivation research specialists they employ. Is it possible that many people in American society have recognized the subliminal game being played by advertisers, but have been unable to verbalize or make conscious this knowledge? Human perceptual defense mechanisms should never be underestimated.

10. The Man Who
Almost Thought for Himself

Cigarette advertising is a fascinating and profitable business. In spite of the cancer and emphysema warnings—medical realities factually established beyond any shadow of a doubt —cigarette sales continue to soar each year. Tobacco companies are showing higher profits than ever before in their history.

The market that was created for so-called low tar and nicotine cigarettes has permitted manufacturers to almost double the number of cigarettes they can produce from the same amount of tobacco. The health-hazard publicity has actually helped increase profits. And, consumption has spiraled upward over the past decade in a dizzying rate of ascent. Tobacco company stocks are still among the American economy's most prized investments. The prodigious profits accumulated during the past ten years have enabled these corporations to diversify their investments. Most are now well on the way to becoming giant international conglomerates.

Smokers, the ones who have purchased the products, made possible these prodigious profits, and supported the diversification of the cigarette companies, have not fared so well. Many have ended their smoking careers with cancer of the mouth, lungs, or larynx; others have fallen to emphysema where they often linger on as vegetables for years; some have gone the route of coronary or circulatory diseases. Many of these degenerative diseases have their roots in smoking. One prominent physician put it this way: "Cancer is probably the most merciful of the diseases related to smoking. It kills—usually in six months or less. And, though there is a significantly higher proportion of smokers who develop cancer than nonsmokers, cancer is still a rather remote statistical probability. Emphysema is different. Any smoker simply has to smoke a large enough quantity over a long enough

171

time and he will develop emphysema. Emphysema patients sometimes struggle on pathetically for five to ten years as vegetables—needing constant care 24 hours a day."

The U.S. Government's involvement with the tobacco industry is intriguing. Government offices such as the Federal Trade Commission; the Surgeon General; Housing, Education and Welfare; and Consumer Affairs have known about the effects of cigarette advertising for decades. They have cautiously walked a tightrope on the issue. Many southern states' tax income depends heavily upon tobacco crops. Tax income from cigarette sales is a staggering emperor's ransom at both state and federal levels. Tobacco companies are, of course, heavy contributors to political parties.

In the face of overwhelming evidence of damage to the national health, the Federal government has merely supported the removal of cigarette advertising from television. Ad budgets for newspapers, magazines, and billboards have skyrocketed—as have cigarette sales. The denial of television advertising turned out to be only a minor inconvenience for the tobacco industry.

In 1970, $84 million was spent by the U.S. Congress to improve tobacco interests. Indeed, in a special report NBC news revealed that the tobacco farmer today could not survive without government assistance. Someone must be getting the money from the tobacco crop. As usual, it isn't the farmer.

The U.S. Government guarantees a minimum price per acre for tobacco crops; it spent $2.7 million in research directed at discovering new, more efficient ways to grow tobacco, and invested another quarter million dollars in foreign advertising for U.S.-grown tobacco. The United States is the world's largest tobacco exporter. The government grants a five cents per pack subsidy to tobacco companies for their exports.

In 1971, the last year for cigarette advertising on television, the industry spent $11.4 million on that medium alone. Ad expenditures increased for cigarettes in 1972, concentrating on print and other media. Sales and profits have never been higher.

There are 44 million smokers in the United States. The U.S. Surgeon General estimated in 1972 that 300,000 individuals die each year as a direct or indirect result of smoking. This annual casualty figure is much higher than American losses in both the Korean and Vietnam wars.

All this, of course, was published long ago. Though everyone knows about the dangers of smoking, more people are smoking today than ever before. Why?

Big Money in Neurosis

The subliminal content of cigarette advertising is a powerful agent—subverting both reason and logic. In effect, subliminal advertising content has initiated and sustained a compulsive neurosis among hundreds of millions of people throughout the world. Psychoneurosis is generally defined as "An emotional disorder in which feelings of anxiety, obsessional thoughts, compulsive acts and physical complaints without objective evidence of disease, in various patterns, dominate the personality" (*American College Dictionary*).

Take cigarettes away from any addicted smoker and his behavior conforms precisely to that of a psychoneurotic. It would be simple just to conclude that smokers were stupid—continuing their habit in the face of overwhelming evidence as to the damage they will experience. Smokers are no more stupid than anyone else manipulated by subliminal mass media content. They are merely acting predictably to what amounts to a posthypnotic suggestion from the advertisers. They are performing what they are commanded to perform by tens of millions of dollars of advertising annually. As these twentieth-century robots puff away their lives and breaths, they should understand at least part of how the advertising industry has been making fools and fortunes out of them for years.

Shortly after the respiratory disease statistics were released during the 1950s, the tobacco industry generally stopped trying to refute the well-documented medical facts. It continued a modest public relations campaign which tried to throw doubt and confusion over the medical research, but it essentially backed off. Trying to argue with scientifically supported evidence is a loser's game. Knowing that people's perceptual defenses will lead them to accept information they are already predisposed to believe, the cigarette advertising agencies came up with a most amazing gimmick—the cigarette filter.

Back in the early days of the filter, tobacco companies actually increased tar and nicotine content of cigarettes to overcome the weakened smoke inhalation sensations produced by the filter. This ruse was eventually discovered and exposed. It really didn't make any difference, as the national market was gradually swinging toward a preference for weaker cigarettes—or at least the illusion of being weaker.

National research on cigarette taste or flavor and aromatics has revealed that very few people can differentiate between brands—or for that matter between filtered and non-filtered brands. Indeed, a sizable proportion of subjects are unable to determine for certain whether or not the cigarette is lit. Brand differences are established primarily through image manipulation in advertising, similar to the techniques used with beer, automobiles, deodorants, and other consumer products.

Carefully supervised tests have shown that no one could perceive a difference in taste between charcoal and cellulose filters. There is also no significant difference in the way these two filters screen out tars and nicotine. One is as ineffective as the other. There is an enormous fictional difference, nevertheless, in filter images. The charcoal filter is believed by some smokers to offer greater protection against cigarette chemicals entering the lungs than the cellulose filter, but both filters are perceived as protection for the smoker.

The reality of this fantasy, supported by an incredible mountain of consumer and public health research, is that filters have no effect whatsoever in reducing the damaging effects of tobacco smoke upon the human respiratory system. The whole thing is just another mass-media-perpetuated fantasy—and one which undoubtedly results in death and suffering for countless people each year who continue to smoke even though they are being irreparably damaged in the process. The phenomenon is shocking: most smokers know exactly what they are doing, but the media-supported image fantasies are so strong, they compel smokers to act against their own best interests. One tobacco company recently featured its brand as the thinking man's cigarette. The truth is that if the programmed robot could think for himself, he would have stopped smoking years ago.

Life Begins with Tasting

Over many years virtually all cigarettes have, at one time or another, been sold on the basis of their "tastes." Consider the significance of the word *taste* in terms of the experiments discussed earlier that measured emotional reactions to words that differ only slightly from certain taboo words.

Significant affective (emotional) reactions were derived in polygraph and electroencephalograph tests of individuals reaction to such words.

"Tastes," changing only the "a" to "e," becomes *testes,* or in the idiom of the days, *balls* or *balling.* With this added dimension, consider the meanings of the following copy quotes on taste:

"In Case of Hot *Taste* Break Open." (Kool)

"Tastefully Cool." (Kool)

"The Great New *Taste*." (Kent)

"A Good Time for the Good *Taste*." (Kent)

"It's A Matter of *Taste*." (Viceroy)

"Taste in her Cigarette." (Eve)

"The Natural Choice for a Lady with *Taste*." (Eve)

"A *Taste* That's Never Harsh or Hot." (Salem)

"Tastes as Fresh as Springtime." (Salem)

"Taste Me! *Taste* Me!" (Doral)

"You Demand Good *Taste*." (Vantage)

In advertising the cigarette usually is illustrated as a phallic symbol. If the cigarette held by the models is *down,* sex has already occurred. If the cigarette is held *horizontally,* the model is warming up. When the cigarette points *upward,* however, the model is turned on and ready to go with a symbolic erection. The possible combinations of up, down, and horizontal cigarettes are virtually endless. A male model's cigarettes might be *down,* the female model's *up.* She lights his cigarette, thereby turning him on, or up, or vice versa.

Sexual innuendoes in ad copy provide additional subliminal reinforcement for smoking. In the modern vernacular, words such as "Come," "Long," "Ball'n," "It," "Holder" (she who holds "it"), "Cool," and "Length" have strong sexual symbolism, especially when transmitted subliminally. Consider, "You can take Salem (males) out of the country (cunt)—but you can't take the country (cunt) out of Salem (males)." When these are used in advertising with sexual implications, the reader can gain some insight into what the unconscious part of the brain is reading into advertising copy. These words, at the subliminal level, can trigger strong emotional reactions within most any individual in our culture. And, the more rigid the morality and the more consciously inhibited the individual, the stronger the subliminal reaction.

Most cigarette advertising is directed at the unconscious for it is here that preferences are usually formed. The cigarette market illustrates well the power of subliminal communication technique, because the products are either identical or very similar and brands cannot be sold on the basis of actual differences discerned through reason or logic. Smokers, in spite of their brand loyalties, are smoking little more than brand images. What is perceived as flavor or aroma can be influenced by the visual response to a package design.

Consider a Kent cigarette ad that was designed to appeal to the woman readers of *Cosmopolitan* (see Figure 24). Kent is a strong masculine name, suggesting a solid and distinguished Wasp heritage. Simply change the vowel from E to U, however, and KENT becomes the phonetic word symbol for the female genital. Keep this in mind as we review Kent ads directed at both male and female smokers.

The white, gold striped Kent package symbolizes cleanliness and purity with a male (gold) richness or royal heritage implied. Prominently displayed is the Federal Trade Commission report of November 1970 which gives the presumably low tar and nicotine levels of Kent. It is incredible that cigarette companies have learned how to use the FTC warnings as part of their advertising strategy, knowing well that most smokers have no idea which cigarettes are high or low in tar and nicotine content. Kent, incidentally, ranks quite high in tar and nicotine content compared with other king-sized cigarettes, according to the latest government analysis.

The ad portrays a woman's hand resting gently upon a man's hand that is holding a cigarette. Notice it is the man smoking, not the woman. The couple is just beginning dinner at an expensive restaurant, suggested by the plates and silverware, which are as yet unused. Their wine glasses are half empty. The evening appears promising—certainly to the woman for whom the ad was designed. But specifically what the evening promises our woman reader if she purchases Kent cigarettes is far more basic than a good meal at an expensive restaurant.

Genital symbolism is introduced by the man's phallic forefinger and cigarette. The woman model's thumb and hand form a vaginal symbol. The frequent reaction to symbol analysis is that a hand and finger could mean anything. Anyone analyzing symbolic content is immediately suspected of reading in his own interpretations. Indeed, this is always a possibility.

Therefore, the doubting reader is urged to hold the Kent ad on its side, with the man's hand pointing upward. In the shadows under the woman's arm and wrist is the outline of a man's torso and legs. The spoon under her wrist projects from between the shadow of legs, forming an erect penis which is aimed at the base of the woman's thumb.

What woman smoker could resist the subliminal appeal of Kent cigarettes?

You Can Find "It" Anywhere

Another Kent ad, appearing full page in four colors in *Look* magazine, was probably directed at both male and female smokers of all ages (see Figure 25). An attractive blonde model relaxes in the warmth of a hot sun. A lazy summer breeze moves wisps of hair across her tanned face. The expression around her mouth is suggestive of euphoric sensuality.

The model has apparently raised her sunglasses to let the warm afternoon rays reach her eyelids. She, of course, is holding a Kent in an upright position, symbolically ready for action.

What is she getting out of Kent? The answer is hidden in her right (the reader's left) sunglass lens. Block off everything in the ad except that lens. Try to find the answer yourself before reading further.

The subliminal trigger which will induce tens of thousands of people to switch to Kents is a finger gently caressing a vagina—masturbating, if you will—in the sunglass lens. The subliminal promise of Kent is therefore a good horny feeling. Who could resist? Kent proves, indeed, to be closely related to Kunt. Remember the ad copy which read, "Football 'n Kent"?

In case the reader's unconscious might miss the full meaning of the sunglass lens, the ubiquitous embedded SEX appears to the left of her little finger; the bottom of the subliminal S is on the cigarette. Another SEX appears, reading from the left side of the page, across the crosslines leading from the edge of the picture into her palm. A large SEX appears in the palm of her hand, an erogenous zone, the E formed by the outline of her thumb and hand against the background, and a large X appears below as two strands of hair against the black background. There is, as well, a SEX in her left sunglass lens and on the porous skin above each of her eyes. If you wish, you can find SEX appearing numerous additional times in the picture.

Benson & Hedges, with its series of broken cigarette ads, may have reached a high point in subliminal selling. The broken cigarette, of course, symbolizes an extra-long penis—suggesting B & H smokers will likely be perceived as excessively masculine. The long-suffering B & H models are always in some situation where their symbolic masculinity has gotten in their way.

The aging sign painter is a classic example (see Figure 14). As he letters away on the shop window in gold paint—gold is archetypally symbolic of masculinity and richness—his concentration has caused him to break his B & H 100 against the display window of the watch shop. This is the logical conscious message—not displeasing, perhaps, but as a sales message hardly justification for a full-bleed, four-color page in *Newsweek*.

What does the kindly old painter have an excess of at the moment? What in the picture is in abundant supply? Think about the question before going on to the next paragraph.

The answer would probably be *time*. The background of the ad is hung with clocks. Then the question becomes, so the old painter has plenty of *time; time* for what?

Of the six letters apparent in the layout, which one is most different from the others? Study the lettering, ATCHES, before proceeding to the next paragraph.

The S, of course. It has not as yet been painted. Only the stencil appears on the window.

The second most different of the letters is E—only half the E has been painted; the remainder of the letter still appears as a stencil.

So, the two most different letters appearing on the window are S and E, in the order of their differences from the other letters. There must be a third letter somewhere. See if you can find it before reading further.

The brush appears poised on the downstroke of the letter E. The eye follows the brush to the finger, hand, wrist, and arm. The arm rest crosses the arm to form the letter X. If the arm rest was actually being used to steady the painter's hand, it would be placed further up on the wrist.

The old painter has plenty of time for SEX. This message presumably reaches instantly into the unconscious psyches of millions of readers throughout North America. Of the hundreds of test subjects who have evaluated the ad, none has consciously perceived the basic sex theme. Should

Philip Morris International, which owns Benson & Hedges, want to make the sex consciously instead of unconsciously perceived, it would have been quite simple.

There is more, however. Assuming the unconscious may miss the major sex theme, the word is embedded throughout the ad. SEX appears on the inside seam of the shirt sleeve, the letter S appearing in the fold just above the letter B in Benson & Hedges. The E and X follow the seam upward, the X appearing just below the arm rest.

Another embedded SEX appears on the palm of the painter's hand. The S appears under the first knuckle of the finger next to the little finger. The bottom of the S is completed by the crossline in the palm. The E begins with the lifeline, the three horizontal lines crossing the base of the thumb. The X is formed by the lifeline extended up the wrist and a crossline on the wrist. Even the old man's hand is full of SEX.

Another SEX is embedded across the right side of the painter's neck, in the shadow. And another SEX appears above his left eyebrow. Still another appears vertically, the S in his right eyeglass—as one looks at the layout with the right side down; the E was developed between eyelid and eyebrow, and the X is above the eyebrow on the forehead. There are probably several SEX embeds in the layout that were missed.

The subliminal message says simply, you can get lots of sex with B & H. Though the cleverly designed ad is humorous, the fact that many people are unable to disobey commands given or implied at a level of unawareness is not funny, not when you consider that this single ad is at least partially responsible for some of the yearly statistics on cancer, emphysema, and coronary disease.

Fun and Recreation with Guilt

One of the most penetrating jobs advertising does on the human psyche is to manage the individual's conflicts between pleasure and guilt. Products such as cigarettes must first be made to appear fun, exciting, sophisticated, or glamorous. Then the smoker must be given moral permission to have fun without guilt. This is not at all easy, considering North America's Puritan-Calvinist heritage.

A Virginia Slims advertisement is a classic example (see Figure 19). Published in many national magazines such as

TV Guide, Glamour, and *Redbook*—a magazine aimed at a
reader market of young, married, lower-middle-class housewives with small children and a high school education or
less—the ad shows the cigarettes are related to sex, and
sex is related to the "new" woman and her right to self-ex-
pression.

The editorial content of *Redbook* suggests that the reader sees herself as neglected, unloved, and envious of women
who are free to do their own thing. The young mothers see
themselves as household drudges, entirely dependent upon
husbands who are out in the world every day. The laboring
scrubwoman in the black and white photograph, grinding
away at her washboard, projects the *Redbook* reader's
self-pitying image of herself. The ad ostensibly offers a
1972 engagement calendar, *A Book of Days,* which will remind her all year long of her unhappy lot as a housewife
with the "added little stories, anecdotes, quotes and facts
about women." These are obvious descriptions of the ad's
primary features. But what is going on at the subliminal
level? If we consider a photograph as time stopped at a
particular instant, what was the attractive, leather-clad young
woman doing or thinking about just before the picture was
taken?

The model is shown in a relaxed, pensive posture—a
thoughtful, reflecting, perhaps even slightly naughty expression on her face. She is obviously pleased with herself over
something.

Her right hand is in an interesting position inside the coat
pocket. The model's finger could be touching her genitals—
likely her clitoral area.

The erect cigarette provides the hand with a phallic symbolism. Red lips, as was discussed earlier, are vaginal
symbols. The model's thumb and forefinger are poised at one
corner of the mouth, symbolically suggesting the clitoral
area. Oral-genital interchangeability is a basic symbolic device in the mass communication industry.

The model's facial expression, posture, and hand positions
now begin to make sense—the kind of sense that would
justify the large-scale expenditures made on the advertisement run in *Redbook* and in other publications.

The copy, with a line break after the key word, gives the
message an additional subliminal impact, "You've *come* a
long way, baby."

The message provides the *Redbook* reader with moral

authority to obtain sexual satisfaction through masturbation. Control over one's own body sexually is the promise of Woman's Liberation and, of course via the ad, Virginia Slims. The V.S. smoker is free, independent, and self-satisfying. Virginia Slims, incidentally, translates at the subliminal level into *slim virgin*. Who needs men, anyway?

As an added motivational feature, subliminal SEXes are embedded in the model's hair and on her suede coat.

They'd Walk a Mile

A very large proportion of ad content, aimed at the subliminal, involves a commercial exploitation of the consumer's secret miseries and self-doubts. Camel cigarette advertising—aimed at males in the lower-middle class, with high school or less education, married with young children, median age 25 to 30, exploits the feared sexual inadequacies of its market.

Some men have, for probably quite natural and justifiable reasons, an excessive fear of impotency or sterility—the fear they will be unable to impregnate women. Though all men share this fear to one degree or another, it would likely be strongest among cultural groups where manhood has been traditionally equated with the ability to make women pregnant. First- or second-generation children of immigrants from cultures where large families were an indication of a man's virility would be especially affected. Also affected strongly would be individuals with moral inhibitions about sexual indulgence—those who need to see sex morally justified only as a means of procreation.

Camel advertising promises a glorious fantasy future of a continually pregnant wife and a houseful of children—a subliminal promise likely to reassure even the most sexually insecure smoker.

What does the "camel" mean? Why is the cigarette-brand Camel one-humped instead of two? The one-humped camel is archetypally symbolic of pregnancy. One image study of smokers indicated the Camel brand image was overwhelmingly connected with strength, masculinity, potency, virility, and —unique for cigarette brands—fatherhood and morality.

Self-idealization, image or identity reinforcement of the Camel smoker was recently emphasized in a series of *image ads* widely published in many national magazines. The se-

ries, "They're not for everybody," projected the Camel smoker's view of himself: exclusive, down to earth, hard-working,
morally righteous, solid citizen, strong, rugged, slightly younger than he actually is, and masculine. The image ads are,
of course, loaded with subliminal SEX embeds.

An entirely different series of Camel ads—which ran con-
currently with the image series—suggests something far more
subtle than merely a strong self-image (see Figure 18). The
first ad in this odd, almost inexplicable series of ads aimed
at the unconscious mechanism in the minds of millions of
smokers, simply showed a pint carton of chocolate ice cream
on top of which is a spoon and at the bottom of which
are two slices of dill pickle. This ad appeared in several very
large circulation national magazines, including *TV Guide*.
How, one might reasonably ask—as we can be certain the
R. J. Reynolds tobacco company, which paid for all this
advertising, must have asked—how can ice cream and pickles sell Camel cigarettes to lower socio-economic level working men?

The answer is actually so simple it should have been
consciously—rather than unconsciously—apparent. Who eats
ice cream and pickles? Pregnant women, of course, going
through the pregnancy stage where exotic appetites drive
their husbands to distraction. And, this pregnant woman is
not just any woman—at least not to the market pursued by
Camel cigarettes—she is the smoker's wife. The promise of
the ad, subliminally, is a pregnant wife. Try not to laugh too
loudly for just a moment. There is still much more to this
idea.

Even though at the conscious level the man might want
very much to avoid a pregnancy, the subliminal implication
of the ad is that Camels would make him capable of implant-
ing another pregnancy—a strong emotional appeal to a sexually insecure man. Remember the constantly reappearing
theme in cigarette advertising—*anyone strongly fearing rejection may seek out means of oral gratification in smoking.*

The ice cream container is archetypally symbolic of woman; the full container means fertility in a woman. The spoon
handle is symbolically phallic.

The subliminal embedding in this ad is curious. Hidden
in the spoon, stuck into the chocolate ice cream, is a fetus.
Several embedded SEXes are floating around in the ice
cream, as well as between the lower pickle and the con-

tainer, where they are made to appear as fingerprints on the page.

As the ad says, "A man needs a good reason to walk a mile. Start walking." Consciously understanding the subliminal mechanics of this ad would make any reasonable man *run* instead of *walk*—but in the opposite direction.

The second ad in the series takes the prospective Camel smoker one step further on the road to seeking sexual security in a large family. The ad shows simply a crushed Camel pack resting upon a pool table cushion with a 10-ball in the background. The ad appeared in *Playboy, TV Guide* and in a number of other national publications.

"Empty" symbolically refers to bodily sensations. In man's most basic, unconsciously programmed context around which meanings accumulate throughout life, the separation of mother and child at birth results in a sensory experience of emptiness for the former and loneliness for the latter. The empty container (in this case, cigarette pack) is archetypally symbolic of birth. In many European cultures, such as Slavic, German, and English, the concept "empty" is symbolically the opposite of "pregnant."[1]

The textured wood, upon which the empty Camel pack rests, is symbolic of woman, according to Sigmund Freud's analysis of dream phenomena.[2] This subliminal message—connected with Camel cigarettes—would reassure the smoker of his sexual potency and virility. He has, at least symbolically, demonstrated his manhood by producing a child in his wife's womb.

The billiard ball is numbered symbolically 10—the "perfect" number used for centuries as a base for mathematics and monetary exchanges, as well as in science, art, and religion. The numeral "1" is symbolic of man, "0" of woman; the two numbers enclosed in a circle symbolizes the union of man and woman in marriage.

Dozens of embedded SEXes appear throughout the ad, further reinforcing the smoker's need for support against his fear of impotency and rejection—around the shadow area of the ball, throughout the green felt on the cushion, and in the finely textured wood of the table. The prospective Camel smoker should have run when he had the chance. It is now too late, symbolically at least.

[1] Theodore Thass-Thieneman, *Symbolic Language* (New York: Washington Square Press, 1966), p. 19.
[2] *Interpretation of Dreams* (New York: Avon, 1970), p. 391.

The third ad, illustrated by a royal flush in hearts, poker chips, ashtray, Camel cigarettes, and curling smoke, completes the trilogy aimed at the sexual insecurities of the North American working-class male.

The royal flush symbolizes that he has finally made it. The King and Queen symbolize father and mother. The Jack, or knave, and the Ace complete the symbolic family —the Ace symbolic of the craftsman child (think about how many service companies are called Ace) and the Jack symbolic of the clown child. The significance of the 10 as a symbol of family unity has already been discussed. The use of hearts has archetypally referred to the true inner self of man (the ego, love, fidelity) and has often been used in symbols as a personal pronoun—in effect, the big I AM. The entire family is in his hands.

The eminent position of the thumb is also highly significant. The hand is symbolic of man's creative or reproductive power. Hands involve very strong emotional meanings and fantasies. "Thumb" was derived from the Latin word meaning "to grow strong and to swell." Greek and German fairy tales and mythology told of creatures known as "thumblings" from whom our legendary Tom Thumb was derived, a small man who accomplished great things! The thumb is symbolically a strong phallic object, significant in the fantasies of early infancy or later childhood when young boys unconsciously identify their thumb with their genitals.

The idea presented symbolically by the ads of pregnancy, birth, and family is essentially an extension of the ego—a reinforcement for the smoker's fear of impotency, rejection, and sexual inadequacy.

Indeed, the Camel smoker now may find it much too late for *walking,* not to mention *running.*

The embedded subliminal words in the royal flush ad are somewhat more imaginative than in the other layouts in the series. The cigarette, symbolic of the male penis, is resting in the circle, symbolic of woman, provided by the ashtray. As the eye follows the smoke up, just above the ashtray rim, the smoke spells KISSES against the felt of the card table. As the smoke rises further above the poker chips, it outlines the shape of a pregnant woman. The poor woman is hooked again in support of her husband's fear of impotence.

SEXes have been sewn with near abandon throughout the felt tabletop and in the hand holding the cards. At the bottom of the ashtray, just below the burning end of the Camel, is written in script the word FUCK, which seems like as good a thought as any with which to end our story about The Man Who Almost Thought for Himself.

11. The Avarice-Entrapped Media of Mass Communication

There is so much more that should have been included in this book—a Hilton Hotel room-service menu, SEX embedded from breakfast through dinner; a Las Vegas Hotel Sahara travel pamphlet saturated with mosaiced SEXes; the paper cover of Eldridge Cleaver's book *Soul on Ice*, SEXed throughout; elementary grade textbooks, designed and marketed for school administrators, loaded with every subliminal trick conceivable; the fascinating perversities of the subliminally loaded Sears catalogue; the U.S. Air Force recruiting ad—full-page four-color in *Life* magazine—which features Scott and LEM on the surface of the moon after he had planted the Stars and Stripes, with moon landscape, dust, flag, and LEM covered in SEX mosaic; the U.S. map behind John Chancellor during the NBC Evening News with SEX embedded across Northern Florida and Southern Georgia; the dark, erect penis that forms the lower jaw of the lion on the paper cover of Robert Ardrey's excellent book *The Social Contract;* these and many, many more. So many more, in fact, that the author has frequently believed, while researching this book, that he might be off on a paranoic delusion of some sort. There appears to be a subliminal dimension in everything that communicates in the mass media. The content presented here was a random selection of what seemed to be typical examples.

The 1972, highly-publicized $1 million research study, sponsored by the U.S. Surgeon General's office—which tried to explore the "impact of televised violence"—is a dramatic example of the intellectual and moral bankruptcy of the so-called social sciences in North America. *TV Guide* referred to the study as the One Million-Dollar Misunderstanding.

The study was performed and analyzed by a large, carefully selected group of the most illustrious names in social science research—a truly blue-book stable of American in-

telligentsia. The findings of this group were pathetic nonsense. The authors summarized the totality of their findings
as, "We have noted in the studies a modest association between viewing of violence and aggression among at least
some children, and we have noted some data which are
consonant with the interpretation that violence-viewing produced the aggression. This evidence is not conclusive, however, and some of the data are also consonant with other
interpretations."

Nonsense!

Media has the proven, completely established ability to
program human behavior much in the same way as hypnosis.
And, if there is one common, dominant theme in American
media that is even more pervasive than sex—it is violence.
The taxpayers' money squandered on the nonsense game
did not find a causal relationship between TV and violence
because it would have produced an embarrassing problem
for the Nixon administration, and three TV networks, and
the advertisers—whose well-being appeared to have been a
major consideration among those alleged scientists who performed the research.

The Surgeon General's TV study highlights the basic dilemma of social science research in America. Investigative
and analytical technique—as well as social and behavioral
theory—have been designed to maintain the system, not
change it. If more money could be made by advertisers
through the elimination of violence from TV as has been
made by including it, a direct causal relationship would have
been established years ago. It is entirely possible that both
educational and governmental institutions—as well as their
so-called experts and scientists—are victims of their own
perceptual defenses which have blinded them to the realities
(the violent realities) of America's past and present. This
does not suggest that the illustrious social scientists, whose
names appeared on the Surgeon General's report, consciously lied to the American people. Far worse than this, they
first deceived themselves into believing in their own highly
repressed fictions and merely passed these along as "scientific
objectivity."

Had the $1 million study produced a firm causal relation-
ship between TV and violence, all hell would have broken
loose. Government, industry, and the media would have had
a lot of explaining to do. Like so many studies of its kind,
the final results were completely predictable long before the

research proposals were even written or the money appropriated. Predictability, of course, is the usual basis for referring to any conclusion as "scientific."

No Easy Answers

The big question, finally, is: *What can be done?* To eliminate advertising would restrict the availability of mass media and have serious consequences in the national economy. Besides, this could provide antidemocratic groups with a tool to completely control mass media. America may yet discover an important role media can play in support of survival and adjustment in a world of growing dangers and complexity. Perhaps the media could be saved from itself.

A "cleanup" of advertising, however, would merely result in a continuation of the same game we have been playing. Even if all known techniques of subliminal persuasion were made illegal, the law would be impossible to enforce. With the enormous pressures in our society behind selling, it would only be a short time until someone figured out new techniques that circumvented the law. Laws, contrary to what the legal profession might claim, have not eliminated crime—they have only caused it to become more highly refined and sophisticated. The number of possible new techniques of subaudible, subliminal, and subtractile stimulation appear virtually endless. As clever, devious, and ingenious as the mass communication media have been in their development of subliminal technology, they have only scratched the surface. And, besides, the subliminal dimensions inherent in human communication has existed since far, far back in evolution. It is most unlikely it could be removed from the human psyche, even if anyone wanted it removed.

Two approaches to the subliminal phenomena must be explored immediately—probably by government or well-endowed private foundations. The explorations must be public, well publicized, and strictly maintained in the public interest by men who have nothing to gain or lose from what they discover, if this ideal is possible. What is already known, together with what will be discovered through additional research, must be integrated into the public educational systems.

There is very little public information available about subliminal influences. Virtually nothing is known at present by the general public, educators, and others who presume to carry a public trust. Industry, commerce, and their research and advertising agencies, on the other hand, possess exhaustive analytical studies on the use and effects of subliminal stimuli. These proprietary studies should be appropriated in the public interest. Every major advertising agency in North America and its research and consultant agencies are known to have sponsored extensive study and research into subliminal perception—dating back as far as thirty years. Government agencies such as the FBI and CIA are also known to have conducted research and extensive investigations into the use and effects of subliminal phenomena.

In American universities, however, thirty years of behaviorist, experimental psychology have produced very little that would shed light upon the question. Virtually all the behavioral and social sciences in America are *verbal-definition* oriented instead of *reality-process-interrelationship-meaning* oriented. This academic compartmentalization of knowledge has defeated rather than encouraged the pursuit of truth. In the real world there is no such thing as sociology, psychology, and the like. These labels only survive as administrative conveniences in public institutions. Psychological assumptions, for example, are totally invalid if they fail to incorporate sociological, historical, economic, political, and other implications. But that is not the way university courses are taught.

Obviously, our so-called educational institutions, like our news and information sources, have unpardonably failed to alert us to what has been going on in the mass media, and very possibly in many other vital areas. The constant accusations that modern university education today is irrelevant are not without justification. One of the first things a young professor must learn when he starts teaching is not to rock the boat. Universities are in business to perpetuate themselves and the private empires of their administrators and political supporters. The socially approved wisdoms found most acceptable in classrooms involve more of a public relations activity for society and its institutions, rather than the source of new discoveries, insights, and conceptualizations.

Who's Been Watching the Store?

Of the public relations oriented educational areas, one of the most intellectually retrograde has been the so-called schools and departments of journalism. These have purpose-

fully disregarded the entire subliminal polemic. Though most
journalism professors have had limited professional experience, many have been aware for years of these subliminal
practices. None has, as far as anyone can tell from the
literature, ever introduced the subject into classrooms.
Roughly 37,000 students in the United States are in training each year at universities that offer courses in mass communication or journalism. Very few of these students, if indeed any at all, are exposed to *ethics* (an area usually taught
in philosophy), and these students have pathetically inadequate knowledge of *human perceptual systems,* what can be
done with them, and the problems of *illusion-reality* (also
usually taught in philosophy as epistemology or philosophical
linguistics). Over ten thousand individuals enter the field
of mass communication each year in America—supposedly
college-trained in the public interest—but actually without
any knowledge of even the questions, let alone the answers.
These young people, however, have been fully prepared or,
if you will, programmed to make money for their employers.
Their education has been a super-automatic, high-speed
brainwashing in behalf of the economy and its institutions.
They have learned to accept any rationalization necessary to
justify the status quo. Certainly as regards manipulation, the
mass media have so far not served the public interest.

If, however, North Americans were to launch a large-scale
educational effort on subliminal techniques, the most important work would be done in grade schools—even kindergar-
ten would not be too early to begin. Language training in
American society is an absurd anachronism. Children pass
through twelve years of the world's most expensive education and emerge totally unqualified to live in the linguistic
and symbolic environments in which they will spend their
lives. They are taught to deal with language in terms of
simplistic dichotomies—truth versus falsity, good versus bad,
rich versus poor, and so on. They are carefully trained
to identify words with things—the word "tree" is the same
as the object "tree"; of course it can never be the same, one
is a *symbol* and the other a *reality.* American children, moreover, are taught nothing about the perceptual abilities
and limitations known to exist within their own bodies, but
are encouraged to grow up mouthing such platitudes as "seeing is believing."

Human motives are rarely, if ever, discussed as a part
of language training in primary schools. Ancient and primi-

tive sensory concepts, such as Aristotle's five senses, are still the basic orientation in most U.S. schools, even universities. Teachers often rationalize that any mention of the thirty-seven known senses might confuse children—an unsupportable argument when you consider that ten-year-olds can easily be taught to read several thousand words per minute.

The whole object of language or symbolism—whether it involves a verbal, a mathematical, a natural, or a physical language—is *meaning*. The major question upon which all language education must be predicated is, *"What does it mean?"* This is the real name of the game. It matters little whether you spell or punctuate correctly if you repress, confuse, or distort meanings without realizing *what* and *why* you are doing so. And, meaning must be considered at both conscious and unconscious levels. We already know quite a lot about our conscious perception. Almost nothing really new has been discovered in this area for a quarter of a century. Cognitive or conscious insights into behavior must now be integrated into knowledge of the subliminal, much of which has been around, even though often ignored by scholars, for centuries. It may well be time for humanists and interpretive psychologists to begin sleeping with behaviorists and experimentalists, in the interest of finding out what is really happening to the world and the people who live in it.

Research is the first major necessity. The first scientifically respectable book on subliminal perception was published in England in the fall of 1971.[1] There have been, of course, a large number of articles in professional journals, but these are unlikely to make much sense to a nonacademic audience.

Back in the late 1950s Vance Packard put together a journalistic treatise on the *hidden persuaders*. Packard was on the right track as he probed the so-called motivation research of his day, only he never pushed far enough. As it turns out, there was a great deal his sources did not tell him. Packard tried to perform a public service by popularly exposing what was going on in the media. He only scratched the surface, but was denounced widely as a shallow sensationalist trying only to make a fast buck. America should have listened more carefully. Two years after his book was published—though it became a best seller—Packard's thesis had been widely discredited by the media, the universities,

---

[1] N. F. Dixon, *Subliminal Perception: The Nature of a Controversy* (London: McGraw-Hill, 1971).

and, of course, by the businesses which control and support both. Everything went quietly and peacefully back to normal.

Those "Voices" May Really Exist

There are a thousand new questions which must be asked in the hope of finding answers. Mental illness, the Twentieth-Century Plague, may be related to subliminal stimuli. What is vaguely called schizophrenia, for example, could be involved with an individual's perception of subliminal stimuli. A review of the schizophrenic theories of R. D. Laing and Karl Menninger—two of the many available—reveals that a surprising number of their adolescent cases testified endlessly about the words or ideas—often dirty words and ideas—older people put into their heads. These were often described as "voices" the patients were surprised to learn other people could not hear. Throughout the history of mental illness these voices had always been thought to be purely products of their illness—produced internally by disoriented mental processes. Maybe not. Could these words really exist embedded in funny books or grade school readers to enhance the sales of marketing-conscious publishers? Could these *imaginary* ideas have been subaudibly implanted in the sound tracks of television programs or commercials, in printed content or advertisements, or perhaps in the grooves of million-seller rock and roll recordings? As it should now be quite apparent to the reader, this is not at all impossible or improbable if you consider the extent to which we are being massaged by subliminals each day.

In both the Laing and Menninger theories of schizophrenia, the young patients talked about the role their parents played in their lives as models for behavior and morality. If the reader of the case studies merely replaced the word "parent," "father," or "mother" with the idea of *media*—making a mental note to include both print and electronic media—the implications are startling. One cannot help but wonder if these children could have somehow confused or combined media (perhaps TV) with parental models and influences, hopelessly losing themselves in the unreality of media and its illusions (*strongly reinforced with subliminal massaging*), which, of course, can never compare with the day-to-day stress and boredom of reality.

What portion—the question is appropriate—of today's mental illness is an escape into a permanent world of ideal-

ized fantasy resulting from the total impossibility of a re-
conciliation between the illusions and fantasies of media with
the complex and frustrating realities of daily life? No one as
yet knows the answers to these questions. But, as a society
which hopes to survive what lies ahead during the next
quarter century, we had better find out and quickly before
the damage—and there is little doubt there has already been
some damage—becomes irreversible.

The effects of subliminal stimulation upon mental health,
especially where young people are concerned, must receive
first priority. But secondly, there could be positive or constructive potentials in subliminal techniques. It appears reasonable to assume that a new theory of aesthetics may be
developed that considers the two levels of human perception, *conscious* and *unconscious*.

What, for example, is the difference between a very
good violin and a Stradivarius? There is an enormous difference, any concert violinist will maintain, but one which
defies conscious empirical description. Is it possible the
Stradivarius violin emits subaudible tonalities which are perceived by audiences as vague undefinable feelings?

Is it further possible that poets such as Milton stumbled
upon verbal symbols, images, or icons which evoked subliminal reactions in the reader? The conscious information in
Paradise Lost can be summarized quite briefly, categorized,
quantified, computer-programmed, and stored on magnetic
tape. It is most doubtful this tape would survive as meaningful literature or as a significant example of human experience. *Paradise Lost,* in its poetic form, will likely have
deep significance as long as there is an English language—
perhaps longer, as was the case with the poems of Homer
and Euripides. How much of sculpture, painting, and other
expressions of profound human meaning or feeling might be
explained or at least partially understood in terms of subliminal stimuli? No one knows at this point, but we can
only hope someone will try to find out.

It would be sad if this exposé of subliminal machinations
—and the manipulative role played by people who have
been trusted by millions of readers and viewers—ended up
with merely a public relations soft soaping by both government and business. They will certainly try. There will be
countless apologists and apologies in behalf of the media
and the businesses whose products media sells. The author
hopes however, enough people will become so indignant and

outraged that they will demand, through their political leadership, immediate and forceful action resulting in intensive research and a widespread educational program.

All the News That Sells

Media has most clearly proven itself socially irresponsible and hopelessly entrapped by its own avarice. The wastelands of television, one might hope, will be irrigated and reseeded with integrity. Some form of large-scale media surveillance, perhaps by government or a private trust, must be instituted —perhaps not with the power of censorship but certainly with the power to expose publicly communication techniques that operate against the public interest. Federal commissions on the press and other forms of public communication have already been proposed and discussed in both the United States and Canada. But, they must be given power, authority, talented and dedicated public servants, adequate financing, and be totally free of partisan favoritism or political pressures.

It is also hoped that subliminal manipulations will provoke an intense public examination of the role manipulation plays or should play in our society. How defensible is mass manipulation?

The *behaviorist* would probably argue, "Yes, why not, as long as it is in a good cause." In other words, if the motives are pure and the end is love, happiness, and goodness, then manipulation is justified. The obvious problem, of course, is who shall decide what is to be considered good or even desirable?

The *pragmatist* business orientation of media and advertising would likely put the polemic in these terms: "What in hell are you complaining about? Look what we have done for you. Americans are better fed, better automobiled, better clothed, and so on and so on, than any other nation in the world. So we use the subliminal devices, to help you decide to do what you already wanted to do. We keep the products and services moving. And, this is no small accomplishment." There are some obvious flaws also in this line of argument— ecological imbalances, resource depletion, possible psychopathological effects, for example. But they are quite correct in one fact: mass manipulation has resulted in an incredible material prosperity for virtually everyone in North America

—even our ghetto inhabitants live better than most of the world's population.

Finally, the *humanist* or *existential* philosophers and psychologists would likely say: "Look! When you manipulate people, regardless of your motives, you take away their right to decide for themselves *what they want to do* and *who they want to be.*" Humanists usually lean strongly on free will as an ideological foundation.

The polemic very likely has no simple, single answer. It is imperative, however, that the whole argument become a public issue. We repress or hide from ourselves these polemics only at great peril.

This book was purposely not written for exclusive academic consumption. With a small mountain of research data from which to draw, it could have been dribbled out, one pedantic article at a time, over a period of several years. In several ways this might have been a preferable procedure. The evidence would have been thoughtfully probed, more exhaustively tested, argued, and further examined as to its significance. One thing appeared quite certain from the research: the subliminal perception issue is of enormous significance to modern man.

This author believes the discussion should not be restricted to the peculiar jargons of academia which often obscure the simplest, most obvious facts or details. The academics have sat unproductively for far too long, unwilling to take on the enormous power concentration behind the media. The issue must go public and quickly. Someone must ask the social and behavioral scientists who were highly paid to develop subliminal techniques for the communications industry —why they said nothing in violation of professional ethics and the public trust.

This book has also been an attempt to examine another form of cultural programming used daily on an enormous scale throughout North America. The programming is invisible and masquerades under the disguises of truth, objectivity, honesty, fairness, morality, virtue, and even love for your fellow man.

Our modern affluent culture urges us to be reasonable. The notion that we will all love each other if only we will be reasonable, communicate, find the right words, and look for a happy, equitable compromise is apparently basic to American life today—as many would like to believe it exists. Being reasonable is not necessarily the road to eternal happiness, as many philosophers have pointed out for a long time. Being reasonable is very often simply an open invitation to be raped. So, this book will pointedly deny the rational premises of being reasonable. It is a studied and premeditated attempt *to be most unreasonable, indignantly unreasonable.* The shattering realization that one has been cheated, lied to, manipulated, exploited, and—on top of it all, the final indignity—laughed at for being gullible is simply too much to endure further without at least trying to fight back.

Symbological Degeneration

There is, of course, more to America's present national dilemma than just the loss of integrity in the language and symbolisms of the society. But, the symbolic dilemma is major, even basic, and as good a place as you can find at which to aim the first rocks. Several modern writers have blamed the exhaustion and perversion of symbolic values, meanings and functions twisted in the interest of commerce and industry, as almost a unique symptom of American corruption. The problem currently appears more intense in America than in any other nation.

In man's slow, painful evolution, symbols acquired meaning and significance over literally centuries of experience. Symbolic values arrived and disappeared very slowly—certainly incorporating as they evolved various survival and adjustment mechanisms. This symbol-making and symbol-sustaining ability is believed to be the primary reason for man's survival as a species.

Today, we use, modify, manipulate, destroy, invent, and exhaust our symbolic languages at a staggering rate. New words and symbolic concepts by the thousands enter our languages each year. Perhaps roughly the same number annually disappear. Nothing symbolic in our society seems to have more than a very transient and superficial dimension of meaning. We no longer believe in our symbols—elements many writers have called the glue which holds together societies, languages, cultures, and human existence. We are cynical, doubtful, alienated, distrustful, and frequently bewildered by the spinning, hypnotic effect of omnipresent media-induced symbolic pressures upon our conscious and unconscious minds.

The general *conscious* versus *unconscious* or *cognitive* versus *noncognitive* polemic has endured well over a quarter of a century between the two academic polarities—psychological behaviorists; and their opposing schools, humanistic, Gestalt, and the rest. Very quietly, however, while the academics have argued over how many angels could dance on the head of a pin, commercial research organizations—sponsored in their confidential proprietary research by large corporations—made enormous progress in learning how the human condition could be molded, used, and controlled in the interest of profit. This research was never made public. Indeed, one research executive who completed over 300 projects during ten years of working for large U.S. companies, never had a single project which he could publish or even publicly discuss. The million dollars, spent in behalf of the corporations by this single executive on research, produced insights and information only meant to benefit individual businesses in their life-and-death struggle for competitive corporate survival.

So, all the power of corporate enterprise, the mass media which it supports, and the government it sustains in power—not to mention the educational institutions supported by this affluent establishment—have a collective interest in pretending subliminal perception is only a romantic notion dreamed up by some radical, irresponsible troublemaker.

In the Most Powerful Office

As this book began to develop, late in 1971, a chapter with illustrations was forwarded to Mrs. Virginia Knauer, Director of the Office of Consumer Affairs in the Washington office of President Richard M. Nixon. Included were the Gilbey's advertisement as well as a dozen or so other simple, clear examples of subliminal advertising. The material was carefully chosen—so simple a child could understand what was going on. At the time, Mrs. Knauer was receiving national publicity over her so-called "deep investigations" into American advertising. In what turned out to be just a superficial public relations and vote-soliciting probe, the President's office was then making another gesture to pacify the American public's growing discontent with the quality of life its country now offers.

Mrs. Knauer's consumer affairs office refused to even discuss the possibility of subliminal perception techniques in advertising. Several of her department's consultants, it was discovered, had reviewed the subliminal materials. They reported that, indeed, something was going on in the advertisements which seemed to involve a "generally unknown technique of persuasion." The entire matter was hushed up. A secretary employed in Consumer Affairs at the time reported that for several weeks after the manuscript had been passed around the office, the subliminal perception material was the main subject of conversation. Suddenly, word was passed that the subject was not to be discussed any further —internally or externally.

Considering the U.S. government involvement with advertising agencies and their media, and the enormous research budgets available, it is simply unbelievable that present applications of subliminal technique are not known within that government. Consider all of the interesting applications which could be made by the CIA and FBI in the development of new techniques for manipulating subversives or converting, which instead of overthrowing governments who disagree with U.S. foreign policy; by the military, which instead of only selling the Pentagon, might be able to include the Brooklyn and Golden Gate bridges; or, by the President's office, which by subliminal SEX embeds might sustain the illusion of virility and youthful dominance far, even farther, into the outer reaches of senility.

It may be reassuring to know that Washington has carefully protected the subliminal technology of mass media so it doesn't fall into the wrong hands.

With Thanks

The author is most grateful to the over 1,500 patient, long-suffering, and persevering students who participated in classroom lectures, discussions, and often heated debate during the three years this book was in preparation. Many of the illustrations will be familiar to these students. In any respect, student support, encouragement, critical discussions, and creative insights were invaluable to the explorations into subliminal mechanisms. The greatest regret is that there was never enough time for long, probing bull sessions with these questioning and critical young minds. But, then, there is never enough time.

Special mention must be made of the contribution of a handful of young scholars who worked long and often unrewarded hours as teaching and research assistants. Included are John Cardiff, who the author hopes will one day publish a rock-shaking probe into the world of popular music; James Johnston, whose powers of perception and intellectual agility are far greater than he yet suspects; Lee Palser, a tough, bright ex-journalist determined to write the great Canadian novel; John and Louise Clutterbuck, two talented young people looking for new mountains to climb; and Peter Stemp, one of the most gifted and creative students of life the author has known. Jean Stone, a very beautiful secretary, contributed a very clean-typed final manuscript.

The author also feels himself honored by the help and encouragement given him by colleagues and good friends with whom he shared long and exciting evenings over glasses of beer, lively discussions of treasured books and authors, vigorous philosophical arguments, and their constant emphasis upon checking over and over again the facts and the theories.

In particular, Professor Marshall McLuhan, whose seminars were exciting intellectual high points during the author's four years in Canada; Professor Williams Hart, art historian and warm friend, who contributed companionship, ideas, and support during the long research months of uncertainty and frustration; and sociologist Professor Orrin Klapp, whose writings and friendship were so important to the background perspectives which provided a door into the world of symbolic value systems.

Most important, however, was the lovely Iris who intimately endured the highs of enthusiasm and the lows of depression during these years of research, teaching, and writing. She was the first to read and critique the rough manuscript. Her love and wisdom have given the author more happiness than he probably deserves.

There are many, many more who should be mentioned. They would, however, fill an encyclopedia. To everyone who contributed—simply, Thank you!

References

Ardrey, Robert. *The Social Contract.* New York: Atheneum, 1970.

Arnheim, Rudolph. *Art and Visual Perception: A Psychology of the Creative Eye.* Berkeley: University of California, 1964.

Berelson, Bernard, and Steiner, G.A. *Human Behavior: An Inventory of Scientific Findings.* New York: Harcourt, Brace, and World, 1964.

Berne, Eric. *Games People Play: The Psychology of Human Relationships.* New York: Grove Press, 1964.

Burke, Kenneth. *A Grammar of Motives and a Rhetoric of Motives.* Cleveland: World Publishing, 1962.

————. *Language As Symbolic Action: Essays on Life, Literature, and Method.* Berkeley: University of California, 1966.

————. *Permanence and Change: An Anatomy of Purpose.* Indianapolis: Bobbs-Merrill, 1965.

Burrow, Trigant. *Preconscious Foundations of Human Experience.* New York: Basic Books 1964.

————. *Science and Man's Behavior.* Westport, Conn.: Greenwood Press, 1968.

Carnap, Rudolph. *The Logical Syntax of Language.* New York: Humanities Press, 1951.

Carpenter, Edmund, and Hayman, Ken. *They Became What They Beheld.* New York: Outerbridge & Lazard, 1970.

Cirlot, J. E. *A Dictionary of Symbols.* New York: Philosophical Library, 1972.

Cleaver, Eldridge. *Soul on Ice.* New York: Delta, 1968.

Dixon, N. F. *Subliminal Perception: The Nature of a Controversy.* London: McGraw-Hill, 1971.

Ehrenzweig, Anton. *The Hidden Order of Art.* London: Paladin, 1970.

Fiedler, Leslie. *Love and Death in the American Novel.* New York: Criterion Books, 1960.

Frazer, J. G. *The Golden Bough.* London: Macmillan, 1967.

Freud, Sigmund. *Interpretation of Dreams.* New York: Avon, 1970.

————. *Leonardo da Vinci.* New York: Norton, 1964.

————. *On Creativity and the Unconscious.* New York: Harper, 1958.

Fromm, Erich. *The Forgotten Language.* New York: Grove Press, 1951.

————, Suzuki, D. T., and de Martino, Richard. *Zen Buddhism and Psychoanalysis.* New York: Harper, 1960.

Hall, Edward T. *The Hidden Dimension.* New York: Doubleday, 1966.

————. *The Silent Language.* New York: Doubleday, 1959.

Hayakawa, S. I. *The Use and Misuse of Language.* New York: Fawcett, 1964.

Innis, Harold A. *The Bias of Communication.* Toronto: University of Toronto, 1951.

Jobes, Gertrude. *Dictionary of Mythology, Folklore, and Symbols* (3 Vols.). New York: The Scarecrow Press, 1962.

Johnson, Richard E. *Existential Man: The Challenge of Psychotherapy.* New York: Pergamon, 1971.

Jung, C. G. *Analytical Psychology: Its Theory and Practice.* New York: Vintage Books 1968.

————. *Man and His Symbols.* New York: Dell, 1970.

————. *Psyche and Symbol.* New York: Doubleday, 1958.

Kahn, Herman, and Weiner, Anthony J. *The Year 2,000.* New York: Macmillan, 1967.

Klapp, Orrin E. *Collective Search for Identity.* New York: Holt, Rinehart and Winston, 1969.

————. *Symbolic Leaders.* New York: Minerva Press, 1964.

Kluckholm, Clyde. *Mirror for Man.* New York: McGraw-Hill, 1949.

Kohler, Wolfgang. *Gestalt Psychology.* London: Boni and Liveright, 1929.

Korzybski, Alfred. *Science and Sanity.* Lakeville, Conn.: Institute of General Semantics, 1958.

Laing, R. D. *The Divided Self.* Middlesex, England: Tavistock, 1959.

————. *Knots.* London: Tavistock, 1970.

————. *Politics of Experience.* New York: Pantheon, 1969.

————. *The Politics of the Family.* Toronto: CBS Learning Systems, 1969.

————, and Esterson, A. *Sanity, Madness, and the Family*. Middlesex, England: Tavistock, 1964.

Lane, Michael (Ed.). *Structuralism*. London: Jonathan Cape, 1970.

Langer, Suzanne K. *Philosophical Sketches*. New York: Mentor, 1962.

————. *Philosophy in a New Key*. Toronto: Mentor, 1951.

Leach, Edmund. *Levi-Strauss*. London: The Chaucer Press, 1970.

Lorenz, Konrad Z. *King Solomon's Ring*. New York, Thomas Y. Crowell, 1952.

McGinniss, Joseph. *The Selling of the President*. New York: Trident, 1969.

Machiavelli, Niccolò. *The Prince*. London: J. M. Dent & Co., 1940.

McLuhan, Marshall. *The Gutenberg Galaxy*. Toronto: University of Toronto, 1968.

————. *The Mechanical Bride*. Boston: Beacon, 1969.

————. *Understanding Media: The Extensions of Man*. New York: McGraw-Hill, 1964.

———— (with Wilifred Watson). *From Cliché to Archetype*. New York: Viking, 1970.

————, and Parker, Harley. *Through the Vanishing Point: Space in Poetry and Painting*. New York: Harper, 1968.

Malinowski, Bronislaw. *Magic, Science, and Religion*. New York: Doubleday, 1954.

Marcuse, Herbert. *Five Lectures*. Boston: Beacon, 1970.

————. *One-Dimensional Man*. Boston: Beacon, 1964.

Maslow, Abraham. *Toward a Psychology of Being*. Princeton, N.J.: Van Nostrand, 1962.

Masters, William H., and Johnson, Virginia E. *Human Sexual Inadequacy*. Boston: Little, Brown, 1970.

May, Rollo. *Existential Psychology*. New York: Random House, 1969.

————. *Symbolism in Religion and Literature*. New York: Braziller, 1960.

Meadows, Donella H., Meadows, Dennis L., Randers, Jorgen, Behrens, William W. III. *The Limits of Growth*. New York: Universe Books, 1972.

Miller, George A. *Human Memory and the Storage of Information*. I.R.E.: Transaction of Information Theory: IT-2: 129-137, 1956.

Mills, C. Wright. *The Sociological Imagination*. New York: Oxford University, 1959.

Moreno, J. L. *Who Shall Survive?* New York: Beacon, 1953.

Morris, Charles. *Language and Communication.* New York: McGraw-Hill, 1951.

―――. *Signs, Language, and Behavior.* Englewood Cliffs, N.J.: Prentice-Hall, 1949.

Ogden, Charles K. *The Meaning of Meaning.* New York: Harcourt, Brace & Co., 1956.

Packard, Vance. *The Hidden Persuaders.* New York: David McKay, 1957.

―――. *The Sexual Wilderness.* New York: David McKay, 1968.

Pears, David. *Wittgenstein.* London: Fontana, 1971.

Perls, Frederick S. *Gestalt Therapy Verbatum.* Moab, Utah: Real People Press, 1969.

Piaget, J. *Language and Thought of the Child.* London: Kegan Paul, Trerich, and Trubner, 1932.

―――. *The Mechanisms of Perception.* London: Routledge & Kegan Paul, 1969.

Rank, Otto. *Art and the Artist.* New York: Agathon Press, 1968.

Read, Herbert E. *Icon and Idea.* Cambridge, Mass.: Harvard University, 1955.

Reich, Theodore. *Myth and Guilt.* New York: Grosset & Dunlap, 1970.

Reusch, Jurgen, and Bateson, Gregory. *Communication: The Social Matrix of Society.* New York: Norton, 1951.

―――, and Kees, W. *Non-Verbal Communication: The Visual Perception of Human Relations.* Berkeley: University of California, 1959.

Russell, Bertrand. *Mysticism and Logic.* New York: Longmans, Green, 1921.

Sapir, Edward. *Culture, Language and Personality.* Berkeley: University of California, 1966.

Schneider, David M. *American Kinship: A Cultural Account.* Englewood Cliffs, N.J.: Prentice-Hall, 1968.

Simpson, George. *People in Families.* Cleveland: World Publishing, 1966.

Storr, Anthony. *Human Aggression.* New York: Atheneum, 1968.

Strelka, Joseph. *Perspectives in Literary Symbolism.* University Park: Pennsylvania State University, 1972.

Stromeyer, Charles F., "Eidetikers," *Psychology Today,* November, 1970.

————, and Psotka, J., "The Detailed Texture of Eidetic Images," *Nature*, Vol. 225 (January 24, 1970), 346–49.

Swartz, Robert J. (Ed.). *Perceiving, Sensing, and Knowing*. New York: Doubleday, 1965.

Thass-Thieneman, Theodore. *The Subconscious Language*. New York: Washington Square Press, 1967.

————. *Symbolic Behavior*. New York: Washington Square Press, 1967.

Toffler, Alvin. *Future Shock*. New York: Random House, 1970.

Watts, Alan W. *Nature, Man, and Woman*. London: Thames & Hudson, 1958.

Weiner, Norbert. *The Human Use of Human Beings: Cybernetics and Society*. New York: Doubleday, 1954.

Westin, Alan F. *Privacy and Freedom*. New York: Atheneum, 1967.

Whittick, Arnold. *Symbols, Signs and Their Meaning and Uses in Design*. London: Leonard Hill, 1971.

Wilentz, Joan Steen. *The Senses of Man*. New York: Thomas Y. Crowell, 1968.

Young, John Z. *Doubt and Certainty in Science: A Biologist's Reflections on the Brain*. New York: Oxford University Press, 1960.

INDEX

There's an epidemic with 27 million victims. And no visible symptoms.

It's an epidemic of people who can't read.

Believe it or not, 27 million Americans are functionally illiterate, about one adult in five.

The solution to this problem is you... when you join the fight against illiteracy. So call the Coalition for Literacy at toll-free **1-800-228-8813** and volunteer.

Volunteer Against Illiteracy. The only degree you need is a degree of caring.